3 0050 06232 7431

30050062327431 -Mar09- DPLG
100 SHO
Shouler, Kenneth A.
The everything guide to
understanding philosophy /

THE EVERYTHING®
Guide to
Understanding Philosophy

Dear Reader,

A love of philosophy can occur slowly or at first sight. For me it happened at once. Its moral, metaphysical, and epistemological questions—about God, the good life, free will, and the rest—spoke to me early on. It didn't matter that the first book I read was a ho-hum sounding text called *A Concise Introduction to Philosophy*. The questions seemed important all the same. The issues came alive. I had to talk about it in class. In fact, I couldn't shut up about it.

Maybe philosophy will shake you in the same way. I hope I have talked to you about the lives and most important ideas for each thinker in this book. Hang with philosophy. Give a tough question the time it deserves and philosophy will reward you with understanding. Philosophy takes the deeper concerns we have about life—the kind that arise every day in casual discussions in our places of business, at home, or out socially—and turns them over and over again and allows us to look at them more profoundly. When we raise philosophical questions and join in discussions we join the great conversation that began nearly 2,600 years ago, when Greek philosophers looked at the vastness of nature and tried to explain it all in a different way.

Kenneth Shouler, Ph.D.

DISCARD

D1279207

Welcome to the EVERYTHING® Series!

These handy, accessible books give you all you need to tackle a difficult project, gain a new hobby, comprehend a fascinating topic, prepare for an exam, or even brush up on something you learned back in school but have since forgotten.

You can choose to read an *Everything*® book from cover to cover or just pick out the information you want from our four useful boxes: e-questions, e-facts, e-insight, e-ssentials. We give you everything you need to know on the subject, but throw in a lot of fun stuff along the way, too.

We now have more than 400 *Everything*® books in print, spanning such wide-ranging categories as weddings, pregnancy, cooking, music instruction, foreign language, crafts, pets, New Age, and so much more. When you're done reading them all, you can finally say you know *Everything*®!

QUESTIONS?
Answers to
common questions

FACTS
Important snippets
of information

INSIGHT
A revealing look at
an issue

ESSENTIALS
Quick
handy tips

DIRECTOR OF INNOVATION Paula Munier

EDITORIAL DIRECTOR Laura M. Daly

EXECUTIVE EDITOR, SERIES BOOKS Brielle K. Matson

ASSOCIATE COPY CHIEF Sheila Zwiebel

ACQUISITIONS EDITOR Lisa Laing

DEVELOPMENT EDITOR Brett Palana-Shanahan

PRODUCTION EDITOR Casey Ebert

Visit the entire Everything® series at *www.everything.com*

DAVENPORT PUBLIC LIBRARY
321 MAIN STREET
DAVENPORT, IOWA 52801

THE
EVERYTHING®
GUIDE TO
UNDERSTANDING PHILOSOPHY

The basic concepts of the greatest
thinkers of all time—made easy!

Kenneth Shouler, Ph.D.

adamsmedia

avon, massachusetts

Copyright © 2008 by F+W Publications, Inc. All rights reserved.
This book, or parts thereof, may not be reproduced
in any form without permission from the publisher; exceptions
are made for brief excerpts used in published reviews.

An Everything® Series Book.
Everything® and everything.com® are registered trademarks of F+W Publications, Inc.

Published by Adams Media, an F+W Publications Company
57 Littlefield Street, Avon, MA 02322 U.S.A.
www.adamsmedia.com

ISBN 10: 1-59869-610-6
ISBN 13: 978-1-59869-610-3

Printed in the United States of America.

J   I   H   G   F   E   D   C   B   A

Library of Congress Cataloging-in-Publication Data
available from the publisher.

This publication is designed to provide accurate and authoritative information with regard to the subject matter covered. It is sold with the understanding that the publisher is not engaged in rendering legal, accounting, or other professional advice. If legal advice or other expert assistance is required, the services of a competent professional person should be sought.

—From a *Declaration of Principles* jointly adopted by a Committee of the American Bar Association and a Committee of Publishers and Associations

Many of the designations used by manufacturers and sellers to distinguish their products are claimed as trademarks. Where those designations appear in this book and Adams Media was aware of a trademark claim, the designations have been printed with initial capital letters.

This book is available at quantity discounts for bulk purchases.
For information, please call 1-800-289-0963.

Dedication

I dedicate this book to my philosophy professors at
St. Bonaventure University—especially Rod Hughes, Len Geller,
Patrick Dooley, Mike Chiariello, Rich Reilly, Tony Murphy, John Hunter,
and Neal Fay. All of them piqued my curiosity for philosophy.

Contents

Acknowledgments

I would like to thank Lisa Laing, my editor at Adams Media, whose encouragement and direction at the outset of this project helped my confidence in carrying through twenty-four chapters. Bob Diforio, my agent, has been a pro from day one. I couldn't have asked for a smoother working relationship.

As ever, praise goes to my wife Rose Marie. She gave me the time and space needed to dig into this project and get it done on time.

Top Ten Interesting Philosophy Quotes

1. **Aristotle:** "Men are good in one way, but bad in many."

2. **Albert Camus:** "Man stands face to face with the irrational. He feels within him his longing for happiness and for reason. The absurd is born of this confrontation between the human need and the unreasonable silence of the world."

3. **Socrates:** "The unexamined life is not worth living."

4. **Plato:** "Philosophy begins in wonder."

5. **Bertrand Russell:** "Every proposition which we understand must be composed wholly of constituents with which we are acquainted."

6. **David Hume:** "The life of man is of no greater importance to the universe than that of an oyster."

7. **Jeremy Bentham:** "A full-grown horse or dog is beyond comparison a more rational, as well as a more conversible animal, than an infant of a day, or a week, or even a month, old. But suppose the case were otherwise, what would it avail? The question is not, Can they *reason?* nor, Can they *talk?* but, Can they *suffer?*"

8. **Immanuel Kant:** "Nothing can possibly be conceived in the world, or even out of it, which can be called good, without qualification, except a good will."

9. **Soren Kierkegaard:** "A crowd . . . in its very concept is the untruth, by reason of the fact that it renders the individual completely impenitent and irresponsible, or at least weakens his sense of responsibility by reducing it to a fraction."

10. **Jean-Paul Sartre:** "Man is condemned to be free."

Introduction

▶ IF YOU ARE a student of philosophy seeking an introductory reference to the subject, then this book is for you. Philosophy is not easy when you first take it on. You may have to read paragraphs over before you can begin turning pages. Reading history, science, and literature is much easier. But philosophy—it's a different matter altogether.

Philosophy takes nothing for granted. Philosophy turns reality upside down and shakes out its pockets. The answers that others assume are correct in discussing God, morality, political issues, medicine, art, business, and sports are scrutinized more thoroughly by philosophers. In this way, they hope to arrive at a deeper understanding of some issue.

Even for people who have been teaching for years philosophy is not easy. If philosophy seems easy to you at some point, it might be that you're missing something. Maybe you're not raising one more essential question, or you've failed to consider another way of examining an important issue. While on trial for his life Socrates said "The unexamined life is not worth living." It may well be the most recognizable sentence in the history of philosophy. Not everyone would give up his life rather than cease philosophizing. Even so, Socrates' seven-word thought captures the spirit of philosophy.

If you are just getting started in philosophy, then this book should work for you. Key ideas are explained thoroughly, leaving nothing to chance. The book is also complete enough for you to get a history of the subject, as most of the major figures are covered.

Naturally, there is no way to include every figure of Western philosophy from roughly 600 B.C. to the present. Still, it seemed important to include all the major philosophers and the most influential ideas. Without them, there would be no way to see the development of the subject and the connections from one era to another.

Philosophy is a love of wisdom, Pythagoras said. You look at the deeper reality of the world and philosophy draws you in, summons your curiosity, and refuses to relax its tight grip. A century after Pythagoras, Socrates said that philosophy was the pursuit of truth. People seek answers and pursue the truth as if truth were a fugitive trying to elude them. You likely come into philosophy seeking answers to fundamental questions about morality, God, immortality, freedom of the will, and other matters. But you soon find out that philosophy suggests as many questions as answers. Socratic questioning helps in eliminating bad answers. But the task of finding truths for the most fundamental questions never seems complete.

So it is best not to assume that philosophy will serve up final answers for its students the way math and the sciences may. The activity of philosophy is an unending give and take, an eternal conversation that allows readers to turn issues over and over in their minds. You end up knowing it better. You should not conclude that your answer is a final one. But at least you have a fuller appreciation of what the issue involves.

Philosophy rewards a vigilant search for truth. Even if the answer does not arise, the inquirer undergoes a significant change in the process of seeking it. In a word, the inquirer—whether student, professor, businessman, or layperson—has joined in the search for truth.

CHAPTER 1

Early Greek Philosophy: The Pre-Socratics

Philosophy in the Western world began in ancient Greece, most likely in Miletus on the Ionian seacoast of Asia Minor. Ionia was a crossroads of ideas where Eastern and Western influences merged. The first three "pre-Socratic" philosophers were Thales, Anaximander, and Anaximenes. They are often referred to as physicists because of their devotion to cosmology—that branch of physics that deals with the "cosmos," or the nature of the orderly universe. In particular, these first philosophers wanted to know the nature of substance, or matter.

Thales (c. 625–c. 545 B.C.)

Thales was a man of broad interests in science and mathematics. He likely traveled to Egypt to learn astronomy, geometry, and practical skills to do with the measuring and management of land and water. This practical knowledge enabled him to navigate ships. Also, according to the Greek historian Herodotus, he predicted an eclipse of the sun that occurred in 585 B.C.

Thales was different from his Egyptian predecessors because he tried to give a rational explanation of the world. He raised the question: What is the source of all things? His answer was "water." He thought water was the cosmic stuff of the universe. All things come into being from water, and the earth floats on water like a log. But why did Thales think water was the ultimate substance? It's not known for sure. The writings of Thales have not survived. In fact, what is known of the Milesian philosophers is so fragmentary that philosophers must supplement it with the reports of Plato, Aristotle, and other philosophers and historians.

You can, however, make intelligent guesses about why he thought water was the primary substance. He might have chosen water because water can take many forms. It exists in all three forms of matter: solid, liquid, and gas. Aristotle thought it was more probable that Thales was influenced by the essential connection of moisture with life, as seen in such substances as semen, blood, and sap.

Thales' knowledge of geometry was practical. For one, he could measure pyramids in relation to the shadows they cast at certain times of the day. Also, the Greek historian Herodotus relates the story of how Thales once overcame the problem of getting an army across a river by diverting the flow of water to run behind the army's encampment until the channel in front of it was shallow enough to be crossed.

Like other Ionian philosophers, Thales believed in the doctrine of *hylozoism*. This theory says that matter possesses life, or sensation. In other words, life and matter are inseparable. Soul is *in* substances. This may be the explanation of another saying attributed to him. A story goes that he saw metal filings being drawn to a magnet. He could not account for how this happened and proclaimed, "Everything is full of gods."

Anaximander (610–545 B.C.)

Born in Meletus, Anaximander was a student of Thales and is regarded as the second of the Ionian naturalists. Like Thales, Anaximander was renowned for his mathematical prowess. He is known for inventing the sundial and gnomon, which is the triangular blade on the sundial that casts a shadow. In addition, Anaximander provided the first map of the Greek world, the first map of the stars and constellations placing the earth at the center as a disk, and determinations of the path of the sun.

FACT

Anaximander also offered the first theory of evolution. His examinations of fossils from cliffs showed that (a) those taken from the lower parts of the cliffs were simpler in structure than those taken from the higher parts, and (b) the fossils were similar in structure and over time became more and more complex. Living forms are not unchanging, but evolve from simpler forms. His thinking was rejected in his own time.

Though he was Thales' student, Anaximander disagreed with his teacher. Anaximander contended that the original substance of the universe was not matter like water, but must be *immaterial*. He thought the fundamental, ultimate stuff of the universe must be the infinite. The Greek word is *apeiron,* meaning something that is "without limit" or "boundless." His thinking was that prior to all perceptible material bodies there must have been an indefinite, immaterial something.

Let's try to understand Anaximander's thinking. He looks out on nature and sees the sky, water, soil, stone, and more. Such variety could not have come from one finite (and therefore limited) substance. From Axaximander's *boundless* all things came or were "separated out." Here Anaximander hit upon an ingenious idea: if the purpose of cosmological investigation is to find a single substance from which all other entities can emerge, what could be better than something infinite, which contains within itself the capacity to produce any other thing? The *boundless* accounts for the multifarious creations and changes we observe. He also called this infinite stuff a "principle." As Aristotle said in his *Physics,* "Everything is either a principle or derived from a principle. But the limitless has no principle—for then it would be a limit. It is ungenerated and indestructible and so is a principle."

Anaximander also believed that the earth, a flat cylinder, hangs freely in space because of its equal distance from all parts of the spherical universe. The sun is the same size as the earth. This concept was the first of all attempts at a rational cosmogony and as such represents freedom from mythical modes of thought.

Anaximenes (580–475 B.C.)

Anaximenes is the third of the Ionian or Milesian naturalists. He was a friend and student of both Thales and Anaximander. Anaximander had said that the infinite was the principle of all things in nature but didn't specify what that principle was; Anaximenes said that the principle is limitless air.

INSIGHT

Hippolytus, a contemporary of Anaximenes, observed: "Anaximenes said that infinite air was the principle, from which the things that are becoming, and that are, and that shall be, and gods and things divine, all come into being, and the rest from its products."

The "Originator" was his other name for the basic substance air. Anaximenes believed that this cosmic air, or mist, extended everywhere, pervading all things in the universe, and was the primordial element for two reasons: (1) air held all things together, as the soul is the air that holds us together, and (2) all things arise from it according to whether forces make them expand (rarefaction) and contract (condensation).

According to Theophrastus, a student of Aristotle, Anaximenes meant that:

Being made rarer (or finer) air becomes fire, being made thicker it becomes wind, then cloud, then when thickened still more water, then earth, then stones; and the rest comes into being from those. He, too, makes motion eternal, and says that change, also, comes through it all.

The Milesian Approach

What is important with each of the Milesians is not this or that specific theory of the universe. Rather, what is significant is their approach. Though the Egyptians and Babylonians held that water is the primordial element, they thought that divine action explained the creation and nature of the world. The Milesians, on the other hand, offered naturalistic explanations. For example, Thales explained earthquakes not by appealing to the actions of some sea God, but by suggesting that they are the result of tremors in the water upon which the earth floats.

The first three philosophers began the search for answers about the nature of the universe. Their quest for knowledge of the physical world remains the centerpiece of the scientific quest right into the twenty-first century.

Pythagoras (c. 570–c. 495 B.C.)

Pythagoras was one of the most celebrated and controversial of the ancient Greek philosophers. He was at once a mathematician and a philosopher, not to mention a kind of cult leader and seer on the fate of the human soul. He was born on the island of Samos, off the coast of modern Turkey. But at the age of forty he left to escape the tyranny of Polycrates and settled in Croton in southern Italy.

The Purification of the Soul

Once in Croton, Pythagoras founded a brotherhood of disciples dedicated to *philosophia* (a term derived from the Greek word *philo,* meaning "love," and *sophia,* meaning "wisdom"). He said philosophers were "lovers of wisdom." He was called a "leader and father of divine philosophy." The

Pythagorean society he led was known for its belief in the purification of the soul. Living by a set of religious and ethical rules was the way to purification and human bliss.

Since Pythagoras believed in a transmigration (or reincarnation) of the soul from human to human and even human to animal, he and his followers were vegetarians. He believed in a brotherhood of all living things. All living things must be interrelated because their souls have each possessed a great number of different bodies during past transmigrations. One writer told the story of how Pythagoras, seeing someone beating a dog, told him to stop, since he had recognized the voice of a friend in the yelping of the dog. Whether the tale is true or not, Pythagoras did believe in a migration of the soul in which the soul survives death.

QUESTION?

Was Pythagoras the first to put forward a theory of immortality?
No. According to the Greek historian Herodotus, the Egyptians were the first to hold this view. When the human body dies, the soul enters another animal as it is being born. When the soul has gone round all the creatures of land, sea, and air, it once more enters the body of a person that is then being born. This cycle takes 3,000 years.

The Pythagoreans also dedicated themselves to certain ritual practices. There were thirty-nine rules in all, most of which were rules of abstinence. The Pythagoreans also believed in prolonged silences as a means to improving their self-control. All such rituals furthered the purification of the soul.

They believed that whereas physical sensuality contaminates the soul, the noblest means of purification is intellectual activity, which liberates the soul, and the greatest intellectual activity is mathematics.

All Things Are Number

Devotion to mathematics is at the heart of Pythagorean philosophy. Pythagoras thought that all things could be expressed numerically. In seeing that points, lines, and surfaces are the real units that compose nature, Pythagoras anticipates Galileo's thinking of the seventeenth century.

The most obvious example of the lawlike numerical structure of nature is the Pythagorean theorem, $A^2 + B^2 = C^2$. But they thought that a mathematical principle could explain all of reality. In this sense, all bodies must be regarded as numbers. It makes sense: in a straightforward way, a large triangle differs from a small triangle in a measurable, numerical way. Even musical pitch depends upon numbers, since the lengths and the intervals on the musical scale may be expressed by numerical ratios. Pythagoras also spoke of a cosmic harmony: he thought that the law-like mathematical relationships between heavenly bodies must have caused a "music of the spheres."

Heraclitus (540–480 b.c.)

Heraclitus was a melancholy man known as "the Dark Philosopher," "the Weeping Philosopher," and "the Obscure." He had an aloof and solitary temperament and was contemptuous of ordinary, unreflective citizens. He was given to amusing and baffling remarks like "Physicians who cut, burn, stab and rack the sick, demand a fee for it which they do not deserve to get," "Man is called a baby by God, even as a child by man," and "Asses prefer straw to gold." Besides these remarks, he was an important philosopher, just as his Ionian predecessors were.

If you put your foot in the Hudson River, take it out, and put it back again, you are disturbing "new waters" each time, as Heraclitus put it. At the same time, the spatio-temporal coordinates of your foot's location are the same. After all, it is still the Hudson River that you put your foot into, not the Nile or the Allegheny. Reality is changing but still one.

"The Philosopher of Change"

Heraclitus changed the focus of early Greek philosophy. He shifted the emphasis away from the ultimate constituents of the world to a new problem, the problem of change. One of his main ideas was expressed in his most popular saying: "All things are in a state of flux." He also said "You cannot step into the same river twice, for fresh waters are ever flowing in upon you." He viewed the world as "an everlasting Fire, with measures of it kindling and measures of it going out." In all of these sayings Heraclitus seems to hold the position that change is the only constant thing in nature.

Reality Is One and Many

But if you stop here, you won't get Heraclitus's complete meaning. For change is not the most important feature of his philosophy. Heraclitus's main contribution to philosophy is his thought that there is unity in diversity. Reality is one and many at the same time. There is identity in difference. Changes from day to night and from summer to winter show the predominance of one kind of matter over another, but only for a time.

We all experience change and yet in some sense we remain the same. So there must be some unity beneath the changes. The world is an everlasting fire—taking on new matter and giving off new matter. The world remains stable because equal measures of matter go into and out of existence.

He was known as "the Riddler," "the Dark One," and "the Obscure" and Heraclitus could be truly bizarre. For example, take this saying of his: "The god: day and night, winter and summer, war and peace, satiety and hunger. It alters as when mingled with perfumes, it gets named according to the pleasure of each one."

Parmenides (c. 515–c. 450 B.C.)

Contrary to Heraclitus, Parmenides thought that all change is an illusion of the senses. The same is true of diversity and motion: they are unreal appearances.

"The Way of Truth" and "The Way of Falsehood"

Parmenides wrote an argumentative poem titled *On Nature*. The first part was called "The Way of Truth" and another part "The Way of Falsehood or Illusion." The way of truth is the way of reason or intellect, unaided by the senses. The way of falsehood is the way of the senses, which Parmenides viewed as inferior to the intellect. If you talk about a caterpillar changing into a moth you say that Substance A, the caterpillar, *changed into* Substance B, a moth. But this must be an illusion caused by our sense of sight, for a change from state A to state B is a change from what something "is" into what "it is not." But you cannot even conceive, much less speak intelligibly about, "what is not." Can anyone form an idea of what is nonexistent? "Just try it," Parmenides seems to be saying.

Parmenides would say that an acorn growing into a tree or a snake molting are illusory changes, since a precondition of anything changing is transition into something that it is not. Variety is impossible, too, since if you claim that there are moons and stars, for example, you are asserting that one entity—the moon—possesses some attributes that the other—the stars—does not have. Being is changeless.

The Use of Argument

To substantiate his points, Parmenides introduced the use of argument—a series of premises to support a conclusion. Here is his argument about the illusion of change:

1. There is no variety, change, or movement in the world, since anything described as having these attributes would be described as changing from a state that it is in into a state that it is not.
2. But we cannot talk about (or even conceive) what is not.
3. It is therefore impossible to talk about variety, change, or movement.

4. Thus, all change is illusion.
5. Therefore, all reality is one.

Despite appearances, despite what our senses tell us, nothing ever changes in the world. The nature of all things throughout the world is fundamentally the same essence. What is real is one object, or Being. Being is symbolized as a sphere, having no beginning and no end. After all, any other shape would involve a difference from one part to the other. It is an uncreated, eternal cosmic substance. Such a being would have no beginning.

In the "Way of Truth" and the "Way of Falsehood and Illusion" Parmenides said: "The one way, that it is and cannot not-be, is the Path of Persuasion, for it attends upon Truth; the other, that it is-not and needs must not-be, that I tell thee is a path altogether unthinkable. For thou couldst not know that which is-not (that is impossible) nor utter it."

Parmenides' argument stands common sense on its head. For your senses tell you that material objects are changing all the time. But opinion is secondary to the activity of reason.

Zeno of Elea (490–430 B.C.)

Zeno was Parmenides' pupil. Zeno defended his teacher's position on the illusion of change. Like Parmenides, Zeno took the view that common sense led to absurd conclusions. Our senses fail to provide any evidence about reality but only about appearances. Therefore, what our senses reveal to us is deceiving.

Zeno's Paradoxes

To illustrate these differences, Zeno came up with several paradoxes. Paradoxes are statements that appear contrary to common sense but are in fact true.

- In the paradox of *The Racecourse* the runner will try to finish the course. But if the course is, say, 100 yards, the runner must first reach the 50-yard marker. And in order to reach the 50-yard marker, he must reach the 25-yard marker. To reach that marker, he needs to reach half that distance, and so on, with the halfway distances being infinitely subdivisible. But since an infinite series of points cannot be traversed in a limited time frame, the race can never really be finished, despite all appearances that tell us that that runners finish races all the time. Thus, motion cannot exist; it is illusory.

- In *Achilles and the Tortoise* the point is similar. In order for the swift Achilles to overcome the tortoise, he must reach a point that the tortoise has already left. The distance between the two can be infinitely subdivided and so Achilles can never really overtake the tortoise. Motion cannot exist at all.

- *The Paradox of the Arrow* also illustrates that motion is impossible. An arrow shot at a target cannot reach its destination, for at every moment, the arrow has to occupy a specific position in space equal to its length. But this is the definition of an object at rest. So the arrow does not move.

In all of these examples, Zeno is showing that a pluralistic universe is impossible. Parmenides had shown that variety and change were illusions of the senses. In his paradoxes Zeno showed the same thing about motion. Parmenides was right.

Evaluation and Significance

In what way do these early Greek scientists merit the title "first philosophers"? There are three reasons why the dozen "pre-Socratic" thinkers from 600 to 400 B.C. deserve the title.

One, they looked at and tried to understand the world in a scientific, rational manner. They were convinced that the world was a systematic, orderly place.

Two, because they viewed the world as systematic, they did not think that all events in nature were determined by the will of god. The pre-Socratics were not atheists, but their view of the gods was different from the traditional view. The poets who preceded them, for instance, might explain natural phenomena in supernatural terms. For example, they might describe thunder as Zeus growling or a rainbow as created by the goddess Iris. For the most part, the pre-Socratic gods, like the gods of Plato and Aristotle to follow, did not interfere with the natural world.

Third, these thinkers can be credited with being the first philosophers because they raised the question of where things came from. In answering this fundamental question, they often sought to identify a single substance from which the world would emerge.

The pre-Socratics made a bold start. Their naturalistic philosophy laid the groundwork for Socrates, the most famous philosopher in the history of the West. In the words of Aristotle, Socrates "called philosophy down from the heavens." Socrates thought that human conduct and how one should live—and not naturalistic speculation—was the true subject of philosophy.

CHAPTER 2

Socrates: The First Moralist

Without writing a single word, Socrates (c. 470–399 B.C.) is arguably the most important philosopher in the history of Western thought. He took to the streets of Athens to reason with and question his fellow citizens. By raising philosophical questions—more often than not about virtue and the nature of the good life—he urged craftsmen, poets, politicians, and citizens of all stations to question their own values and the very purpose of living.

Socrates and His Questioning Profession

In 399 B.C. Socrates would ultimately defend himself in a trial before 501 Athenians, explaining to them that "The unexamined life is not worth living" and that he would not cease philosophizing even to save his life. But what was it about Socrates' life that brought him to an Athenian courtroom at the age of seventy?

The details of Socrates' early life and education are unclear. What we do know of him comes from several sources. We have the dialogues of his student Plato (428/27—348/47 B.C.), which provide an affectionate, lively, three-dimensional account of Socrates' character and thinking. In addition, we have the accounts of Xenophon, a contemporary philosopher; Aristophanes, a satirical dramatist; and Aristotle, a philosopher and historian of Greek philosophy.

Socrates was born in either 469 or 470 B.C., based on available evidence that he was seventy years old when he died in the spring of 399 B.C. His father, Sophroniscus, was a sculptor and his mother, Phaenarete, was a midwife (Oddly: Socrates would later describe himself as a kind of "philosophical midwife," seeking to give birth to others' ideas with his well-placed questions). Socrates was likely a sculptor and stonemason before he turned to philosophy.

FACT

Socrates was a soldier, serving as a "hoplite" (the word meant "heavyfoot") during the Peloponnesian War. In fact, he distinguished himself for exceptional bravery three different times. The first was at the siege of Potidaea (431–430 B.C.), then at Delium (424), and a third time at Amphipolis (422).

Socrates is known for some incredible feats of physical endurance, like walking barefoot across ice in one military campaign. On another occasion he stood in a trancelike state and meditated for thirty-six consecutive hours, as described in Plato's *Symposium*. Both events testify to Socrates' ability to ignore physical discomfort in order to achieve some greater mental or spiritual objective. These are some of the amazing acts that have built the legend of Socrates.

Socrates' legend owes more to his profession, however. His philosophical mission began with an oracle, or divinely appointed authority. It was customary for Greeks to bring their difficult questions to the city of Delphi, where the god Apollo relayed the answers to an oracle, who at Delphi was the priestess Pythia. In the *Apology,* Socrates explains that his vocation as a philosopher goes back to the time when the oracle answered the question of Socrates' friend Chaerephon, who inquired, "Is there any living person wiser than Socrates?" The priestess answered "no." Socrates at first doubted the response, for he knew that he had "no wisdom, great or small."

QUESTION?

What did Socrates mean by calling himself a "gadfly"?
A gadfly is a large fly that pesters livestock and other animals with its stings. Likewise, Socrates was an irritant to his fellow citizens. He likened Athens to a large steed and he peppered Athenians with questions, causing them to think about how to live their lives.

He set out to disprove the oracle, going about Athens questioning others. He posed questions about virtue and goodness to poets, religious authorities, generals, and craftsmen. But he found that these and other citizens with the greatest reputations for knowledge had none. So he concluded that "Real wisdom is the property of God, and this oracle is his way of telling us that human wisdom has little or no value." Socrates was wisest in one respect: others thought they had knowledge, but didn't. By contrast, he had no knowledge and knew it. To be aware of one's own ignorance is true wisdom.

Socrates in Death

In 399 B.C. Socrates was brought to trial on the charges of (1) not worshipping the gods whom the State worshiped, but introducing new and unfamiliar religious practices, and (2) of corrupting the youth of Athens. Why did Socrates suddenly find himself in such dire circumstances?

Socrates' philosophical vocation had not changed but political realities in Athens had. The protracted Peloponnesian War—sometimes referred to as "Athens Vietnam"—began in 431 and ended in defeat for Athens in 404. Socrates had lived freely during much of his time in Periclean Athens. (Pericles (495–429 B.C.) was an Athenian statesman and general noted for his oratory and leadership skills. He championed democracy and presided over Athens's "Golden Age," sending out colonists and building its empire.)

But now the climate was different. The Athenian politician and general Alcibiades turned out to be a traitor, aiding rival Sparta's victory. Many Athenians knew that Alcibiades was Socrates' pupil and concluded that Socrates must have had a hand in his corrupt actions. In addition, Critias and Charmides, friends of Socrates, were involved in the Commission of Thirty, a violent oligarchy executing anyone having to do with the democratic Athens of Pericles' time. For Socrates it was another example of guilt by association.

Prior to his trial, Socrates could have gone into exile. He also could have hired a lawyer, or "rhetor," to defend him in court. Instead he chose to defend himself before 501 jurors, which was a snapshot of a diverse Athenian society. In his defense he challenged the trumped up charges against him, showing that the real grounds for bringing him to trial were political. But he was found guilty by a vote of 280 to 221.

FACT

Defendants had from morning until evening to conduct their defenses and there were no appeals. Some people have commented that Socrates might have swayed more jurors to his side if he had more time. But this is doubtful. After all, between the verdict and penalty phases of his trial a second count was taken and Socrates lost eight-one people who were previously on his side.

In the penalty phase of his trial the prosecutor Meletus proposed the death penalty. As was customary, the defendant proposed a counter-penalty. Socrates offered to pay a meager fine of thirty minae, which he said his friends in the court would put up. He then argued that he should be maintained publicly in the Prytaneum, an elegant residence, as a reward for his years of service philosophizing for the State. This was an honor bestowed upon eminent generals, Olympian winners, and other outstanding people.

As for holding his tongue or going into exile, both were unthinkable. He said that he would not stop philosophizing, since to cease and desist in this way would be tantamount to agreeing with the court that he had harmed his citizens rather than helped them.

During his trial Socrates considered whether he should cease philosophizing. Ultimately he decided that he could not, for he believed on Apollo's authority that the philosophical pilgrimage of his life had been a good choice, and at no time during his trial had his inner voice instructed him to change his views.

Socrates had irritated his audience further. Affronted by his arrogance, a second vote was taken. Now the tally was 361 to 140 for the death penalty. Some four weeks after the trial Socrates faced death in jail. Crito, as described in Plato's dialogue of that name, tried to persuade Socrates to escape. But Socrates refused. He argued that escaping would be unjust, since it would nullify the verdict of the court. The jailor brought Socrates a cup of hemlock. He drank it and died.

QUESTION?

How does hemlock kill an individual?
The cup of hemlock (obtained from a poisonous hemlock tree) that Socrates drank would numb his lower extremities and make its way up his body. He was told that if he kept moving about and getting overheated, the poison would work more quickly. He drank from the cup, before sitting and then lying down to die.

Crito used other arguments to convince Socrates to escape. The reasons he offered were that Socrates had duties to his children and that the reputation of his friends would suffer if he didn't escape, since it would appear that they refused to spend the money to spring him from jail. Socrates replied that it is always wrong to do wrong. Further, all revenge is a kind of wrongdoing and escape is a kind of revenge. It follows, therefore, that it is wrong to escape.

"Calling Philosophy Down from the Heavens"

The pre-Socratics were the first philosophers, raising questions about the cosmos and its origins. Socrates brought philosophy down from the skies. His predecessors' speculations about the origins of matter didn't preoccupy Socrates. He thought that philosophy ought to be concerned with practical questions about how to live and the nature of the good life. Because of these concerns about values, he essentially invented the field of philosophy known as "ethics." He is deserving of a distinctive title in the history of thought: the first moralist.

The Objectivity of Values: Socrates Against the Sophists

One of Socrates' primary goals was to show that values can be known and are objective. People are born into different times, come from different places, and embrace different customs. So is it possible to arrive at a universal concept of goodness? This was the subject of the debate between the Sophists and Socrates.

FACT

The word sophistry entered the English language with a decidedly negative definition courtesy of the Sophists. These ancient figures were the equivalent of self-help gurus and had more in common with motivational speakers than philosophers. For a fee, they would help people use tools of rhetoric and debating skills to help advance their career.

The Sophists were traveling teachers. They hailed from places beyond Athens and were ready to help Athenians rise to influence in this open society with a new democracy. Their greatest skill was the ability to teach rhetoric, or persuasive speech, to the masses. But their skepticism about values and objective truth could lead them to argue any case, even in an attempt to make the "weaker argument appear stronger." They developed reputations for taking young people from good upbringings and leading them to question and reject their own traditions in ethics and religion. Further, they weren't in keeping with the images of philosophers as disinterested seekers after truth. Rather, they charged fees for their teaching, and they sought out the rich who were able to pay these fees. Socrates couldn't afford to pay them because of his poverty and Plato disparaged them as "shopkeepers with spiritual wares."

The Chief Sophist: Protagoras

Protagoras (c. 490–c. 420 B.C.) was the most influential sophist to arrive in Athens. Protagoras famously said, "Man is the measure of all things; of the things that are, that they are, of the things that are not, that they are not." This makes each individual the standard of what is true and false. This would be true of ordinary perceptions of physical things—you may taste wine as sweet while someone else may find it bitter, so it must be both of these things—but also about ethical values.

Protagoras's skepticism affected his view of the Gods: "Concerning the gods I have no means of knowing either that they exist or that they do not exist nor what sort of form they have. There are many reasons why knowledge on this subject is impossible, owing to lack of knowledge and shortness of human life."

Taken to the extreme in ethics, this would imply complete *relativism,* or the view that each person must decide the truth for his or her self. But in Protagoras's case, he also espoused that the laws of a land are to be obeyed. So people should uphold the customs, laws, and moral rules that their tradition has carefully nurtured. But this relativism would make it impossible to criticize the immoral practices of some societies or even one's own. Thus, if you favor relativism, there are no objective rights or wrongs. The ideology of Nazism and slavery aren't objectively bad, but were true for groups at different times of history. In ethics, as in other things, there are no absolutes.

Socrates held a very different view than the Sophists. Socrates thought that certain moral knowledge could be arrived at through the pursuit of truth, rather than persuasion. Unlike the Sophists, he engaged in philosophical debate not for the purpose of destroying notions of truth or of developing worldly skills in lawyers and politicians. He was trying to establish a solid basis for morality.

Ethical Doctrines

Any student of philosophy looking through Plato's Socratic dialogues will find evidence of some of the same moral views. Two doctrines in particular are staples of Socrates' thought. Chief among these doctrines is the view that knowledge and virtue are the same thing; in other words, that to know the good is to do the good. For instance, if a person really knows it is bad to smoke cigarettes or cigars, then he won't do it. A second ethical doctrine is that wrongdoing harms the doer more than it harms the recipient of the wrongdoing.

Knowledge Equals Virtue

According to Socrates, if a person fully understands what the good is, then he will do that good. Put another way, he identified goodness and knowledge, saying that to know the good is to do the good. Vice or evil is the absence of knowledge. So just as knowledge is virtue, vice is ignorance. In his mind "knowing" is necessarily linked with "doing." Anyone who knows what goodness is will automatically do it. Socrates thought that anyone who failed to act courageously or justly simply didn't know what it meant to be courageous or just, otherwise they would not have failed to act.

If a person understands that abstaining from drugs is the right thing to do, then such a person would follow through and shun drug use. This concept presents the idea that performing a good action or choosing a good life course—or avoiding an evil action or life course—is an intellectual matter.

This may be another of those famous Socratic paradoxes. It seems as if people fail to do what they set out to do all the time. They resolve to diet, to stop drinking, to give up smoking, but they backslide and do these things, which bring bad results. According to Socratic thinking, the person who has the cigarette or uses the steroids lacks self-knowledge; that is, he confuses his *apparent* good with his *real* good.

INSIGHT

It sure seems like Socrates is wrong in saying if you know the good you will do it. How could he have missed a point so obvious? He didn't. If a person claimed he knew it was wrong to smoke cigarettes but did anyway, then he didn't really know. But what kind of knowledge was Socrates speaking of? Self-knowledge, the most important kind of knowledge there is.

Wrongdoing Harms the Doer

After Socrates was sentenced to death, he explained to the jury why he did not fear death. He described death as either one of two things: a state of unconsciousness—a kind of dreamlike state of sleep; or a "migration of the soul from this place to another." In this other place, he believed he would meet his "true judges" like Homer, Hesiod, and others who were "upright in their earthy lives."

Thus, he said his physical death would not be a great evil. For even if he met his physical death, it wouldn't follow that he would suffer harm to his soul.

You too, gentlemen of the jury, must look forward to death with confidence, and fix your minds on this belief, which is certain—that nothing can harm a good man either in life or after death, and his fortunes are not a matter of indifference to the gods. . . . For my own part I bear no grudge at all against those who condemned me and accused me, although it was not with this kind intention that they did so, but because they thought that they were hurting me; and that is culpable of them.

Now it is time that we are going, I to die and you to live, but which of us has the happier prospect is unknown to anyone but God. (Apology)

Socrates turned the tables: the harm will be greater for those jurors and ambitious prosecutors who sentenced him unjustly than it will be for him. Those who have put him to death will suffer greater harm, for their souls will endure the mark of wrongdoing.

Inductive Reasoning and the Socratic Method

Looking back on the philosophical career of Socrates, Aristotle would say that Socrates' great contributions were his quest for definitions and inductive reasoning. Aristotle (who St. Thomas Aquinas would later praise as "the master of those who know") was surely right about Socrates. Socrates sought definitions of terms like justice and virtue, love and piety. He thought that unless one could define these terms that one didn't know what love and virtue were. He used inductive reasoning, starting with particular statements like "This generous action is virtuous," hoping to establish more important generalizations like "All generous actions are virtuous."

Inductive Reasoning

Socrates thought that a definition of a philosophical term provides a needed objective basis. For without the definition of an ethical term, there is no foundation for making ethical judgments. Plato's early dialogue *Euthyphro* provides an excellent example of this through Socrates' cross-examination of Euthyphro in an attempt to elicit a definition of piety.

Euthyphro is a prominent religious figure about to bring charges of impiety against his own father, who has been involved in the death of one of his servants. At the same time, Socrates must also concern himself with the definition, since someone has brought an indictment against him for impiety. In both cases, a vote of guilty on the charge of impiety could be a capital offense. Socrates decides to learn what piety is from Euthyphro and use that knowledge in his own defense before the court.

Socrates adopts his usual position of ignorance, saying that he needs Euthyphro to explain what it means to be pious or holy. Euthyphro first answers Socrates by defining piety as "prosecuting the wrongdoer," as he is doing with his father. Impiety would be not prosecuting him. To this Socrates replies, "I did not ask you to tell me one or two of all the many pious actions that there are; I want to know what the concept of piety is which makes all pious actions pious." In other words, Socrates is saying, "Don't give me an example of piety; I'm asking for a definition."

Euthyphro tries to offer a second definition. This time he says, "What is pleasing to the gods is pious." But Socrates replies that the Greek pantheon of gods often quarrel with one another about right and wrong, better and worse. As a result, the same act will be pleasing to one god, but not to others. So Euthyphro's own definition has led to self-contradiction. After two tries at a definition, it is apparent that Euthyphro doesn't know the meaning of the term. But shouldn't he know what piety and impiety are before he prosecutes his own father on the grounds of impiety?

Euthyprho amends his previous definition, this time saying, "Piety is what all the gods love, and impiety is what they all hate." This definition, more general than the first, is an improvement, for it says what "all" Gods like and dislike. But Socrates asks, "Do the gods love an act because it is pious or is it pious because the gods love it?" The latter cannot be the case, for this would mean that what causes or makes the act to be pious is the god's love of it. This would mean that if god loved murder, murder would be pious. So it must be that god loves it because it's pious, not the other way around. But even if Euthyphro accepted this formulation, he would be giving an *attribute* of piety, not a definition of it. We need the "essence" of piety.

INSIGHT

Socrates placed high regard on the correct definition of terms. In Plato's *Cratylus,* he says, "If we assign names as well as pictures to objects, the right assignment of them we may call truth, and the wrong assignment of them falsehood. . . . There may also be a wrong or inappropriate assignment of verbs; and if of names and verbs then of the sentences, which are made up of them."

Socrates asks again. But Euthyphro says, "Another time, then, Socrates, for I am in a hurry, and must be off this minute." Euthyphro cannot stand the test of Socrates' rigorous cross-examination. The dialogue ends without a definition of piety. But Socrates has shown his dialectic method and the importance of definition in ethics. Behind his quest for the definition is the idea that if you cannot define the term, you shouldn't use it.

What Socrates is interested in when it comes to definitions is a general account.

Socratic Method

Like other dialogues, *Euthyphro* shows that one of Socrates' lasting contributions to philosophy is his skillful method of cross-examination. What is now known as the "Socratic Method" is his manner of attaining knowledge. The method was designed to force one to examine his beliefs and the validity of such beliefs. In fact, Socrates once said, "I know you won't believe me, but the highest form of Human Excellence is to question oneself and others."

The *Euthyphro* ends in skepticism and irony. If Euthyphro is so sure that he is doing a pious act by prosecuting his father, then why is it that he cannot even describe what piety is?

The dialogue also shows something about the effect Socrates had on his fellow citizens. Socrates can be seen as a nuisance, constantly irritating others with his logical inquiries. Euthyphro handled the cross-examination with a good spirit, but not everyone did. With his questioning Socrates is a slayer of idols. At times, nothing of a conversant's original position is left standing, as the search for truth clears away false opinions like a scythe clears away unwanted brush. All opinions must stand the test of critical examination.

QUESTION?

How did Socrates compare himself with his mother?
His mother was a midwife, a woman trained to assist women in childbirth. Socrates thought that he, too, acted as a kind of "midwife" in seeking to help others give birth to ideas through engaging in philosophical discussions with them. In a manner of speaking, the questions he puts to Euthyphro cannot elicit the correct answer. His dialectic, however, eliminates some of Euthyphro's bad offspring.

Evaluation and Significance

In terms of content and method, Socrates is one of the most important philosophers in the history of the West. The Socratic method of questioning is a tool used by many effective teachers.

Because of his preoccupation with the good life, he essentially invented the concept of the self. According to Socrates, the care of one's self, or soul, turns out to be the most important task in life. He did not think, as many of his predecessors did, that the soul accompanied the body, was useless without it, and had no bearing on the thoughts or emotions of the person. An excellent soul is well ordered, has wisdom, and maintains control over the emotions and bodily desires.

The question-and-answer method was one of Socrates' most important contributions to Western thought. He would apply his dialectical method of inquiry, known as the "Socratic method," to key moral concepts such as goodness and justice. The definitions of such terms are elusive, but Socrates used his approach to peel away bad answers and get closer to the truth.

Socrates did, however, accept the idea that the soul is immortal. In the *Phaedo* he jokes with Crito that when he dies "You must catch me first," meaning that his real immaterial soul will be active, not dead like the body.

Above all, Socrates stands the test of time as a person of great integrity. He did not surrender his values, even when he was facing death. He didn't just discuss philosophy with curious listeners. He lived his philosophy.

CHAPTER 3

Plato: Dramatist of Reason

Plato (428/27—348/47 B.C.) was twenty-nine years old when his teacher Socrates died. In the course of his lengthy life Plato used dialogues, an inherently dramatic form, to pour forth a complete system of philosophy. Plato was a polymath at work. He was equally comfortable writing on ethics, epistemology, metaphysics, political philosophy, and aesthetics (philosophy of art). He made contributions to every branch of philosophy, leaving behind a system of thought that is breathtaking in breadth and depth.

The Life of Plato

Plato was born about 428 or 427 B.C. and died at the age of eighty or eighty-one in 348 or 347 B.C. Other dates have been offered, notably by Diogenes Laertius, a biographer of Greek philosophers, but the dates given here have been accepted as accurate. Plato was born to a distinguished family—his father Ariston and mother Perictione were said to have been descendants of the god Poseidon. It is likely that Plato had two older brothers and a sister, Potone. The brothers, Glaucon and Adeimantus, are significant interlocutors in the first two books of his dialogue the *Republic,* believed by many to be his greatest work and believed by some to be the single greatest work of philosophy ever written.

The year Plato was born, Socrates was forty-two years old. It is evident from Plato's writings that Socrates' life and thought served as inspiration and foundation for Plato's philosophy. He became a pupil of Socrates, one of the youths who followed Socrates around Athens to hear him converse with citizens. He was also present at Socrates' trial. Under Athenian democracy he had witnessed the collapse of Athens and the execution of Socrates. As a result, he conjectured that perhaps democracy was not the correct form of government and the State should be ruled by one person with adequate knowledge, what Plato would call "philosopher-king."

QUESTION?

Did Plato ever attempt to put into practice his idea of the philosopher-king?
Yes, Dionysius II, a young tyrant from Syracuse, invited Plato to help him become a philosopher-ruler of the sort described in the Republic. But the blueprint Plato had envisioned did not work, for the philosopher-king Plato envisioned had to be concerned above all with knowledge and not with his own power, as Dionysius II was.

In 387 B.C., twelve years after the execution of Socrates, Plato founded the Academy in Athens for the study of philosophy, mathematics, and logic, the sciences, and legislative, political and ethical ideas. The Academy lasted for several centuries after his death and is regarded by many to have been the first university.

Plato's Dialogues

The character, personality, and ideas of Socrates are front and center in Plato's earliest dialogues. For this reason, these have been called his Socratic dialogues. Most of them explore one or more of Socrates' ethical notions. They read at once like devoted portraits of his teacher and argumentative forays into fundamental moral issues, including the definitions of fundamentally important terms like courage, piety, friendship, and self-control. In his Seventh Letter Plato described Socrates as "the justest man alive." Though Socrates is clearly much beloved by Plato, the latter throws no whitewash on his teacher. Socrates is revealed as an inquirer and provocateur, relentless in his cross-examination and holding his opponent's arguments to the highest critical standards.

Ordering the Dialogues

Though finding the precise dates when Plato wrote his dialogues is an inexact science, it is accepted practice among scholars to divide his writings into three main groups. For decades, scholars have used "stylometric" considerations—like noting the frequency and timing of Plato's technical terminology, usage, phrases—to help determine the order of the dialogues.

The first group includes those early dialogues where the subject matter under consideration is moral excellence, including a pursuit of the definitions already mentioned. It is believed that these dialogues represent the ideas of the historical Socrates. It is agreed that *Apology, Crito, Euthyphro, Charmides, Laches,* and *Lysis* are among the earliest of Plato's dialogues.

The middle group of dialogues sets out ideas that Plato and not his teacher Socrates actually held. These ideas include his theory of forms and accompanying theory of knowledge, his account of the human soul, his political ideas, and his ideas about art. Most notable among the middle dialogues are *Meno, Gorgias, Protagoras, Symposium,* and the incomparable *Republic.*

Finally, the third group of writings bears a more abstruse character. Several of Plato's later dialogues are what now might be called *meta-philosophical*. These dialogues are highly technical, showing a concern for logical and linguistic issues. Chief among the later dialogues are the *Sophist*, the *Statesman*, the *Timaeus, Critias* and the *Laws*. In addition, the later dialogues witness what might be called an "eclipse of Socrates." Socrates is no longer active in the dialogues, but is instead a quiet bystander.

Theory of Knowledge: Opinion Versus Knowledge

The inquiries of the early dialogues lead naturally to Plato's view of knowledge. Plato distinguishes between opinion and knowledge. One might look at figures like Euthyphro, Laches, and some of the other main characters in the early dialogues as having opinions about piety, courage, and other qualities. Opinion about some matter is not the same as ignorance. But it is not philosophical insight either. Opinion is most people's state of mind. Euthyphro has seen pious actions but does not know what piety is. Laches knows soldiers who are courageous but cannot rise to the more philosophically challenging task of defining courage. You might have seen a beautiful work of art or looked at a person and proclaimed him to be beautiful. But you lack the philosophical acumen to define beauty in its essence. Why is this?

The Allegory of the Cave: Different Levels of Knowledge

Plato makes use of a symbolic story to explain ignorance. In the allegory of the cave the prisoners have been chained in a cave since childhood. They are chained by their necks and can only view the wall of a cave right in front of them. Behind them is a fire and other people. The fire casts shadows on the wall before the prisoners, but the prisoners can never see those people or other objects causing the shadows; they know only the shadows.

Imagine that one of the chained persons was set free from his chains and forced to walk toward the fire, past the objects whose shadows he had just seen, and up to the sunlight coming from outside the cave. His eyes, which had been fixed on shadows only, would be unfamiliar with these new sights. He would rather return to his comfortable world of shadowy images on a wall. After a time, however, he would understand that he was looking at the real objects, not just shadows of things and that the sun illuminated these objects. He would understand that the shadows he had previously seen on the wall did not possess the reality of the objects themselves.

But if he was forced down into the cave again and instructed to tell his fellow prisoners what he had seen, they would mock him and think that he was lying or deranged. He might persuade them to come up and see as he had, but he might not be successful in liberating them, for they would be comfortable where they were. Plato says that they might kill him for even trying to free them and show them the truer nature of things.

Plato's symbolic story suggests that most people dwell in the darkness of the cave, happy to live in a world of shadows and appearances, like the kind found on television. They might take the artificial world of fleeting images to be a world of reality, but it is not. Until they turn their eyes toward the fullest reality—symbolized by the light of the sun illuminating the world outside the cave—they will not have a true education. For those liberated from the cave, the highest knowledge is attainable by contemplation. But they cannot remain in such a state. They must come down and educate the others. Plato was convinced that persons could discover a higher reality.

The Divided Line

Plato's Divided Line corresponds with his allegory of the cave. The line symbolizes different levels of being and the mental faculties used to know them. As such, the divided line is a metaphysical and epistemological affair: it lays out four levels of reality and four faculties used to know those realities. The four levels of being are images, objects, mathematical objects, and forms. The faculties used to know them are imagining, belief, thinking, and understanding.

Let's look at examples of each. Images are the tools of artists and poets. The artist who does a watercolor painting of the Empire State Building doesn't capture the reality of the building itself, but presents an image of the object. In creating that image—which has no more reality than the shadow the prisoners see on the cave wall—he uses his imagination. His created image of the building is a level removed—and a level lower—than the actual brick and steel structure standing in New York. We recognize that structure with our senses, especially sight. These two levels and the faculties utilized to know them are in the realm of opinion.

The realm of knowledge does not depend upon sense knowledge. In the realm of knowledge the faculties employed to know things are thinking and reasoning. At the level of thinking, the thinker employs mathematical hypotheses to understand the Empire State Building. One application is that an engineer or architect looks at a building differently than an ordinary citizen does.

When Plato talks about the mathematical level of knowing, the influence of Pythagoras is apparent. Like Pythagoras, he thought that the world at a deeper level was mathematical in nature.

But applied and pure mathematics were not the highest levels of reality. Plato thought that the highest level of reality was the world of ideas or forms.

The forms are pure ideas. Applied to objects like the Empire State Building, the forms are a higher level than the object itself, a pure idea of what the essence of a skyscraper is. Only the highest intelligence can grasp reality at this level. Here understanding works on pure ideas alone, not objects. At this level, a person looking at a beautiful tree or understanding a just action is no longer thinking of those particular things alone.

Understanding is the activity of the philosopher who is thinking of the true nature of beauty or justice in itself. Here one doesn't contemplate holy or courageous or self-controlled persons or actions, but the form or nature of those concepts.

Metaphysics: The Forms

The culmination of the philosophical quest for understanding is knowledge of the world of forms. In a kind of intuitive knowledge the philosopher, who has left behind the world of murky objects and shadowy realities of this world, understands the highest world of ideas in a flash. For the philosopher it is the only knowledge deserving of the name.

If there is a faculty of reason that represents the highest kind of understanding, there must be some corresponding level of reality that is universal and unchanging. The forms are changeless, eternal, and nonmaterial essences, such as eternal patterns of beauty or justice. By comparison, the beautiful objects and just actions you see in your daily life are just copies of the forms. Objects in experience may become beautiful and then cease to be beautiful, but beauty itself has a separate existence from the changing things of this world. Plato maintains that the actual objects of the visible world are only copies of, or "partake" of, the world of forms. Thus every act of goodness, or every triangle you see, is but a copy of the form of the Triangle.

You have already seen the influence of Socrates and Pythagoras on Plato. With the forms you see how the influence of Heraclitus comes into play. In Plato's view, the world of our senses was a world of "becoming;" only the realm of forms was one of complete being. Plato thought that if Heraclitus was right in maintaining that all reality was in flux, then the only faculty appropriate to knowing the world would be opinion. Therefore, there must be an unchanging world that is known.

INSIGHT

Plato said philosophers desire to know the true being of things, or forms. The person holding opinions cannot describe the essence or real being of justice. Knowledge seeks what truly is—it is concerned with Being. Our phenomenal world known by the senses is a world of change and "becoming." The forms have an independent existence in a realm of "being."

According to Plato, our souls were acquainted with the forms before being united with our bodies. Our minds discover the forms in at least three different ways. First there is *recollection.* Before our souls were united with our bodies, the soul was acquainted with the Forms. People thus recollect what their souls knew in a prior state of existence. Visible things remind them of essences previously known. Education is actually a process of reminiscence. Second, people arrive at the knowledge of forms through the activity of *dialectic,* which is the process of abstracting objects and discovering the relations of all divisions of knowledge to each other. And third there is the power of *desire,* or love (eros) which leads people step by step, as Plato described in the *Symposium,* from the beautiful object to the beautiful thought and then to the very essence of Beauty itself.

The theory is metaphysical, but it explains more than that. When people talk about beauty or goodness, they are not talking only about this or that beautiful object or some good action. For to raise the question of whether a philanthropist's generous action is good we first need to (in Socratic fashion) solve a more general question about what goodness is. Knowledge involves more than seeing. It involves understanding.

Political Doctrine

According to Plato, political theory is married with moral theory. In his masterwork, the *Republic,* Socrates searches for the nature and value of justice. The dialogue progresses by following an analogy between the soul of individual men and the constitution of the State. Indeed, Plato held that the State is like a giant person. As justice is the general virtue of the moral person, so also it is justice that characterizes the good society. "We should begin," he says, "by inquiring what justice means in a state. Then we can go on to look for its counterpart on a smaller scale in the individual."

As souls are best when reason governs appetite and spirit, so those states function best where the ruling class governs the soldiers and guards of the State (the spirited class) and the farmer and artisan class (appetites). If such a state functions with this kind of order, it follows the "order" of a well-functioning soul. Plato concluded that this is what we mean by a just state.

Justice Large and Small

So a consideration of justice in the political realm is inseparable from justice in the individual soul. In ethics Plato follows Socrates, taking many of the same positions. For one, Socrates had argued against the Sophists, who maintained that the good life is pleasure. Plato agreed with his teacher's idea that "Knowledge is virtue." In fact, he agreed with Socrates' view of morality in general, accepting Socrates' concept of the soul and the concept of virtue as function.

Plato showed that the idea of virtue as a fulfillment of function is indispensable to his moral and political ideas. Just as things, like hammers and cars, have functions, so Plato also thought the soul had a function. If doctors and musicians and craftsmen are acting well when they are performing their arts correctly, so too a soul is acting well when it is living properly. Living well is a kind of art.

Plato saw a close parallel between the art of music and the art of living. In both cases the art consists of recognizing and obeying the requirements of limit and measure. A musician can only tune his instrument so far and get the right sounds from it. So, too, a sculptor must know how much stone to chisel, else he too will fall short of good art.

So the soul must operate within the limits set by intelligent living. The soul has appetite, spirit, and reason.

The appetites ought to be kept within limits, avoiding excess so as not to usurp the authority of the other parts of the soul. If a person can moderate his love of pleasure and his desires, then he is temperate and possesses the virtue of *temperance.* If he drinks too much or does drugs to excess or engages in sexual activity without restraint, then, Plato says, he is "like a leaky sieve." For just like a person trying to hold water in a vessel with holes in it that water runs through, a person seeking pleasures without control can never get his fill. He is *intemperate,* or lacking in self-control.

Then there is the spirited part of the soul, which is a person's energy of will, but this too must be kept within limits. If such a person is rash, he runs without looking, speaks aggressively without knowing the situation, or acts excessively in some other manner. He has spirit, but his spirit is disconnected to the requirements of the situation. There are people in battle who run recklessly toward the enemy and there are countries that do the same thing. But the person who runs out of his foxhole during infantry battle increases his chances of being shot. His foxhole is for his protection; it increases his chances of survival. If the foxhole is used properly, a soldier can shoot out of it and expose only his helmet, thereby decreasing the chances that the enemy can strike him. But if he acts with just the right amount of spirit, with the right measure, then he is *brave*.

The virtues are interconnected. *Temperance* is the rational control of the appetites, and *courage* is the rational ordering of the spirit. So reason comes into play, reigning over all of them. Only when each part of the soul fulfills its own function is a fourth virtue, *justice,* attained. *Justice* is the general virtue. It reflects a person's well-being and inner harmony, which is achieved only when every part of the soul is fulfilling its proper function.

QUESTION?

Do tragedies result when the appetitive element in the soul overrules reason?
Yes, that would be Plato's interpretation of many personal conflicts. Reason informs the person that he should eat enough to remain healthy, and even to enjoy what he eats. But reason also informs him not to overeat, use drugs, or drink excessively. But the appetites are in armed conflict with reason and often win out.

The Philosopher-King and the Decline of the Idea State

Plato has said that a state governed by reason—a state with justice—is an ideal state.

Individuals and states with out-of-control drives and appetites end in strife, that is, internal anarchy. For harmony to prevail, the rational element must be in control. Who should be the captain of the ship? Should it be the most popular person, or the one who knows the art of navigation? Come to that, who should be a shoemaker or a shipbuilder or a flute player? Isn't the expert the one who is a master in each of these functions? Likewise, who should rule the State?

For Plato there is just one answer: the philosopher-king is the one whose education has led him up step by step through the ascending degrees of knowledge of the Divided Line until at last he possesses knowledge of the Good, that synoptic vision of the interrelation of all truths to one another. To reach this point the philosopher-king requires the right education—mostly in mathematics, metaphysics, and dialectic—right up to the time when he has the vision of the Good and is then ready for the task of governing the State.

States not governed by their most reasonable element will suffer declines. Plato argued that if "there are five forms of government, there must be five kinds of mental constitution among individuals." The five forms of government are *aristocracy, timocracy, plutocracy, democracy,* and *despotism.*

Plato considered the transition from aristocracy to despotism (or rule by a tyrant who wields power oppressively) as a step-by-step decline in the quality of the State corresponding to a gradual deterioration of the moral character of the rulers and the citizens. His ideal state was an aristocracy, since here the rational element embodied in the philosopher-king was supreme and people's reason controlled their appetites. Plato was disenchanted with all governments, especially Athenian democracy because of how it had treated Socrates. "I saw clearly with regard to all states now existing that without exception their system of government is bad." Still, the norm for a state is aristocracy (or rule by a hereditary or noble class; *aristos = best,* + *kratos = rule*).

Less desirable is a *timocracy.* Plato describes this as a state governed on principles of honor and military glory. Timocracy would result from the first stage of decline from an aristocracy. Timocracy represents a love of honor. The problem is that some ambitious members of a ruling class will be insatiably self-seeking and love their own honor more than the common good. In Platonic terms, the spirited parts of their souls will have usurped (overpowered) the role of reason. Timocracy begins a process whereby the irrational part assumes a progressively larger role. It is a short step from love of honor to the desire for wealth, which means allowing the appetites to rule.

Plato said that the ideal society he described in his Republic "can never grow into a reality or see the light of day, and there will be no end to the troubles of states, or indeed of humanity itself, till philosophers become kings in this world, or till those we now call kings and rulers really and truly become philosophers."

Under a timocracy there would be the beginning of a system of private property, and this desire for riches paves the way for a system of government called *plutocracy* (or government by the wealthy *plutos = wealth + kratos = rule*), where power resides in the hands of people whose main concern is wealth. And Plato says, "As the rich rise in social esteem, the virtuous sink." Plutocracy is problematic, primarily because it breaks the unity of the State into two contending classes, the rich and poor. Also, the plutocrat is like the person who seeks constant pleasure. But pleasure is momentary and must therefore be repeated. There can never be a time of perfect satisfaction; the seeker of pleasure can never be satisfied once and for all, any more than a leaky pail can be filled. Still, the plutocrat is torn between many desires because he knows how to distinguish three sorts of appetites: (1) the necessary, (2) the unnecessary, and (3) the lawless. "His better desires will usually keep the upper hand over the worse," and so the plutocrat, Plato says, "presents a more decent appearance than many."

Democracy is a further degeneration still, Plato said, for its principles of equality and freedom reflect the degenerate human characters whose whole range of appetites are all pursued with equal freedom. To be sure, Plato's concept of democracy, and his criticism of it, was based upon his firsthand experience with the special form of participatory democracy in the small city-state of Athens. Here democracy was direct in that all citizens had the right to participate in the government once past the age of eighteen. But this direct popular government violated his notion that the rule of a state should be in the hands of those experts with the special talent and training for it.

Democracy is rule "by the many," Socrates argues in the *Apology*. The problem is that experts, in technical matters and in moral and political matters, are not the many but the few. It is the many who put Socrates to death, so how wise can a democracy be?

Democracy emerged from plutocracy. It started with the sons of the more restrained father-plutocrats, where the goal of life was to become as rich as possible. "This insatiable craving could bring about the transition to democracy," said Plato, for "a society cannot hold wealth in honor and at the same time establish self-control in its citizens." It is when the rich and poor find themselves in a contest under plutocracy that the turning point is reached, for "when the poor win, the result is a democracy." Thus, "liberty and free speech are rife everywhere; anyone is allowed to do what he likes." As a result, Plato concluded, "you are not obliged to be in authority, or to submit to authority if you do not like it."

QUESTION?

Democracy is favored in America and in other countries throughout the world. So why is Plato so critical of it?
It most likely goes back to his theory of knowledge. If ordinary citizens lack the requisite knowledge of certain crafts, like shipbuilding and flute playing, then how will they possess a more difficult kind of knowledge: namely, what is good for the State?

Plato's Ideas about Art

What is the place of art in Plato's ideal state? In both the *Republic* and the *Laws* Plato maintains that art is subordinated to the good of the State. As such, if art needs to be censured for the betterment of the State, it will be.

Plato defended art that imitated Ideal realities, not the photographic imitation of that which can be sensed and individual experiences. He wrote in the *Symposium* that all beautiful things participate in the Idea of beauty.

Attack on Art

Plato's attack on art is that it often presents images that stimulate illusory ideas in the viewer. If people know only these images, they will have a distorted view of the way things really are. The watercolor image of the Empire State Building, the movie that only gives a rough approximation of its bio subject—these fail as works of art because they are so far from the reality they seek to depict.

The *Republic* also introduces Plato's notorious critique of the visual and imitative arts. These arts trade in appearances merely, not realities. Words are even more serious sources of illusion, especially in speechmaking and in rhetoric in general, whether written or spoken. Someone gifted in word usage could certainly deceive one's listeners and pull him away from the truth.

In Book X of the *Republic* Plato spells out what he thinks is wrong with painting and poetry. Both kinds of artists are ignorant of the true nature of their subjects. Defenders of art respond that one can be ignorant and still be a splendid poet. But Plato says ignorance of medicine is inconsistent with being regarded as an expert doctor, but Homer's ignorance shows that one can be a poet without being knowledgeable.

In the earlier dialogues, Socrates contends that the poets lack wisdom, but he also grants that they "say many fine things." But by the time of the *Republic,* it seems there is little that is fine in poetry or any of the other fine arts. Most of poetry and other fine arts will be censored out of existence in Plato's "ideal state," the republic. Another reason Plato opposed the arts is that they arouse excessive and unnatural emotions and appetites.

Why is Plato so opposed to works of art, especially poetry? Since poetic imitation can be accomplished without appeal to the facts, it cannot be an imitation of a thing's true nature.

Evaluation and Significance

Plato's importance in his own time and for centuries to come is beyond dispute. He went beyond Socrates, his teacher, in developing a system of knowledge that includes every area of philosophy. His ideas about the

Forms—and the different faculties to know realities—the soul, his political doctrines, and art are well-argued philosophies.

It may be that no greater praise has been given to a philosopher than that which the American philosopher Alfred North Whitehead (1861–1947) bestowed on Plato. "The safest general characterization of the European philosophical tradition is that it consists of a series of footnotes to Plato," Whitehead said.

In addition, Plato would influence two millennia of rationalists who, like him, viewed reason as the primary means to understanding reality. Plato's student Aristotle took a different philosophical turn. An empiricist and naturalist whose philosophical grounding was in biology, Aristotle opposed Plato's doctrine of the Forms. With such different orientations, the two were bound to clash fundamentally over the issues of what exists (metaphysics) and how we know it (epistemology).

CHAPTER 4

Aristotle: "The Master of Those Who Know"

Beginning his study of philosophy under Plato at the age of eighteen, Aristotle would become one of philosophy's greatest polymaths. He delved into every area—including but not limited to metaphysics, logic, aesthetics, ethics, and political thought. No wonder, then, that St. Thomas Aquinas would later refer to him simply as "The Philosopher." More than two millennia after his death his work is widely read by students of ethics, politics, rhetoric, and theater and every conceivable branch of philosophy. Aristotle is one of the greatest philosophers that ever lived.

The Life of Aristotle

Born in Stagira in the northwestern region of the Aegean, Aristotle (384–322 B.C.) was the son of Nicomachus, a physician to the Macedonian king, Amyntas II. When he was eighteen, Aristotle left for Athens to study and became a member of Plato's Academy. He was in constant contact with Plato, teaching and studying until Plato's death. During the next twelve years, Aristotle taught and conducted research in biology, zoology, botany, and physiology in various places. It was during this period that he taught the boy who later became known as Alexander the Great. With his pedagogical activity at an end, Aristotle left for a time to Stagira, his native city, which Alexander rebuilt as a payment of debt to his teacher.

In 335 Aristotle returned to Athens. For the next twelve years he founded and directed a school, the Lyceum. It was also known as the "Peripatetic School," since people studied while walking about. In 323 Alexander the Great died, and the reaction in Greece against Macedonian suzerainty led to a charge of impiety against Aristotle, who had been closely connected with the leader in his younger days. Aristotle left Athens, "lest the Athenians sin against philosophy a second time," he said, a remark made in clear reference to Socrates. He went to Chalcis in Euboea, where he lived on an estate of his dead mother until he died in 322.

Logic

Aristotle was the first person to systematize the rules of logic. He thought of logic as "a study of proof." His work on logic is found in his *Organon*. This is the title given to the logical works of Aristotle, implying that logic is an "organ" or "tool" used to acquire philosophical knowledge. In other words, logic is for practicing philosophy and is a kind of preparatory study for students of philosophy. There are two principle forms of logical inference: deduction, which yields certain conclusions, and induction, which yields probable conclusions.

Deductive Reasoning

Since Aristotle was chiefly concerned with the form of proof, he was most interested in syllogism, which he assumed provided certain knowledge concerning reality. For instance, in the syllogism "All men are mortal, Socrates is a man, therefore Socrates is mortal," it is not merely that the conclusion is deduced according to the formal laws of logic; Aristotle assumes that the conclusion is verified in reality. With syllogisms, one reasons from the universal (e.g., a principle like "All men are mortal" or "All kindness is good") to a particular instance (e.g., "Bill is mortal" or "Giving to the poor is good").

These are called "categorical syllogisms," since he is referring to categories like "men," "mortal," and a particular man, "Socrates." If the placement of these terms is imperfect, then the form of the syllogism will not work. For instance, if one says, "All Men are Mortal, Socrates is Mortal, so Socrates is a Man," the syllogism has bad form. For reasoning from the first two premises one can only conclude that Socrates is a man, not that he is mortal. Since the form of reasoning is in error, the syllogism commits a formal fallacy and is *invalid*, which means its conclusion does not "follow." Aristotle observed that there are 256 different varieties of syllogism, but only 24 of them are valid, meaning that their conclusions follow with certainty.

Besides syllogistic deductive reasoning, there are three laws of thought that are also known with certainty according to Aristotle. The first is the *principle of contradiction*. This law, or principle, asserts that a statement cannot be true and false at the same time. For example, a person could not logically make the statement "It is raining and it is not raining." Statements of this form are internally contradictory and can never be true.

The second law is the *principle of the excluded middle*. This law says that a statement must be true or false. "It is raining *or* it is not raining" is an example. It is called the principle of the "excluded middle" because it is either raining or not; there is no third or "middle" possibility.

The third law is the *principle of identity*. This principle asserts that everything is equal to itself. The statement "X is equal to X" is true without exception. As with the first two principles, one immediately apprehends this principle. That is, one has an intuitive grasp of its truth, quite apart from any knowledge about the facts of sense experience.

Inductive Reasoning

In the *Analytics* Aristotle considers not only deductive scientific proof or demonstration, but also induction. "Induction proceeds through an enumeration of all the cases," he says. Induction, then, proceeds in the opposite direction, enabling one to reason from a particular instance, like "This swan is white" to a general conclusion like "All swans are white." Proceeding from the particular to the general is just one way in which inductive arguments differ from deductive ones. They are also distinguished by being probable as opposed to being certain. But Aristotle's ideal for reasoning is deduction, or syllogistic, demonstration.

Aristotle's Square of Opposition is one of the most useful educational tools available for anyone trying to develop, attack, or defend a thesis. Someone might contend that "All stealing is wrong." But the square reminds us that to defeat such a universal affirmative thesis we only need one example—in this case "Some stealing is not wrong."

In everyday life, however, few arguments are deductive. There are times when the best one can do in arguing is to arrive at conclusions that are probable. So you might reason: "Whenever I have set my alarm for 6 A.M., it has sounded off at 6 A.M. Therefore, the next time I set it at 6 A.M., it will sound off at 6 A.M." Now it may be true that your alarm will once again sound at 6 A.M., and you hope that it does. The probability that it will sound off is high—close to a probability of one, which is to say close to a certainty. But you cannot be certain that it will; it is a *probability*. So, inductive arguments are those whose conclusions follow with probability. Most of the conclusions about your everyday life would seem to be probable in a similar way.

You expect that it will take you thirty minutes to drive to your job from your home because it *usually* takes thirty minutes. In addition, since your car was running fine yesterday and the day before, you expect that it will run reliably today and tomorrow. Notice that the probability of your getting to work in thirty minutes depends on several factors that are also based on probabilities: the traffic, the weather, the condition of your car, road accidents, and so on. You could calculate the probability of getting to work in thirty minutes by multiplying the probabilities of each of these events.

QUESTION?

Can facts about experiences ever be certain?
It is tempting to think so. For instance, the sun has always risen, so you may conclude that the sun will rise tomorrow. Similarly, since penicillin has always healed your strep throat in the past, you infer that it will help the next time. But both conclusions are merely probable; that is, their probabilities are less than one.

Probabilities play out frequently on the field of sports. In years past, if you have seen a baseball player, say Boston's David Ortiz, hit for a batting average of .300. (equivalent to 30 hits for every 100 at bats), you might expect him to hit .300 this year. In all reasoning of this kind, your conclusions are established by the evidence with a *degree of probability* (with probabilities landing on a spectrum somewhere between 0 and 1) and so are *inductive*. One of the characteristics of such inductive arguments is that you expect that the future will resemble the past.

Metaphysics: Philosophy Begins in Wonder

Aristotle said "All men by nature desire to know." It is intellectual curiosity that drives people to wonder about the nature of reality and the origin of the universe. His statement might have applied to the pre-Socratics (discussed in Chapter 1), with their quest to find the ultimate principles and origins of the universe.

That the love of knowing is what drives metaphysical knowledge is made clear early on in Aristotle's *Metaphysics*:

That it is not a science of production is clear even from the history of the earliest philosophers. For it is owing to their wonder that men both now begin and at first began to philosophize; they wondered originally at the obvious difficulties, then advanced little by little and stated difficulties about the greater matters, e.g. about the phenomena of the moon and those of the sun and stars, and about the genesis of the universe.

Even if there is no material reward in wondering, these men "philosophized in order to escape from ignorance," Aristotle asserts. They were "pursuing science in order to know, and not for any utilitarian end."

Metaphysical knowledge is the science of first principles, or first causes. The earliest philosophers wanted to know the explanation of the things they saw, and so philosophy arose out of the desire to understand. Aristotle thought that the true philosopher is one who desires knowledge about the ultimate causes and nature of reality and desires that knowledge for its own sake, not for any practical use.

Aristotle declares at the beginning of Book IV that metaphysical science is concerned with being as such or being *qua* being. But Aristotle differs with his teacher Plato on the kinds of being there are. Plato had argued for a transcendent world of forms, which existed apart from the world of sensible things that people inhabit. This disagreement brings out their different approaches to knowledge. Plato was the rationalist, claiming that all knowledge could be arrived at using reason and intellect. By contrast, Aristotle was an empiricist, who claimed that all knowledge comes from experience, beginning with sense experiences.

Aristotle's Criticism of Plato's Theory of the Forms

Aristotle's most celebrated difference with his former teacher is his attack on Plato's Theory of the Forms. You will recall from Chapter 3 that Plato argued that besides this *phenomenal* world of sights and sounds and objects that we live in there is a *transcendent* world of absolute, perfect, unchanging ideal forms or eternal essences. Since there can be no knowledge of this changing world of material objects that are revealed to your senses (you can only exercise "belief" and "opinion" about it, as he shows in his Divided Line schema), Plato argues that knowledge can only be of unchanging ideas or forms.

Aristotle makes several objections to his mentor's prized theory. His disagreements stem from Plato's assertion that the forms exist in a separate, transcendent world, outside of the very things that they were supposed to be causes of. This leads to three problems:

1. If forms are essences, they cannot be outside of things; they must be "in" the things of which they are the essential nature. In other words, Aristotle is asking how the essence of a triangle or a beautiful statue can be outside the entities themselves. By contrast, Aristotle insists that the forms of objects are in the objects themselves, as the form of this baseball—its spherical shape, roughly two-inch diameter—is connected to the matter of the ball; that is, its horsehide cover, stitching, and cork center. In sum, form is always coupled with matter—there is no such thing as unmattered form or unformed matter.

2. If forms are static, unchanging entities, as Plato asserts, then, Aristotle asks, how can they be used as "causes" to explain change in the phenomenal world of changing entities? More simply put, how can unchanging entities impart change—for example, motion or change in substance—to phenomenal things?

3. According to Aristotle, it is unclear what it means for the particular objects or things sensed in this world to "participate" in the Forms, or imitate the Forms, as Plato maintains they do. "To say that they (i.e., sensible things) are patterns and the other things share in them, is to use empty words and poetic metaphors," Aristotle replies.

In sum, Aristotle has claimed that Plato's forms are but a purposeless doubling of visible things. The forms are useless for our knowledge of things. "They help in no wise towards the knowledge of the other things."

According to Aristotle, form is always married to matter. There is no unmattered form, nor is there unformed matter, as Plato thought. The water bottle in front of you has matter of plastic, paper, and ink. It also has form or shape, however, since it is cylindrical in nature. It is impossible to talk about either matter or form without talking about the other.

The high-level exchange shows Aristotle's greater interest in the visible universe. Plato was not really concerned with the things of this world for their own sake, but only as stepping stones to the Forms. Aristotle's training was in biology. As such, he saw that form and matter were "in things" and so he placed Plato's doctrine of transcendent forms with his idea of "immanent" forms.

Ethics

Aristotle's ethics are teleological. The Greek root *telos* means "end," "goal," or "purpose." Aristotle sounds the keynote of his moral philosophy in the very first line of the *Nicomachean Ethics:* "Every art and every inquiry, every action and choice, seems to aim at some good; whence the good has rightly been defined as that at which all things aim." But what is the aim or "end" of human behavior? Aristotle says that it is happiness. The means to that end is a state of character he calls virtue. Simply put, a person who lives a virtuous life will have a better chance at attaining happiness than one who lives without virtues.

Happiness

Aristotle explains that the doctor's art aims at health, and the shipbuilder's craft aims at a safe voyage. You could go further and say that the musician's art aims at pleasing melodies and the sculptor's art aims at a fine statue. But these kinds of ends have further ends or goods in view. But there must be some end that is ultimate. This ultimate good will be one you desire for its own sake. Men agree that this good is happiness, he says.

This means that a "right" action is one that promotes happiness. A wrong action is one that is opposed to the attainment of happiness.

But people understand different things by happiness. Some people identify happiness with pleasure, Aristotle says. But surely pleasure is not identical with happiness. For pleasure is fleeting and ephemeral; happiness is a more lasting good. Further, beasts can experience pleasure, so it is not a peculiarly human good. Others equate happiness with honor, like the honor attained by a statesman. But this sort of honor depends more on the giver and is not really our own. By contrast, happiness must be something you can attain by your own activity. Nor can happiness be the activity of growth or reproduction, since even plants can do that much. Nor can happiness be equated with sensation, because even animals are capable of sensations.

Happiness must be an activity of that which is peculiar to man among natural beings—activity in accordance with reason. Now the excellence or virtue of each thing lies in the efficiency of its peculiar function; therefore "human good turns out to be activity of the soul in accordance with virtue, and if there are more than one virtue, in accordance with the best and most complete." In other words, the criteria of the good for man are finality and self-sufficiency—it is valued for its own sake—and its achievement will leave nothing to be desired.

FACT

Aristotle uses the ideas from biology to understand ethics. He studied over 500 different species. He noticed that each has its own end. Tadpoles become frogs and not snakes. So, too, humans have their own proper functions or ends. This is Aristotle's teleological idea of nature applied to ethics.

The good must be found in man's own function as a man. Aristotle turns to his metaphysics and his position on matter and form, potentiality and actuality. The usual illustration is that of the acorn. Relative to the tree the acorn is matter, an unrealized possibility that will eventuate in the actuality of form, the oak tree. Thus the end or "telos" of the acorn is integral to its nature, and its "good" is to fulfill its formal function well—to become a strong well-shaped tree.

For man, this activity will be virtuous, since there are intellectual virtues, like reasoning, and moral virtues, like self-control and courage. So, happiness consists of virtuous activity, not only for brief periods but over the course of a life. This kind of happiness will be incomplete without some external goods. Aristotle says you are aided in the pursuit of happiness by having good parents, friends, a modicum of material well-being, even good looks.

Virtue and the Mean

More than anything, one will be aided in the pursuit of happiness by having virtue. Aristotle defines virtue as a disposition. A disposition is developed over time. For instance, you are not born with courage. You develop a disposition—or capacity—for courage by doing courageous acts. The same is true of cultivating other virtues. You cannot have the disposition to self-control without having practiced discipline on some matter. You cannot keep from acting like a buffoon without some instruction or experience in the matter. All this indicates that the virtues are acquired, not innate.

Aristotle's mean is not an exact mathematical term. He says the mean is "relative to us." Therefore, the mean amount for a wealthy person like Donald Trump to give at a wedding is different from the mean amount for a person of average wealth. Naturally, the mean is affected in other ways, too. A parent of the bride and groom will probably not observe the same mean in giving that a mere acquaintance or coworker would.

A love of proportion and order can be seen in Greek art and drama. And in discussing virtue Aristotle adopts a very Greek notion of proportion. Good actions must have a certain proportion. A virtuous action is a "mean" between two extremes. *Mean* is a mathematical term meaning "a midway point." Each of the extremes is a vice. For example, in the act of giving money, the good action will be to give the right amount, which lies between giving too much on the one hand, and not giving enough on the other. You cannot give so much to the bride and groom on their wedding day that you have nothing left for yourself. That is the vice of excess. On the other hand, you cannot give so little that your giving is stingy—that is the vice of defect. There is a mean amount to give.

Aristotle's concept of the midway point between excessive and defective actions has been referred to as the "Golden Mean."

Having a virtuous character is a means to the end of human happiness. People with the vices stand less of a chance of attaining happiness than those without them.

QUESTION?

Can there be a mean for activities like stealing, adultery, and cheating?

No, for Aristotle, there can never be a proper amount of adultery, cheating, stealing, or other inherently bad activities. A mean is between extremes, both of which are vices. The mean between them is virtues. But with bad things even the mean is inappropriate.

Political Thinking

The State forms the basis of Aristotle's political thinking. When Aristotle writes about the State, it is the Greek city-state or "polis" that he has in mind. The State comes into existence for the bare ends of life, but it continues in existence for the sake of the good life. So the State is a necessary means to a valued end. The goal of the State is providing a good life for its citizens, a life of happiness based upon virtue. In the absence of such a state, citizens cannot live moral lives, since man is a political or social animal by nature.

Like every other community, the State exists for a purpose or end. In the case of the State this end is the supreme good of man, allowing for the cultivation of citizens' moral and intellectual life. In order to fulfill himself in this life, man must activate his social life, which requires existence within society. The State must be considered the instrument by which man may attain his goal. So the purpose of the State is that of ethical training for the benefit of its citizens.

Just as the highest virtue of the individual is intellectual activity, so the highest duty of society is that of achieving and making the proper use of a state of peace. Man's natural condition is not one of war, as the Spartans thought, but one of peace.

Different Types of Government

Like Plato, Aristotle declared his preference for aristocracy, which literally means "rule by the best or excellent." This would not be a government based on the arbitrary rights of an individual—as with the divine right of kings—but a government under the leadership of one person who is by nature and education best qualified for the task of governing. But Aristotle added the qualification that the actual *form* of government is not crucial. Any form of government is good whose primary consideration is public welfare. Corrupt governments are those that, on the contrary, place the private concerns of the rulers above the public interest.

Aristotle again shows the influence of his teacher Plato in the types of government he chooses to discuss. Aristotle discusses six types: monarchy, aristocracy, polity, tyranny, oligarchy, and democracy. He maintained that the first three forms of government were good and laudable for having the welfare of their citizens at heart. By contrast, the other three are defective: in these rulers seek their own personal gain first. This is the reason that Aristotle ultimately prefers control by one or more intellectually and morally superior person (monarchy) or by a few such persons (aristocracy).

Government Not for the Good of All

As commonsensical as Aristotle made his preference for aristocracy seem, whole sections of the population would of necessity be excluded from his government. Since women, children, and slaves were considered inferior, they were shut out from the process of government. Aristotle regarded slavery as a natural phenomenon and thus condoned the practice.

In fact, he saw the justification for slavery as being rooted in nature rather than nurture. He regarded slaves as those who lack intellectual endowment and so prefer to be ruled rather than command. The slave also prefers to follow rather than think for himself. The master, on the other hand, thinks and acts for himself. He is also executive in nature, not passive, and he issues orders and assumes responsibility. Together, each augments the happiness of the other. Apart, unhappiness results, for they work together in unison and they must work harmoniously in their respective, natural roles.

Aesthetics

Like his ethics and political philosophy, aesthetics is seen by Aristotle as a practical art, concerned more with action than with theorizing. The core of his aesthetic theory can be found in two books: his *Rhetoric* and *Poetics.* He spells out his actual theory of art in the *Poetics,* writing that all art is imitation. The purpose of art is to stimulate man's emotions in such a manner that he will be able to find release from emotional stress and regain his poise and serenity.

Similarly, even amusements and recreational activities are imitative arts, releasing pent-up pressures which put a strain upon the soul. Aristotle called this relaxation *catharsis,* a purification of the soul by relieving or healing it or its intense passions. In this way, it is hoped that all the intense feelings become relaxed. Were Aristotle alive today, he would argue that sporting events such as soccer matches, boxing, and football have value for spectators, because they experience an emotional release.

QUESTION?

Do violent sporting events always provide a catharsis, or purging for spectators?
Aristotle thought that the purification spectators felt during tragedies purged or purified them by relieving intense passions. But evidence shows that this is not always so at sporting events, where fans sometimes riot in the grandstands and in the streets before and after games.

Art as Imitation: Plato and Aristotle

Aristotle accepts that art is imitation. The visual arts like paintings and sculptures mimic objects like beautiful buildings or religious figures. It is the artist's job to copy the essence or form rather than the individual object as such. In so doing the artist idealizes the subject matter rather than simply making a direct copy.

Plato would agree with Aristotle that art is imitative. But that is where the agreement ends. For Plato, art is not only a copy of reality, but an inferior copy. The form of David in Michelangelo's status is several levels away from the form David. The marble statue is an entity once removed from the actual man. The actual David is in turn once removed from the ideal man. So Plato maintained that art was thrice removed from what is real. It is ontologically inferior to the world of forms.

Because Aristotle disagreed with Plato on the location of the forms, he didn't accept Plato's conclusion about the inferior imitative nature of art. The form, or essence, of David is captured by the artist and is married to the material marble. The watercolor of the Empire State Building that Plato would protest against might capture the essence of the majestic skyscraper, according to Aristotle.

Aristotle thought that tragedy was imitative, too. Tragedy imitates serious events, often events of life and death, by employing beautiful language. Music, painting, and poetry are similar forms of artistic expression. Whereas Plato thought that these art forms engaged the emotions of the viewers and corrupted their appreciation of the truth, Aristotle thought that tragedy was cathartic. The audience identifies with the characters through sympathy and thereby relieves their fear and grief over the tragic events. The playgoer, liberated from such intense emotions, regains his tranquility.

Evaluation and Significance

Soon after Plato's death, Aristotle praised him as a man "whom bad men have not even the right to praise and who showed in his life and teachings how to be happy and good at the same time." Despite this unparalleled respect and affection for Plato, Aristotle was an independent and innovative thinker. He was not merely happy to repeat the ideas of his beloved teacher. He modified some ideas and rejected others.

The philosophy of Aristotle cast such an enormous shadow, that for centuries after, right through the modern period two millennia after his death, philosophers either fell into the empiricist camp of Aristotle or the rationalist camp of Plato.

There were also vast stylistic differences between the two. Plato is commonly described as idealistic, otherworldly, inspiring, and as a perfectionist. By contrast, Aristotle is described as realistic, scientific, this-worldly, and pragmatic.

CHAPTER 5

Stoics: The Practical Philosophy

After the death of Alexander the Great in 323 B.C. and Aristotle in 322, several social shifts in Greece led to the emergence of different philosophies. Political life in Greece changed dramatically. Wars between Greek city-states robbed their independence, alienating the average citizen from participation in government. With this disillusionment over institutions such as government came a decline in popular religion. People now longed for more individual, practical philosophies of life. The two most popular philosophies to emerge during the Hellenistic (or quasi-Greek) period were Epicureanism and Stoicism.

History of Post-Aristotelian Greece

With the end of the free and independent Greek city-states like Athens, Corinth, and Sparta, it would not be long before Greece was to become a province of the Roman Empire. Plato and Aristotle were born into the Greek city-state. In their minds, free men could only flourish in the life of the city, and the life of the city could only flourish with free men. In the language of Aristotle, free citizens could only attain their "ends" (or goals or purposes) if they partook of the richness of city life.

After the death of the great conqueror Alexander, the East opened up to the influence of the West. It was now more appropriate to speak of Hellenistic (as opposed to National-Hellenic) than of Hellenic civilization. Greece could no longer remain uninfluenced by this new state of affairs. The free city was joined with a more cosmopolitan whole. Cosmopolitanism and individualism were to be fused. The individual was no longer tied to his city-state identity, but cast into a larger whole. The result of this fusion was Stoicism and Epicureanism, each of which had an ethical and practical emphasis. The study of metaphysics and cosmology had receded into the background.

The post-Aristotelian schools of the Roman period were more interested in practical, moral matters than they were in metaphysical speculation. The old Romans had insisted on attention to character and a code of living to build that character. Now that the ideal of the old Roman Republic had been replaced, it was the calling of philosophers to come up with a code for living. With this emphasis on practical and moral standards of living, philosophy gained more popular appeal among the cultured classes of the Hellenistic-Roman world.

Philosophy in the Roman period became more and more part of the regular course of education, in its own manner becoming a rival to Christianity when the new religion began to lay claim to the allegiance of the empire. Philosophy, as a kind of secular religion, could play a part in satisfying the religious aspirations of mankind. After all, disbelief in popular mythology at this point was common. Adherents of an ethical philosophy like Stoicism could find religious elements there. When Neo-Platonism arises, where the last remnants of ancient philosophy are manifest, philosophy and religion mesh. Philosophy passes over into religion with Plotinus's

Neo-Platonism, for it is a kind of mystical ecstasy that represents the highest point of that philosophy.

Lives of the Stoics

Stoicism was a Greek school of philosophy founded around 300 B.C. in Athens by Zeno of Citium. In little time it would develop into the dominant philosophy of the Roman Empire. The word *stoa* from which "Stoic" derives is the Greek word for "porch." This owes to Zeno delivering his lectures from the "painted porch," which was a public building in the Greek agora, or marketplace. The essence of the Stoic belief was that one should resign oneself to fate, perform one's appointed duties faithfully, and thereby acquire tranquility of mind.

The most famous Stoic was also a Roman emperor. Marcus Aurelius was a prominent Stoic whose collection of journal entries entitled *Meditations* is a quintessential distillation of Stoic thought and practice.

Zeno of Citium

Zeno was born around 336 or 335 B.C. and died about 264 or 263 B.C. in Athens. He likely followed his father in commercial activity. It appears that his first philosophical influences were at the age of twenty. He read the *Memorabilia* of Xenophon and *Apology* of Plato and was filled with admiration for Socrates' character. In approximately 300 B.C. he founded his own philosophic school, where he lectured. Of his writings only the smallest fragments remain. He is said to have taken his own life.

Cleanthes of Assos took over Zeno's leadership of the school and Cleanthes in turn was succeeded by Chrysippus of Soloi in Cilicia, who was known as the second founder of the school because of his systematization of the Stoic doctrines. All told, he wrote some 705 treatises, which were better known for their dialectical method than their style of composition.

Epictetus

A later Stoic, Epictetus (A.D. c. 50–c. 138) was born a Greek slave in Asia Minor. He was crippled in slavery, which no doubt influenced his spirited motto: "Bear and forbear." He was freed sometime after the death of Nero in 68. He was known as a kind man, who was humble and charitable, especially to children. He embraced Stoicism and taught that people should submit to fate as God's sacred gift and design. Epictetus did not write down his philosophy, but Flavius Arrianus, a student at his school at Nicopolis, composed eight books based on Epictetus's lectures. Of these eight books only four remain. He also published a small catechism, or handbook, of his doctrines, the *Encheiridion.*

Zeno: A Virtuous Life

Because so little of what Zeno wrote survives, little is known of his philosophy. Contemporary knowledge of the Stoics who followed is greater. But the beginnings of what could be referred to as a Stoic ethic is seen in his work.

According to Zeno, nature has implanted in all people an instinct for self-preservation, which might mean self-perfection or self-development. Humans have reason, which animals lack. So one must live a life "in accordance with nature," Zeno said. By this he meant life in accordance with "our" nature, which is reason. Reason leads to virtue.

Some people are turned off by the philosophy of Stoicism. They dislike the viewpoint that God shapes their lives and that little can be done about it. When trials and tribulations occur, the Stoics seem to be saying that there is a divinely ordered reason that these things happen and there isn't much people can do. If this is true, why make any effort at all?

There is also a larger meaning to "living in accord with nature," according to Zeno. Our nature is part of the nature of the universe. Here the ethical lesson for us is to do nothing that nature would forbid, nothing that goes against the reason that is part of all things and is identical with Zeus, the guide and governor of the universe.

Epictetus

Despite his severely compromised physical condition, Epictetus's philosophy is unfailingly positive. According to Epictetus, all men have the capacity for virtue. God has given to all men the means of becoming happy, which requires steadfast character and self-control. The kind of self-control he stresses has two chief parts: the control of your own attitude toward reality and the control of your senses.

The Stoics sought happiness through embracing the wisdom to accept whatever happens in life. Centuries after Socrates met his death with courage and equanimity, Epictetus wrote, "I cannot escape death, but I can escape the dread of it." You cannot control all events but you can control your attitude toward what happens. It is possible by an act of will to control your fear.

Epictetus revealed this part of his philosophy in several portions of the handbook:

5. It is not things that upset people but rather ideas about things. For example, death is nothing terrible, else it would have seemed so even to Socrates; rather it is the idea that death is terrible that is terrible. So whenever we are frustrated or upset or grieved, let us not blame others, but ourselves— that is, our ideas. It is the act of a philosophically ignorant person to blame others for his own troubles. One who is beginning to learn blames himself. An educated person blames neither anyone else nor himself.

In a similar vein he said,

8. Don't seek for things to happen as you wish, but wish for things to happen as they do, and you will get on well.

And again,

10. Whatever occasion befalls you, remember to turn around and look into yourself to see what power you have to make use of it. If you see a handsome boy or a beautiful girl, you will find the relevant power to be self-controlled. If labor is heaped on you, end; endurance is what you need; if abuse, forbearance. And thus habituating yourself, you will not be carried away by impressions.

*41. It is the sign of a weak mind to spend too much time on things hav-
ing to do with the body, such as exercising a lot, eating a lot, drinking a lot,
excreting, sex. Such things should be done incidentally; let your attention be
concentrated on your mind.*

Epictetus's basic ideas keep getting repeated. People have the necessary degree of self-control to not be overwhelmed by events, even ultimate
events like death. Regarding the control of the senses, individuals also have
the strength to refrain from the pleasures of food, drink, and sex. You can
see how Epictetus's underlying philosophy of "bear and forbear" keeps
appearing in his ethic.

Ethics and the Human Drama

According to Epictetus moral philosophy rested upon a simple insight,
wherein each person is an actor in a drama. What Epictetus meant when
he used this image was that an actor does not choose a role, but on the
contrary it is the author or director of the drama who selects people to play
the various roles. God determines what each person shall be and how he
or she will be situated in history. The Stoics thought it was wise for people
to recognize their role in the drama.

The Stoics tell you that as an actor, you may not be able to tell the story.
You can sulk because you play only bit parts or be consumed with jeal-
ousy if someone else is chosen to be the hero in the drama. But if you can
control your attitude and emotions and remain free from these feelings, or
develop what the Stoics call *apathy,* you will achieve a serenity and happiness that are the mark of a wise person.

The Problem of Freedom

If actors do not choose their roles in whatever drama they are acting
out, how can they know that they will choose their attitudes? The Stoics
held to the notion that attitudes are under the control of a person's choice,
but this may be a mere hope. For if providence rules everything, how can
it not rule a person's attitudes? The closest Stoics came to accounting for
this is to say that while everything in the universe behaves according to
divine law, happiness is not a by-product of choice; rather, it is a quality of

existence, which follows from agreeing to what has to be. Freedom, therefore, is not the power to alter your destiny but rather the absence of emotional disturbance.

QUESTION?

Will a person who practices Stoicism think about death at all?
Most people think about death eventually. But Stoics detach themselves from it emotionally, knowing that it must come. The question illustrates one of the problems at the heart of Stoicism: Divine Law rules all, leaving you to control your attitudes toward challenging events.

For Epicurus freedom was especially problematic. This is because Epicurus, like Democritus (460–371 B.C.) before him, was an atomist who believed the finest components of things were atoms that moved regularly in parallel lines.

Democritus contended that all things are composed of atoms and the void. He maintained that reality was composed of being (itself composed of atoms) and not-being (the void), which must exist for any motion of atoms to be possible. Democritus distinguished between "obscure knowledge" obtained by the senses, and "genuine knowledge," which, if it were attainable by humans, would be knowledge of atoms and the void. Democritus thought that sense perception and even thought itself depended on the movements and amassing of atoms.

But Epicurus changed Democritus's materialism by insisting that some atoms "swerved in the void" from their course by a spontaneous act of free will. This random swerve allowed Epicurus to accept the world as mechanistic but still reject determinism as an explanation of human behavior. Free will was preserved.

Epicurus: The Life of Pleasure

Epicurus (341–270 B.C.), a Greek philosopher who was born on the isle of Samos, lived much of his life in Athens, where he founded his successful school of philosophy, called the "Garden," because of the meeting place of the school. To Epicurus the chief aim of human life is pleasure. This is mistakenly linked today with gluttony and an "eat, drink, and be merry" approach toward life. Epicurus distinguished various types of pleasures. For example, some are intense but last only a short time, and others are not so intense but last longer. Also, some pleasures have a painful aftermath, while others offer a sense of calm and repose.

According to Epicurus, all people have an immediate feeling of the difference between pleasure and pain. "We recognize pleasure as the first good innate in us," he said, "and from pleasure we begin every act of choice and avoidance, and to pleasure we return again." But he distinguished between various kinds of pleasures. Some desires are natural and necessary, like food. Others are natural but not necessary, as in the case of some types of sexual pleasure. Still others are neither natural nor necessary—for example, any type of luxury or popularity.

QUESTION?

What might a Stoic say about caring deeply about a fine car and other luxuries?
Stoics believe that it is appropriate to enjoy beautiful things, both material things and things in nature. But someone who has a dependency on such things gets completely out of sorts when the car gets ruined in an accident or stolen off the street. So Stoics would counsel that you give material things only the status they deserve and not let them rule your life.

The Greatest Pleasure Is Freedom from Pain and Distraction

The philosophy of Epicurus is not what Epicureanism stands for today— a sensuous, profligate lifestyle or the elaborate tastes of a gourmet. In fact, he believed almost the opposite. The true life of pleasure consisted in an attitude of imperturbable emotional calm, which required only the simpler things of life. The Epicureans turned in the direction of an ideal for living, which they called *ataraxia,* or tranquility of soul.

The ultimate pleasure humans seek is repose, Epicurus said. By this he means the absence of bodily pain and the gentle relaxation of the mind. This sense of repose can best be achieved by scaling down your desires, overcoming useless fears, and, above all, turning to the pleasures of the mind, which have the highest degree of permanence.

You need a basic but healthy diet, a prudent moral life—where people keep their agreements—and good friends. In the interests of well-being, you must constrain your pleasures. What should you fear? Only the things you know. Since only good or bad sensations (pleasures or pains) should concern you, and death is not a sensation, you should not fear death.

In his *Letter to Menoeceus* Epicurus wrote:

When we maintain that pleasure is the end, we do not mean the pleasure of profligates and those that consist of sensuality, as is supposed by some who are either ignorant or disagree with us or do not understand, but freedom from pain in the body and from trouble in the mind. For it is not continuous drinkings and revelings, nor the satisfaction of lusts, or the enjoyment of fish and other luxuries of the wealthy table, which produce a pleasant life, but sober reasoning, searching out the motives for all choice and avoidance, and banishing mere opinions, to which are due the greatest disturbance of the spirit.

Does it look like Epicurus had returned to that typical Greek idea of shunning excesses? Yes, he believed in a life of moderation. The most virtuous among us realizes which pleasures are the most satisfying and chooses to shun those pleasures which produce pain. The safest and most desirable life is one of simple pleasures. The wise person has learned to need little and lives prudently.

Epicurus was not a prude or a puritan. He did not say that people should seek only tranquility of the soul. According to him, physical pleasures are fine and people should not avoid them completely. In fact, he said, "Pleasure is the starting-point and the end of living blissfully. For we recognize pleasure as a good which is primary and innate."

Individual Pleasure Versus Social Duty

For Epicurus one does not find the good life through service to human beings, but in the pleasant, decent company of intellectually fascinating friends. He would as readily detach himself from the company of poor people, whose needs are many, as he would from the tyranny of exotic foods.

Evaluation and Significance

Stoicism has lived more than two millennia, with the best evidence of its survival being recent books about how to maintain tranquility in the face of turmoil. Despite its staying power, Stoicism has had to fend off several criticisms. For one, some read Stoicism as recommending a life of apathy or indifference to circumstances, including the pain of others. If you cannot alleviate the suffering of another human being, even a child, you should not feel awful. If you did what you could to help but failed, then what happened was meant to be. So Seneca, the Stoic philosopher, said pity is not a virtue but a "mental defect." As quoted by Bertrand Russell in *A History of Western Philosophy*, Seneca said:

Pity is the sorrow of the mind brought about by sight of the distress or sadness caused by the ills of others which it believes comes undeservedly. But no sorrow befalls the wise man.

This led Bertrand Russell, surely one of the greatest philosophers of the twentieth century, to conclude that there is "a certain coldness in the Stoic conception of virtue. Not only bad passions are condemned but all passions."

One of the reasons that Stoicism had such appeal for 500 years was that it coincided with the Christian tradition, even as it was waning as a philosophical movement. Stoicism provided comfort for the Christians, who were under the yoke of a cruel and corrupt Roman government. Like the Stoics, the Christians could derive freedom from detachment, since they knew that the pains of this world are ultimately insignificant in the course of eternity. A purpose can be found in even the most horrible of evils.

CHAPTER 6

Early Medieval Philosophy: St. Augustine

Following the practical ethics of the Stoic period, the era of Christendom dominated Rome. The medieval period in philosophy wouldn't begin until 529 when Justinian I closed the Academy in Athens. Until that time, St. Aurelius Augustine (354–430) was the chief representative of "patristic" philosophy, so-called because it was a set of philosophical doctrines accepted by the Fathers of the early church. Patristic thought was preoccupied with "apologetics," or defending Christian faith against the claims of secular philosophy. When a conflict arose between faith and reason, Augustine resolved the conflict in favor of faith.

The Life of St. Augustine

Augustine was also known as Aurelius Augustinius and Augustine of Hippo. He was born in Tagaste, a provincial Roman city in Algeria in North Africa. His upbringing exhibited a dual influence, since his mother, Monica, was a Christian and his father, Patricius, was a pagan. At age seventeen he headed to Carthage to pursue an education in rhetoric. He also lived a hedonistic lifestyle for a time. In Carthage he developed a relationship with a young woman who would be his concubine for over fifteen years, with whom he had a son. Before the age of twenty he had turned his back on Christianity, since his Christian ideas seemed inadequate to him. In particular, he was perplexed by the problem of moral evil. The Christians said that God is the creator of all things and that God is good. How, then, is it possible for evil to arise out of a world that a perfectly good God had created?

Because Augustine could not find an answer, he turned away from Christianity and toward the Manichees. His mother was horrified. Their philosophy of Manichaeism said that two principles—those of darkness, or evil, and the principle of light, or good—worked together in the universe. The two principles were equally eternal, but eternally in conflict with each other. Things grouped under evil—like excess sensual desires—could be attributed to this external power of darkness.

His mother kept after him to return to Catholicism, but it was the bishop of Milan, St. Ambrose, who exerted the greatest influence in this regard. A master rhetorician like Augustine, Ambrose was also older and more experienced. Influenced by Ambrose's sermons and other studies, Augustine turned from Manichaeism. His search for truth brought him to Plotinus (205–270), a neo-Platonic thinker and Christian who in his *Enneads* argued that man has cut himself off from God and must return to him to find eternal blessedness.

FACT

A turning point in Augustine's conversion to Christianity was the voice of a small girl he heard at one point telling him in a sing-song voice to *tolle lege* (take up and read) the Bible, at which point he opened the Bible at random and fell upon a passage from St. Paul.

Augustine's mother hankered for him to return to Catholicism. Her efforts bore fruit in 386. When Augustine was 32 he underwent a conversion experience and decided to enter the Christian church. His *Confessions* reveal how he now rejected his libertine ways in Carthage and his life of debauchery, "seduced and seducing, deceived and deceiving in divers lusts."

He returned to North Africa and lived in a monastic community for two years. After he was ordained he became assistant to Valerius, the Bishop of Hippo, and eventually succeeded him in the bishopric. He performed his clerical duties, preached, and travelled until his death in 430.

Overcoming Skepticism

As a thinker, Augustine had a great affinity for Plato and his doctrines. While Plato thought of the philosopher's vision of the forms, Augustine referred to religious vision, a theory of illumination. "There is present in us the light of eternal reason, in which light the immutable truths are seen," he said. For Augustine, this illumination comes from God just as light comes from the sun. It is the illumination of your judgment whereby you are able to discern that certain ideas contain necessary and eternal truths. But the skeptics of the Platonic school, especially Pyrrho of Elis (360–270 B.C.), expressed doubts that human beings could know anything at all with certainty. Augustine thought that skepticism must be laid to rest before any knowledge could be attained.

In his early work *Against the Academics* he addressed himself to the skeptics of the New Platonic Academy (a period in the Academy dominated by Carneades, 213–129 B.C.) The skeptics held two theses: (1) Nothing can be known, and (2) assent should not be given to anything. For Augustine, it wasn't just pursuit of the truth that made someone happy—it was the finding of the truth; therefore he believed a way out of skepticism must be found.

Skepticism and Logical Truths

Augustine sought to answer the skeptics. He did this by showing that they were mistaken in assuming that certain knowledge was impossible.

When the skeptics say, for example, that you cannot attain certainty and that only probable knowledge is possible, they fail to realize that probability is a step toward certainty. So Augustine's tactic is to use the experience of uncertainty and doubt against the skeptics.

Human reason does indeed have certainty about various concepts. You know, for example, that the principle of contradiction, as stated by Aristotle, is true. That is, a thing cannot both be and not be at the same time. Can it ever be true, for example, that it is raining and not raining at the same time and in the same respect? No, it can never be. So the skeptics are wrong to say that no knowledge is certain, since logical principles are certain.

FACT

A minority hold the opinion that Augustine is a heretic because of his acceptance of the filioque clause (meaning "and from the son") that was added to the Nicene Creed. The original creed reads "We believe in the Holy Spirit . . . who proceeds from the Father"; the amended version reads "We believe in the Holy Spirit . . . who proceeds from the Father *and the Son*" (italics mine). The addition is accepted by Roman Catholic Christians but rejected by Eastern Orthodox Christians.

I Doubt; Therefore, I Am: Si Fallor Sum

An extreme skeptic, Pyrrho (360–270 B.C.) had declared that sense experiences can never yield knowledge. All you can know are your private sensations. You can never know that your sensations agree with their objects. For instance, if you see a silver quarter, you can say, "The quarter *appears* silver to me." But you can never *know* that it is.

That example refers to sight, but the same applies to taste. You can say, "The honey *appears* sweet to me or *tastes* sweet to me." But you cannot say for sure "The honey *is* sweet." To the Skeptic, therefore, the prudent approach is to suspend judgment and assume nothing at all. The same would hold for moral judgments. Since you cannot know anything for sure, you should stop striving for absolute moral truth—and probably be more tolerant of a variety of viewpoints.

Augustine's book *The Confessions* is a landmark in spiritual literature. It is the first western autobiography and is a brutally honest record of Augustine's own spiritual journey. It reveals his bouts with spiritual doubts and is a confession of his own hedonistic lifestyle before his conversion to Christianity.

As with his example of the principle of contradiction, Augustine replied by trying to show that there is at least one thing you can know with certainty. The skeptic may doubt that the coin is silver or the wine is bitter, but they cannot doubt the existence of perception itself. A person who doubts all truths is thus caught in a logical dilemma. For even the act of doubting is a form of certainty. The individual remembers what he is doing in the very act of self-doubt. If you doubt that it's now seven o'clock at night, at least you cannot doubt that you are doubting.

Surely, *you must exist* in order to doubt. In other words, you can prove the absolute reality of your own soul. Augustine said *Si Fallor sum:* if one can doubt then one surely is. You cannot doubt that you live and understand either. So Augustine shows skepticism can be defeated.

Faith and Reason

From the apologetics of the patristic period through the medieval period, philosophers tried to understand the proper mix of the two faculties of reason and faith in a person's life. Which of the two should someone use to understand the world? According to Augustine, philosophy must include both.

Augustine believed that reason can never be religiously neutral. Reason is not one independent approach to the truth while faith is another. Reason is a function of the whole person and is affected by the orientation of your heart, your passion, and your faith. As he puts it, "Faith seeks, understanding finds; whence the prophet says, 'Unless ye believe, ye shall not understand.'"

The faith and reason issue also applies to moral knowledge. Contrary to the Socratic dictum that "Virtue is knowledge," and that knowing leads you to pursue the truth, Augustine maintained, as a result of his own moral struggles, that knowledge does not produce goodness." According to Augustine, "Faith goes before; understanding follows after."

"I Believe That I Might Understand"

Augustine used reason to work out his own doctrines and to agree with or refute the doctrines of others. He was also a man of faith. As a philosopher, however, he had to inquire and pursue the truth. True philosophy had to join faith and reason, he thought. But according to Augustine, faith was primary.

Augustine embraced the dictum *Credo ut intellegium*—"I believe that I might understand." If one first believes, understanding will come. To Augustine, wisdom was Christian wisdom. In fact, there could be no distinction between theology and philosophy. You cannot philosophize until your wills are transformed; that type of clear thinking is possible only under the influence of God's grace.

Thomas Aquinas would later write, "Whenever Augustine, who was imbued with the theories of the Platonists, found in their writings anything consistent with the faith, he adopted it; and whatever he found contrary to the faith, he amended."

Creation Ex Nihilo

Augustine believed in a supreme being who created the world *ex nihilo*, literally "from nothing." Against Plotinus and Plato, Augustine stressed that the world is the product of God's free act, whereby he brings into being, out of nothing, all the things that make up the world. All things, then, owe their existence to God. Plato thought that God was a "Demiurge," or craftsman, who gave form to already existing matter. And Plotinus, a Neo-Platonist, saw the world as the overflowing and continuation of God.

But for Augustine matters are different. There is a sharp distinction between God and the things he created. Augustine speaks of God as bringing into existence what did not exist before. He could not have created the world out of existing matter, because matter, even in a primary form, would already be something. Everything, including matter, is the result of God's creative act. Matter is essentially good in nature since God creates matter, and God cannot create anything evil. This affects his theory of God and evil, which we will cover in the next section.

Augustine accepted the notion of Creation as recounted in *Genesis*. There it is explained that God created the world from nothing. He therefore rejected the Greek notion that the world was formed out of pre-existing matter. Further, he believed that reason confirmed this. Augustine insisted that everything is form and matter and likened his idea of form and matter to Plato's. But he did not accept Plato's idea that the forms exist independently. Rather, the forms exist in God's mind. He also rejected Plato's conception of the "Demiurge" as a craftsman or architect imposing order on pre-existing matter. Augustine contended that such formless matter would require a creator to cause it to exist.

Augustine said that if the heavens and earth could speak they would cry out, "We did not make ourselves, we were made by him who abides for eternity."

Augustine's View of God

Augustine has already explained his notion of God as the being who created the universe *ex nihilo*. There are several other components to this view. First, Augustine provided an argument for the existence of God. More famously, he gave an explanation of how God's goodness could be explained in light of the evils in the world.

Augustine's Neo-Platonism

Augustine was a Neo-Platonist, meaning he accepted Plato's notion of a world of physical realities knowable by the senses and a world of eternal objects known only by thought. Physical realities are particular, temporal, and changing, and they are known from experience. By contrast, mathematical laws and numbers are universal, eternal, unchanging, and discovered only through the intellect.

Though Augustine is in the Platonic tradition, he had several points of disagreement with Plato. Augustine didn't devalue the senses as much as Plato, since he believed that God created them, along with the natural world they reveal. Also, Plato believed that the mind retains knowledge from a previous existence before this life. Augustine could not accept this view, since there is no mind with information prior to birth when beings are "ensouled."

To explain how the human mind knows higher truths, Augustine invokes his theory of illumination. "There is present in us the light of eternal reason, in which light the immutable truths are seen," he wrote. For Augustine, this illumination comes from God, just as light comes from the sun.

Neither does Augustine believe that these truths are known via the natural intellect, as the philosopher knows Plato's forms. Rather, Augustine claimed that you discover these eternal truths through the illumination of the divine light. He believed that the divine light is to the mind as the sun is to the eyes—a metaphor straight out of Plato's allegory of the cave. Every human mind needs God's light to uncover the forms or to see the truth. If a person thinks she has discovered this on her own, she simply misunderstood the source of their light.

He also includes ethical truths among those higher truths known by the intellect. Truths like "We should live justly," "The worse should be subordinate to the better," "Equals should be compared with equals," and "To each should be given his own" are also "immutable truths of reason," according to Augustine. They are not human creations but objective truths that we discover.

Notice that this is a "causal" argument for God's existence. It might be recapitulated with two premises and a conclusion:

- Persons have ideas of eternal truths.
- They could not have arrived at these truths on their own.
- Therefore, to arrive at these truths they need the illumination that comes from God.

The eternal truths in the human mind are like effects. These effects require causes, and that cause is God.

God and the Problem of Evil

When he was a young man, Augustine's Christian ideas seemed inadequate to him. He was flummoxed by the ever-present problem of moral evil. The Christians said that God is the creator of all things and that God is good. How, then, is it possible for evil to arise out of a world that a perfectly good God had created? Because the young Augustine could not find an answer to this question, he turned away from Christianity.

Ever since the time of Augustine, more than 1,500 years ago, one of the most difficult problems facing believers is the problem of evil. What is the problem of evil and in what ways does Augustine try to solve it? If God is all-knowing, all-powerful, and all-good, how is it that evil exists in the world? Breaking it down further, if God is all-knowing, he knows *how* to stop evil. If he is all-powerful, he *can* stop evil. Finally, if he's all-good, he *cares* to stop evil. Why then is there evil in the world? These evils can be divided into willed evil, which results from the free choices of human beings, and natural evils, which include hurricanes, mudslides, tornadoes, and so on.

In responding to how both kinds of evil occur, Augustine showed his Platonic influence. When it comes to willed evils, Augustine argued that God does not cause such evils. Moral evils can be traced to the absence of goodness. It results from something gone wrong with the will. As disease is the absence of health in the body, so sin is the absence of health in the will. Plato had used the same analogy to describe the soul in the *Republic*.

There are two parts to Augustine's doctrine about the will. One part is that the universe itself is the result of God's free and sovereign will in making it. With respect to humanity, everything is to be explained on the basis of the will. So Augustine is unlike the Greeks in thinking that will and not reason is primary. The intellect follows the will, not the other way around.

But what determines the will? Augustine's contention is that nothing determines the will. The will is completely free.

To explain how natural evils occur, Augustine made use of Plato's thought. In this world of changes—what Plato called a world of "becoming"—change gives rise to natural processes, and these give rise to famines, diseases, plagues, and so on, which in turn give rise to human suffering.

From Plotinus Augustine acquired the idea that evil is not a positive reality but a privation—that is, the absence of good. The world is imperfect. But this does not imply that God is imperfect or responsible for the imperfections of the world.

Morality

The previous section spoke of Augustine's thoughts about God, free will, and evil. Implied in the development of those ideas are his ideas about morality. If humans are free, it follows that they are responsible for their moral choices. Not all of their choices are moral ones, for they often misuse their free wills.

Augustine wrote that God's "foreknowledge" of all events, human and natural, does not preclude human freedom. "God knows all things before they happen; yet, persons act by choice in all those things where you feel and know that you cannot act otherwise than willingly." There are two ideas here. Whether you choose to do action A or action B, God knew beforehand what you would do. Second, when you choose you are doing so freely.

Morality and "Loves"

Because people choose freely—unlike nonrational beings that simply fulfill their natural desires—people have the capacity to make moral choices but also the capacity for immoral choices. The theme of love comes into play here. The will is moved in the direction of what it chooses to love. Like a physical object that is pulled by its weight toward the center of the earth, so every person is pulled by the affections of their own hearts toward that which is the center of their lives. As Augustine says, "My weight is my love. Wherever I am carried my love is carrying me."

On the one hand, you can turn your attention to those matters that represent your true happiness. True happiness requires that you go beyond the natural to the supernatural. Augustine expressed this view both in religious and philosophical language. In his *Confessions* he wrote, "Oh God you have created us for Yourself so that our hearts are restless until they find their rest in you."

FACT

Augustine was canonized by popular acclaim and later recognized as a Doctor of the Church in 1303 by Pope Boniface VII. His feast day is August 28, the day on which he died. He is still regarded as the patron saint of theologians, printers, sore eyes, and a number of cities and dioceses.

A life of virtue is one in which a person is able to evaluate and order "loves" in accordance with their true worth. A person must discover the truths latent in the human mind that are eternal and unchanging. Such persons know that "Their lives are the better and the more sublime in proportion to the degree of perfection of their contemplating it [God's law] by their minds and keeping it in their lives." So the understanding and enactment of God's law is the achievement of philosophic wisdom.

But just as people can love God's law, they can love things in the wrong way. Since Adam and Eve people have been slaves to sin. People achieve true moral freedom only when they are given the gift of grace. Though everyone expects to find happiness through love, one can also find misery and unhappiness in love because love is "disordered" and it results in the failure to devote one's ultimate love to God. An individual can love the wrong person. A person can love tobacco or alcohol or excessive eating or gambling, and if he does, he has chosen wrongly.

Augustine thought that progress in wisdom is made when the mind turns upward toward God, away from the things of this world. This is the Platonic element in his thinking. Though for Augustine this movement away from the sensible world to the spiritual world can only be accomplished if the mind has been purified by faith.

Evaluation and Significance

Augustine is regarded by many as the most original of the patristic and medieval thinkers. He addressed a series of philosophical problems—such as the problem of evil, the problem of God's foreknowledge and human freedom, the freedom of the will, doubt and knowledge—and offered his own solutions to each. As such, he points the way to a problems-and-solutions approach to philosophy. In addition, he was an unrepentant Platonist. As Aquinas (some 800 years after Augustine) would meld his own Christian thinking with the naturalism of Aristotle, so Augustine had undertaken the same synthesis with Plato and Christianity. But any conflict that arose between the rationalism of Plato and the revealed theology of the Scriptures—as with the account of Creation—Augustine came down on the side of Scripture.

CHAPTER 7

St. Anselm and Other Significant Medieval Thinkers

The period known as scholasticism dominated the eleventh to thirteenth centuries. Two fundamental problems persisted for the better part of a millennium, from 529 to 1453. The first was the problem of universals. Briefly put, the problem was whether ideas like "triangle" and "purple" could exist apart from actual triangles and purple things, or whether they had no existence apart from things themselves. The second problem was devising logical proofs for the existence of God. The significant philosophers of the period addressed one or both of these problems.

The Life of St. Anselm

St. Anselm (1033–1109) was an Italian, born in Aosta. After his mother's death he began to travel to avoid quarreling incessantly with his father. By 1059 he had arrived at the Monastery of Bec in central Normandy. Anselm probably chose the monastery because he heard that Lefranc (then its prior) was teaching there. It was not unusual for a student "wandering scholar" to attach himself to any master he chose.

By 1060, after much reflection and self-examination, he became a monk at the monastery. By 1063 Lefranc had left Bec to become abbot of the abbey of Saint-Etienne at Caen, leaving Anselm as the principal teacher at Bec. Henceforth Anselm changed the character of the school. He intended to teach the monks in ways that would foster both their intellectual and spiritual development. His first major work, the *Monologion,* was a meditation on the "divine essence," a subject Anselm frequently took up with his pupils. The work came about when they asked him to record his teaching for them. His next book, the *Proslogion,* contains his arguments for God's existence.

By 1085 he was the abbot of Bec and people were reading both his works in France, England, and Rome. In 1089 Guanilo, a monk, challenged his proof of God's existence in the *Proslogion,* which sparked a famous exchange. Anselm gave instructions that Guanilo's argument and his own response should always be copied at the end when the *Proslogion* was circulated.

Against his inclinations, Anselm was chosen in 1093 to be the archbishop of Canterbury in succession to Lefranc. At the time of Easter 1107 he was seriously ill and working on the *De Concordia,* and he said that he wanted to live long enough to write a study of the origin of the soul, but his health failed him. He died "as dawn was breaking on the Wednesday before the institution of the Lord's Supper, on 21 April in the year of our Lord's Incarnation 1109, which was the sixteenth year of his pontificate, and the seventy-sixth of his life," as described in *The Life of St. Anselm* by Eadmer.

The "Ontological Argument" for God's Existence

Like Augustine before him, Anselm tried to provide rational support for the doctrines of Christianity, assuming no boundaries between reason and faith. He thought that faith and reason could lead to the same conclusions. He thought that natural theology—that is, basing conclusions about God's existence on logical arguments—could provide a rational version of what he already believed. He was also Augustinian in another way, meaning that he was not trying to discover the truth about God through reason alone; rather, he wanted to employ reason in order to understand what he already believed.

"I Believe in Order That I May Understand"

Anselm was a teacher of other monks, so his method was one of seeking understanding through faith. "I do not seek to understand in order that I may believe," he said, "but I believe in order that I may understand." He made it particularly clear that his enterprise of proving God's existence could not even begin unless he had already believed in God. His argument is better known as the "ontological argument." In the second chapter of his *Proslogion* he writes:

And so, O Lord, since though givest understanding to faith, give me to understand—as far as thou knowest it to be good for me—that thou doest exist as we believe, and that thou art what we believe thee to be. Now we believe that thou are a being than which none greater can be thought. Or can it be that there is no such being, since "the fool hath said in his heart, 'There is no God'"? (Psalms 14:1; 53:1) But when this same fool hears what I am saying—"A being than which none greater can be thought"—he understands what he hears and what he understands is in his understanding, even if he does not understand that it exists. For it is one thing for an object to be in the understanding, and another thing to understand that it exists. When a painter considers beforehand what he is going to paint, he has it in his understanding, but he does not suppose that what he has not yet painted already exists.

But when he has painted it, he both has it in his understanding and under-stands that what he has now produced exists. Even the fool, then, must be convinced that a being than which none greater can be thought exists in his understanding, since when he hears this he understands it, and whatever is understood is in the understanding. But clearly that than which a greater can-not be thought cannot exist in the understanding alone. For if it is actually in the understanding alone, it can be thought of as existing also in reality, and this is greater. Therefore, if that than which a greater cannot be thought exists in the understanding alone, this same thing than which a greater cannot be thought is that than which a greater can be thought. But obviously this is impossible. Without doubt, therefore, there exists, both in the understanding and in reality, something that which a greater cannot be thought.

Distinguished from the kind of arguments based on experience that St. Thomas Aquinas would employ later, Anselm employed a conceptual, or *a priori,* argument. The proof of Anselm's argument does not depend upon experience, but can be known independently of experience. In fact, when Anselm defined God as "a being than which none greater can be thought," he thought that the existence of God followed from that concept alone.

Anselm is writing in the tradition of Plato, and like Plato is a rationalist. Ideas of perfect things have existence. In this case, a single premise about God's nature functions like a given in a geometric proof, from which God's nature can be deduced. Once the idea of God is in a person's understanding (just as the idea of the painting is in the painter's mind before he paints it), it must follow that it also exists in "reality."

Guanilo's Reply to Anselm's Argument

Anselm argued that God equals a being of which a greater cannot be thought. Anselm contended that once this concept is allowed as a defini-tion of God, then his existence follows with necessity. Bishop Guanilo, a Benedictine monk and contemporary, challenged Anselm with two argu-ments. Guanilo argued that Anselm's proof was inadequate in two ways. One, the fool, or any doubter or anyone else cannot form an adequate idea of such a being, since there is nothing in his experience from which this reality could be formed. If the mind could form such a concept, no proof would even be necessary, since one would then connect existence with an aspect of this perfect being.

FACT

Anselm was proclaimed a "Doctor of the Church" in 1720 by Pope Clement XI. This designation is reserved for saints (thirty-three so far) whose writings benefit the whole Christian Church. The title requires that "eminent learning" and "great sanctity" be attributed by the proclamation of a pope or of an ecumenical council. The honor is given rarely, only posthumously, and only after canonization.

Two, you often think of things that do not exist. You can, for example, imagine the greatest conceivable island—the "Isle of the Blessed"—but there is still no proof that such an island exists anywhere.

Is this a successful criticism of Anselm? In reply to the first argument, Anselm claimed that persons are able to form a concept of the greatest conceivable being, doing so by comparing different degrees of perfection in things and moving upward to the maximum perfection, that which there is no more perfect. Second, the rebuttal by Guanilo using the idea of the "perfect island" is no rebuttal at all. It misses the point of the argument: a "greatest conceivable island" is conceptually flawed. Islands by nature are limited; thus, while they may be greatest among their kinds, as islands, they in no manner qualify as the greatest conceivable being. So a greatest conceivable being and a finite island can have little in common, since the latter's finitude doesn't imply its existence, not as the greatest conceivable being implies its existence.

Muslim Philosophy: Avicenna and Averroes

It was through the Muslim philosophers Avicenna (980–1037) and Averroes (1126–98) that Europe came to know the works of Aristotle. From the ninth through the twelfth centuries the Muslim world was far more advanced in its knowledge of Greek philosophy than the West. The Muslim world had access to the chief works of Aristotle before Western Europe finally received them. The significance of Muslim philosophers was therefore twofold: they were transmitters of Aristotle and other Greek philosophers to the West, and they were also the authors of interpretations of Aristotle that became the basis of controversy in medieval philosophy.

Avicenna (which is a Latinized name for Ibn Sina) was a veritable polymath, with interests in logic, geometry, theology, and the Koran. Born in Persia, he was a child prodigy; he learned all the disciples and great works of literature as a young boy. He was extremely prolific: even while traveling a great deal, he wrote 160 books about a broad range of topics. At age sixteen he was influenced most by the Neo-Platonists and Aristotle.

God's Necessary Creation and Opposition to the Idea

Like Anselm, who argued that the definition of God as a "greatest conceivable being" implied his existence, Avicenna also thought that God's essence necessarily implied his existence. He coupled Anselm with Aristotle to arrive at his own doctrine of Creation.

According to Aristotle, everything that begins to exist must have a cause. Things that require a cause Aristotle called "possible beings." A cause that is also a possible being must be caused by a prior being. This too must have a cause, and so on. But there cannot be an infinite series of such causes. There must therefore be a first cause, whose being is not simply *possible* but *necessary*, having its existence in itself and not from a cause, and this is God.

God is at the apex of being, has no beginning, is always active (i.e., in the Aristotelian sense of never being merely potential but always expressing his full being), and therefore has always created. According to Avicenna, then, creation is both necessary and eternal. Here came his controversial conclusion.

Since God was a "necessary being" and was without a beginning, Avicenna concluded that all God's attributes were necessary and without a beginning as well, including his status as the creator of the world. Thus God was not free in creating the world, for divine creativity is just another kind of activity and a necessary feature of his being.

If God and all his attributes are eternal, as Avicenna argued, then his creation of the world must have occurred from all eternity. Therefore, the world is eternal, although from all eternity it has depended on and emanated from God. Every creature is a necessary feature of a world system that could not be otherwise. Every existing thing is part of a logically determined chain of causes.

This conclusion struck Bonaventura in the thirteenth century as a serious error and in conflict with the biblical notion of Creation. According to Bonaventura, two chief features of Creation are that it is a product of God's free will, not of necessity, and that Creation occurred at a point in time, not from eternity. Aquinas would agree, however, that philosophically there is no way to decide whether Creation occurred in time or from eternity, that this must ultimately be a matter of faith.

A Muslim Who Defended the Philosophers

Averroes (Ibn Rushd) of Cordova was commended for defending the right of Muslims to study and incorporate Greek philosophy into the Islamic tradition. He was the most distinguished Arabian philosopher of the period. In fact, Averroes was renowned for trying to reconcile Aristotle's system of thought with Islam. Al-Ghazali (1058–1111) wrote an influential book called *The Destruction of the Philosophers* (sometimes translated as *The Incoherence of the Philosophers*). Ghazali argued with great passion that the philosophers contradict the Koran, each other, and themselves. He believed philosophical writings should be kept from the public, for "just as the poor swimmer must be kept from the slippery banks, so must mankind be kept from reading these books."

Averroes held that there is no conflict between religion and philosophy. They are just different ways of reaching the same truth. He said there are two kinds of Knowledge of Truth. The first is the knowledge of truth of religion being based in faith and being untestable; the second knowledge is philosophy, which was reserved for an elite few who had the intellectual capacity to undertake its study.

Averroes responded strongly to Al-Ghazali's *Destruction of the Philosophers* with a thorough refutation in his work titled *The Destruction of the Destruction.* Elsewhere he had argued that Aristotle represents the apex and culmination of the human intellect and that his philosophy did not conflict with the Koran. For instance, he pointed out that the Koran presents the world as God's handiwork and concludes that this lets one demonstrate God's existence by showing God as the cause. In particular, Aristotle's logic, physics, and metaphysics provide people with the tools for such a demonstration, and Averroes cites Aristotle's argument for an Unmoved Mover as an example.

Despite such sound reasoning, Averroes's quarrel with religious traditionalists led to his being ostracized. His books were burned in Islamic Spain. To prevent any repeat instances of such "heresy," a suppression of Greek philosophy was instituted. In 1195, at the age of sixty-nine, he was tried and exiled from his native Cordoba. But his reputation remains. His knowledge of Aristotle's texts was so respected by Christian scholars that he was given the honorific title "the Commentator of commentators" by late medieval philosophers.

Jewish Medieval Philosophy: Moses Maimonides

In one major respect, Jewish thinkers of the medieval period were no different from Islamic philosophers: they were interested in reconciling their philosophy with their faith. The greatest medieval Jewish philosopher was Moses Maimonides (1135–1204), born in Cordova at Spain.

In his major work, entitled *Guide of the Perplexed,* he addressed all those readers who studied philosophy but were unsure of how to get philosophy to harmonize with faith. Maimonides, like Avicenna and Averroes before him, was heavily influenced in his thinking by the works of Aristotle. Nonetheless, he recognized an inconsistency in accepting both Aristotle's belief in the eternity of the world and revealed theology that maintained that the universe was created by God. After all, Scripture claims that the world had a beginning. Maimonides' "solution" was to show that Aristotle's arguments are inconclusive and needn't be accepted.

Despite Maimonides, attempts to remain faithful to the *Talmud* on the issue of the eternity of the world while interpreting Aristotle, he was still branded a heretic by conservative Jewish scholars. His philosophical works were thus condemned and neglected by Jewish scholars until the nineteenth century.

A century before Thomas Aquinas, Maimonides anticipated three of Aquinas's proofs for the existence of God. Using portions of Aristotle's metaphysics and physics, and relying on concepts like possible and necessary beings, Maimonides proved the existence of a Prime Mover, the existence of a necessary Being (relying here also on Avicenna), and the existence of a primary cause.

In his commentary on the Mishna Torah, Maimonides formulated his thirteen "principles of faith." They summarized what he viewed as the required beliefs of Judaism with regards to:

1. God's existence
2. God's unity
3. God's spirituality and incorporeal essence
4. God's eternity
5. God alone as the object of worship
6. Revelation through God's prophets
7. The pre-eminence of Moses among the prophets
8. God's law given on Mount Sinai
9. The immutability of the Torah as God's law
10. God's foreknowledge of human actions
11. The reward of good and retribution of evil
12. The coming of the Jewish Messiah
13. The resurrection of the dead

Unlike Aquinas, he said one could not say what God was like; no positive attributes can be ascribed to God. Rather, one can only use negative descriptors, by saying what God is not like. This was his "via negative," or negative way.

Peter Abelard

Aside from his controversial personal life, Abelard (1079–1142) is noted in the history of philosophy for his dialectical ability, his philosophy of universals, and his defense of what would later be called "the divine command theory" of morals.

Abelard's Life and Doctrine of Nominalism

Abelard was born near Nantes, France, into a noble Parisian family. He studied philosophy and theology and soon achieved a reputation as a contentious and brilliant student. It was his nature to be controversial: he challenged ideas and people, including his professors. After taking courses, he would go on to teach the same subject in competition with his teachers.

Most renowned of all the events of Abelard's life is his seduction of Héloise, niece of Canon Fulbert of Notre Dame, when he was thirty-five years old. When their child was born they married secretly. Her uncle was furious at Abelard. Héloise's brothers broke into his room at night and castrated him. Subsequently Héloise became a nun and Abelard a monk in an abbey outside of Paris.

The scandal followed him, however. His book *On the Divine Unity and Trinity* was condemned and burned at the ecclesiastical council at Soissons in 1121. Twenty years later he was summoned to a council at Sens and was prosecuted for heresy because of his *Introduction to Theology*. It was his position on universals, known as nominalism, that led him to be condemned in 1140, and he died on his way to Rome to defend himself.

FACT

The remains of Peter Abelard and Héloise are presumed to lie in the cemetery of Père-Lachaise in eastern Paris. Their remains were transferred there in 1817 and contributed greatly to the popularity of that cemetery. Lovers and lovelorn people still leave letters at the crypt, in tribute to the couple in hope of finding true love.

Abelard engaged in the debate about universals, one of the abiding controversies of the time. A universal, such as "redness," or "squareness," is something that is common to many particular things. The problem about universals is trying to figure out what kind of realities they are. In other words, what is their metaphysical status? What relationship do universals such as "goodness" or "sweetness" have to reality?

Porphyry (c. 234–c. 304), the Neo-Platonic philosopher, had already posed three questions about universals:

1. Whether universals
   a. exist in reality independently
      or
   b. exist in the understanding alone
2. If they exist in reality, whether they are
   a. immaterial
      or
   b. material
3. Whether they
   a. are separate from sensible objects
      or
   b. are not separate from sensible objects

For Abelard, universals such as beauty and goodness and rectangularity exist a) in the understanding alone, are b) immaterial, and c) are separate from sensible objects. This alone was controversial, since it implied that universals existed mentally, but not in any objective sense. In particular, Abelard maintained that universals existed "nominally," or in name only. Nominalism holds that you can utter words such as *redness* and *circular*, but that these terms exist only mentally, not extramentally. That is, universals do not exist as things in the real world. The universal "redness" is predicable of many different red things and may capture what red things bear in common. That is what justifies the use of the term.

Morality and Divine Commands

In *Ethics* or *Know Thyself* Abelard addressed the concepts sin, vice, and evil. Acts are good when they are in agreement with what God wills for people, and they are evil or wicked when they express disregard for God or go against what he commands, according to Abelard. It is neither the act itself nor the will that led to it which is sinful. "God considers not what is done, but in what spirit it is done; and the praise or merit of the agent lies not in the deed, but in the intention." What makes actions sinful is that they are contrary to God's will.

But if you act with a sincere conscience and do what you believe is right, you might act in error but not in sin. Abelard cites the words of Jesus about his persecutors, "Father, forgive them, for they know not what they do." In fact, Abelard maintained that even prohibited acts—such as sleeping with another man's wife—are sinless if they are done in ignorance. So acts themselves are neutral, until you learn that they accord or fail to accord with God's will.

FACT

Over time, life in a monastery became intolerable for Abelard. He was finally allowed to leave. In a deserted place near Nogent-sur-Seine, he built himself a cabin of stubble and reeds, and became a hermit. As his retreat became known, students flocked to him from Paris, spreading over the wilderness around him in tents and huts. He found consolation in teaching.

Abelard's Dialectic

Abelard's most famous work was *Sic et Non* (Yes and No). Here Abelard exhibited a style of dialectical discussion that was to become familiar in Scholastic times. He set out more than 150 questions on which Church Fathers offered conflicting views. His goal was to challenge students to resolve these theological disputes. "By doubting we come to questioning, and by questioning we perceive the truth," Abelard said.

Thomas Aquinas later modified Abelard's method. An added feature of Abelard's methodology was his resolution of the opposing disputes. Even in employing this technique Abelard stirred controversy. He upset those traditionalists because he viewed theology as an opportunity for vigorous debate and questioning instead of meditation and acceptance. But there was no doubt where his allegiance lay. After his condemnation in 1141, he wrote to Héloise: "I do not want to be a philosopher if it is necessary to deny Paul. I do not want to be Aristotle if it is necessary to be separated from Christ."

Abelard is now known as a philosopher who had an ill-fated love affair with Héloise. In addition, he was known as a poet and composer. He composed love songs for Héloise that are now lost and remain unidentified. Héloise praised the songs in a letter: "The great charm and sweetness in language and music, and a soft attractiveness of the melody obliged even the unlettered."

William of Ockham

More than any other element of his philosophy, William of Ockham (c. 1280– c. 1349) is known for "Ockham's razor," or the principle of parsimony: "Entities are not to be multiplied beyond necessity." The principle reflects the idea that if you possess two different theories explaining some scientific data, you should choose the one that puts forward the minimum number of entities. Ockham, like Abelard, is also known for his nonrealist theory of universals.

An English Franciscan, Ockham was dubbed the "more than subtle doctor." He was excommunicated for his defiant defense of Franciscan poverty against Pope John XXII. He fled to Munich after being called to defend his views in front of a papal commission at Avignon in 1324. He spent the rest of his career under the protection of Emperor Louis IV of Bavaria, and promoted a separation of church and state in which the authority of neither is subordinate to the other. He died in 1347, probably from the Black Death that was raging in Munich at around that time. At the time of his death he was still hoping for reconciliation with the church.

Ockham's Razor

The reason Ockham's theory is known as the "razor" is that he cuts away unnecessary entities. It is hard to justify why a simpler explanation is preferable to a complex one, but his "razor" retains great intuitive appeal. It encourages people to cut out unnecessary complexity in favor of simplicity. Why would I assume two causes of something when one is sufficient? "It is vain to do with more what can be done with fewer," Ockham said. Ockham's principle of parsimony is adhered to in scientific thinking today.

FACT

William of Ockham died, most likely of the Black Death, on April 9, 1348 in the Franciscan convent in Munich, Bavaria. In the Church of England, his day of commemoration is April 10.

Ockham's Position on Universals

One example of Ockham's razor at work is his theory on universals. According to Ockham, universals like "man" and "redness" exist only in our minds. In reality, everything is singular. There are only real particulars like "this red ball" or "this man," but beyond such singular entities there are no really existing universals. Therefore, when your mind picks out some feature like "yellowness" and "fuzziness" when you look at a tennis ball, all that you know as existing is the yellow and fuzziness of this tennis ball. You cannot say that yellowness and fuzziness exist independently of yellow and fuzzy things. Thus, Ockham, like Abelard before him, does not attribute real existence to universals and is thus opposed to Plato's theory of a realm of ideas in which abstract, universal forms exist. But Ockham is sometimes referred to as an advocate of conceptualism rather than nominalism, for nominalists contended that universals were merely names; that is, words rather than existing realities. Conceptualists held that universals were mental concepts that do exist, although only in the mind.

Evaluation and Significance

The medieval period was referred to as "the Dark Ages" for not advancing the state of learning in the world. But this tag is probably undeserved. The debates about the existence of God between Anselm and Guanilo were carefully argued and passionate. The same insight can be found in the philosophies of Avicenna, Averroes, and Maimonides, all of whom tried to reconcile the claims of faith and reason. The importance of the metaphysical issue of universals is shown by Abelard and Ockham, who argue strongly for their contrary positions.

Late Medieval Thought: St. Thomas Aquinas

8

St. Thomas Aquinas (1225–74) was a prolific writer. Though he lived to just forty-nine years old, he produced a philosophy as broad and systematic as Aristotle's. In fact, Thomas's reputation is based largely on his ability to take Aristotle's philosophy—by the thirteenth century translated into Latin across Europe—and join it to Christian thought.

The Life of St. Thomas Aquinas

St. Thomas Aquinas was born in Roccasecca, not far from Naples in 1225. At the age of five he was placed by his parents in the Benedictine abbey of Monte Cassino as an oblate (layperson dedicated to religious life). He made his first studies, remaining in the monastery from 1230 to 1239, when Emperor Frederick II expelled the monks. From there he went to the University of Naples in the autumn of the same year, being then fourteen. At the age of nineteen Aquinas joined the Order of Preachers of the newly formed Dominican order. By 1245 he was attending the University of Paris and still in the Dominican order. There he met St. Albert the Great, who was his teacher. Aquinas edited St. Albert's lectures on Aristotle's Ethics.

He eventually taught theology at the University of Paris. He left Paris for Italy in 1259 and taught theology at the stadium curiae attached to the papal court until 1268. Thomas's views on the compatibility of Aristotle and Christianity met great opposition but eventually prevailed. In 1274 Pope Gregory X summoned him to Lyons. He died on the journey to Lyon.

FACT

St. Thomas Aquinas was known as the "Dumb Ox," not because he was stupid, but because he was a quiet and very large, rotund person. In class he would sit quietly and absorb information and not get involved in vigorous discussion. He wrote some twenty-five volumes in his short life.

His life had been devoted to study, to teaching, and the pursuit and defense of truth. In 1323, within a half century of his death, he was officially declared a saint by the church. In 1879 Pope Leo XIII recommended the philosophy of Thomas Aquinas as a model for Catholic thought. He now enjoys the status of "Church Doctor."

Only Augustine has had an equal influence on the thought of the Western church. In his Encyclical of August 4, 1879, Pope Leo XIII stated that Aquinas's theology was a definitive exposition of Roman Catholic doctrine. Thus, he directed the clergy to take the teachings of Aquinas as the basis of their theological positions. Also, Leo XIII decreed that all Roman Catholic seminaries and universities must teach Aquinas's doctrines. If Aquinas did not speak on a topic, the teachers were "urged to teach conclusions that were reconcilable with his thinking."

Did St. Thomas Aquinas ever have a mystical experience?
Yes, he had a mystical experience while celebrating mass on December 6, 1273, just months before he died. The importance of the experience dwarfed everything else in his life. "I can write no more"; he declared to a friend. "All that I have written seems to me like so much straw compared to what I have seen and what has been revealed to me."

Synthesizing Scripture and Aristotle

It could be argued Thomas Aquinas's greatest contribution to the medieval era and the history of philosophy is his synthesis. He married classical philosophy with Christian theology. By Aquinas's time, there were two major paths in philosophy, Platonism (with disciples such as Plotinus, Augustine, and Anselm) and Aristotelianism (with adherents such as the Islamists, Jewish philosophers, and many other medieval figures).

Aquinas's philosophy is grounded in Aristotle. In fact, the language Aquinas speaks is much the same language Aristotle spoke. The terminology of form and matter, substance and accident, actuality and potentiality is the very framework Aristotle employed to express his ideas about objects in nature. For instance, the distinction between actuality and potentiality is between what something actually is and what it is possible for it to be. So a piece of coal at a given time might be actually black, cold, shiny, and hard, and potentially gray, hot, powdery, and soft, since it can be heated in a fire and become ash.

The distinction between substance and accident can be illustrated in the same example. To heat a piece of coal to the point at which it is merely warm is to bring about an accidental change in it but to crush it with a hammer until it is broken into bits is to bring about a change in substance. Thus, in an accidental change the object's substance remains the same; in a substantial change it becomes another kind of substance.

Changes in entities take place by means of changes in forms. Accidental forms are involved in accidental changes such as the change in the coal from cold to warm. On the other hand, substantial forms are involved in changes of substance, such as the change from coal to ash.

Aquinas also takes Aristotle's notion of "matter" and uses the term for anything capable of substantial change. Aquinas believed that everything terrestrial partakes of both matter and form. He maintained that angels are noncorporeal (immaterial) beings, but each angel has its own form and can be distinguished from *all* other angels by that particular form. By contrast, human beings—composed of both matter and form—are differentiated from each other by being dissimilar parcels of matter.

Aristotle did not acknowledge the existence of angels, but Aquinas's treatment of angels shows how he used Aristotelian categories to explain spiritual phenomena. Aquinas achieved the expression of the Christian theology in Aristotelian terms and utilized Aristotelianism as an instrument of theological and philosophical analysis and synthesis.

Faith and Reason

It can be said that Thomas Aquinas synthesized faith and reason to a greater extent than any other philosopher. Unlike Augustine—who had made a sharp distinction between the natural and divine world in his City of God—Aquinas made no sharp distinction between the natural and divine worlds. He thought that all of creation—natural and supernatural—and all truth, revealed or rational, emanated from God. The two sources of knowledge, reason and revelation, do not conflict. Revelation does not contradict reason.

Aquinas thought that philosophy and science both lead to the truth. In fact, he tended to equate the truths of philosophy and science with the work of "the Philosopher," Aristotle. He believed that Aristotle's philosophical and scientific conclusions were true for the most part, and therefore must be in agreement with the revealed truths of religion; that is, with the contents of the Bible.

Theology begins with faith in God and interprets all things as God's creatures. While philosophers based their conclusions on reason, theologians base their demonstrations upon the authority of revealed knowledge. Still, philosophy and theology are two separate and independent disciplines. Wherever faith is capable of knowing something, faith, strictly speaking is unnecessary. And what faith knows through revelation cannot be known by natural reason. Both philosophy and theology deal with God, but the philosopher can only infer that God exists and cannot by reflecting upon the objects of sensation understand God's essential nature. There is a connection between both disciplines, however, since they are both concerned with truth.

Thomas Aquinas did for Aristotle what Augustine did for Plato, making the "pagan" philosopher appear to seamlessly blend right in with the teachings of the Christian Church. Aquinas is regarded by many as the thinker who overcame the discrepancy between faith and reason.

Aquinas distinguished theology from philosophy. Theology gives you knowledge through faith and revelation, and philosophy gives you knowledge through the natural powers of the intellect common to all men.

Prior to Aquinas, Plato was widely available to early medieval readers. But Aristotle's writings didn't become available until the twelfth and thirteenth centuries. Aristotle's philosophy served up a great system, but it was a system that contradicted Christian doctrine on some crucial matters.

First, he thought that the world was eternal and uncreated. In addition, he denied personal immortality. On both matters, reason does not point to the world being created or eternal. So Aquinas thought one must side with revelation or Scripture.

Aquinas's Five Arguments for God's Existence

Aquinas thought that reflection on familiar features of the physical world affords evidence of God's existence. So he attempted five proofs to demonstrate the existence of God. Recall that Anselm had begun his ontological proof with the idea of a "greatest conceivable being," from which he inferred the existence of that being. By contrast, Aquinas said that all knowledge must begin with the experience of sense objects.

Before addressing Aquinas's five arguments for the existence of God, one thing is worth noting. The question of God's existence is a metaphysical and epistemological concern, since it raises the question of what kind of reality God is and if you can know—and how you can know—whether that reality exists.

Like Aristotle, Aquinas was an empiricist, claiming that knowledge comes from experience. By contrast, Anselm was a rationalist. For Aquinas, sense experience tells you that this universe is a system of causes and effects and lawlike behavior. This world system, this cosmos, requires a *transcendent* cause. Aquinas's five arguments fall into several categories. It is instructive to examine arguments one, two, and five.

Aquinas rejected Anselm's ontological argument. "Even if it be granted that everyone understands this name 'God' to signify what is said, viz., 'that which a greater cannot be thought,' it does not follow that what is signified by the name exists in the nature of things, but only that it exists in the apprehension of the understanding" (*Summa Theologica*).

Causal Arguments

In the first way, Aquinas writes that "it is certain, and it is clear from sense-experience, that some things in this world are moved." Aquinas, like Aristotle, understood the term *motion* to be reduction from a state of *potentiality* to one of *act*. If something is in motion, it must have been moved by another, and that by another, and so on. But this series of motions could continue infinitely, according to Aquinas, "for then there would be no first mover." And then there would be no subsequent movers, since subsequent movers move only inasmuch as they are moved by the first mover; "the staff moves only because it is moved by the hand," Aquinas explains. "So there must be a first mover, moved by no other; and this everyone understands to be God."

From the first argument one can observe a feature that appears in all five. Aquinas ends each of the arguments with the conclusion that God is the cause of some reality, since without God the reality would not be explainable.

Aquinas had a fresh understanding of the problem of evil. He said evil denotes the "absence of good" but it is not every absence of good that is called "evil." For instance, evil in the negative sense—as when a man cannot run like a cougar—is not evil. Rather, it is absence of good in the privative sense that is called evil, as with privation of sight, which is called blindness.

"The second way is from the nature of efficient cause," Aquinas begins. "There is no case known (neither is it, indeed, possible) in which a thing is found to be the efficient cause of itself; for so it would be prior to itself, which is impossible." Imagine that you look outside your window and see a tree branch moving. That branch is being moved by the wind. That wind has its causes, and so on. But as with motions, you cannot go on to infinity in a series of causes. If there is no first cause, there will no be intermediate causes, like the wind and the swaying tree branches. "Therefore it is necessary to admit a first efficient cause, to which everyone else gives the name of God," Aquinas concludes.

These first two arguments are cosmological, since they show features of the world order, like motions and causes, and claim that these realities require an explanation from a divine reality outside the world order.

Teleological Argument

Aquinas's fifth way, or argument, is a teleological argument for God's existence. It is sometimes referred to as his "design argument," and it is his most renowned one. Stated in its entirety, it reads:

The fifth way is taken from the governance of the world. We see that things which lack knowledge, such as natural bodies, act for an end, and this is evident from their acting always, or nearly always, in the same way, so as to obtain the best result. Hence it is plain that they achieve their end, not fortuitously, but designedly. Now whatever lacks knowledge cannot move toward an end, unless it is directed by some being endowed with knowledge and intelligence; as the arrow is directed by the archer. Therefore some intelligent being exists by whom all natural things are directed to their end; and this being we call God.

Here Aquinas, an empiricist, shows his "teleological" understanding of nature (the word *teleology* means "purposes, goals, or ends"). This religious view of the physical world says that nature acts as if it were following a purpose or aiming at some mark. Aquinas's analogy of the arrow being directed by the archer suggests intelligent design. How else could an arrow move toward its target unless someone directed it that way? Likewise, since nature exhibits regularity—as in the motions of planets, the regular succession of seasons, and so on—this regularity must have been caused by an intelligent designer.

If you came into a classroom where the chairs were all in neat rows, would you assume that their "order" came about accidentally or designedly? If you conclude that some "intelligent designer"—like a custodian or teacher—must have ordered the rows neatly, then you are thinking right along with Thomas Aquinas.

Aquinas designed the five proofs not to satisfy the critical minds of mature philosophers, but as introductory material for "novices" in the study of theology. Still, one finds in his *Summa Theologica* (the "sum of theology") that he speaks of proof, or demonstration. And by demonstration he means in this context what he calls *demonstration quia,* namely a causal proof of God's existence, proceeding from the affirmation of some empirical fact, for example that there are things that change, to the affirmation of a transcendent cause.

The proofs remind one of Aquinas's position on faith and reason. The realm of human knowledge can be divided into two areas:

1. Truths known to us in revelation and known by faith
2. Truths revealed in nature and known by reasoning from experience

His proofs of God's existence fit this last category. In so doing, he shows his allegiance to the empiricism of Aristotle. In *Summa Theologica,* quoting

Aristotle, he says that prior to experience the mind is like a blank tablet. In contrast to Plato and his followers, Aquinas does not accept the idea that there is innate knowledge. Even the idea of God is not written on the mind. But sensory cognition is not enough to explain our knowledge. "The intellect knows many things which the senses cannot perceive."

Ethics

Like Aristotle's ethics, the ethics of Thomas Aquinas are teleological. This means he believed that a good life is directed toward some "end" or goal. But for Aquinas the proper end of human activity is different than for Aristotle.

In his *Nicomachean Ethics* Aristotle argued that happiness (the Greek word is *eudemonia,* meaning something like "a good spirit") is an "activity of soul in accordance with virtue." Happiness is the proper end for all men, though people have also disagreed over what that happiness was. Some said it was honor, others said it was pleasure. Aristotle said it was neither, since the former is ephemeral and the latter depends upon the opinions of others. Two characteristics of happiness, he continued, must be its being "final" and "self-sufficient." In other words, happiness needs nothing further to complete it. Surely external goods like wealth, having friends, and even good looks help in its attainment.

But a funny thing happened in Book X of his *Nichomachean Ethics*. For nine books "the Philosopher" (as Aquinas called him) said happiness was man's proper end and virtue the only means to that end. In Book X, however, he says that *theoria* (or contemplation), and not virtue, is man's greatest activity, since contemplation is what is "highest" in us. He meant that the activity of contemplation is most godlike. And what is God thinking of? God never fixes on the mundane events of this world but is contemplating metaphysics, mathematics, and other theoretical sciences. In Aristotle's haunting phrase, "God is thinking about his own thinking."

The Virtues and the Ultimate End

Aquinas agreed with Aristotle that good human activity must pursue some purpose. As Aristotle spoke of virtues, so Aquinas addressed the cardinal (or "hinge") virtues. These are prudence, justice, temperance, and courage. Since the human will requires rational direction to overcome appetites and anger, persons will need to cultivate virtues. The development of these virtues—which are habits—is necessary to achieving human fulfillment. But Aquinas thinks that by themselves they are not enough. This is even true of contemplation, which is the highest activity of theoretical reason, according to Aquinas.

Aquinas distinguished between an imperfect happiness achievable in this life and the perfect happiness of the next life. He thought that our ultimate end is eternal blessedness, which results from a union with God in the next life. If the purpose of life is the possession of the supreme good, the *sonnum bonum,* this cannot be found in the natural world, which is temporal and not eternal. Moreover, happiness is not found in mere knowledge *about* God but in acquaintance *with* him, achieved in the vision of the divine essence. Since knowledge of God attainable in this life is always imperfect, the natural desire of humans for ultimate fulfillment points to the necessity of an afterlife.

In fact, Aquinas insisted that Aristotle was at least vaguely aware of the imperfect happiness of this life. Aquinas cites a passage in Book I of the *Nichomachean Ethics* where Aristotle writes, "We shall define as 'supremely happy' those living men who fulfill and continue to fulfill these requirements (namely possessing complete virtue), but blissful only as human beings." Because Aquinas believed that Aristotle understood that the happiness achievable in this life is imperfect, he had no quarrel with Aristotle.

Evaluation and Significance

At various times St. Thomas Aquinas has been ridiculed for being "Aristotle baptized." To his detractors, Aquinas forced Aristotle to fit into his own Christian assumptions about nature and morality. Some of this kind of criticism is inevitable. After all, the ideas of Aristotle's naturalism and Aquinas's Christianity are not the same. Nonetheless, the two philosophers agreed on more matters than they disagreed. Aquinas sought to combine reason and revolution and the resulting fit was a good one, save for those instances where reason did not bear fruit and only Scripture could be trusted.

CHAPTER 9

The Renaissance Period: Leaving Scholasticism Behind

During the medieval period philosophy was often viewed as "the handmaiden of faith." By making use of reason and argument, philosophy could be used to help establish beliefs. When conflict arises between the claims of faith and the claims of reason, that conflict gets "resolved" in favor of faith. But the credo of the two periods of the Renaissance is different. The arts and philosophy in the humanistic period of the Renaissance (from 1453 to 1600) were human-centered, emphasizing the place of humans in the universe. Philosophy during the natural science period (from 1600 to 1690) was cosmos-centered.

The Renaissance

The word Renaissance means "rebirth." In a historical context it refers to a period of revival of interest in classical culture, specifically the arts and literature, which began in mid-fourteenth-century Italy. In philosophy, the Renaissance covers the period from 1400 to 1600, when Plato and Neo-Platonism were revived due to the availability of Latin translations, and witnessed the revival of ancient systems of thought such as Stoicism and skepticism. The key thinkers of the early Renaissance are Desiderius Erasmus and Martin Luther. By the end of the Renaissance, however, the significant figures were scientific thinkers, especially Nicolaus Copernicus, a mathematician and astronomer, and Galileo Galilei, a central figure in the scientific revolution.

The Humanistic Period: Cultural Developments

The cultural movement of the Renaissance began in Italy in the fourteenth century. Philosophically it began as Latin translations of Plato's dialogues became available. Plato seemed like fresh air compared to the logic-chopping and disputes of Scholastics more associated with the works of Aristotle. Philosophy could now be enjoyed for itself, not just for its use to bolster and defend religious orthodoxies.

Technology was essential to the Renaissance. The invention of the printing press in the mid 1400s made the works of great authors widely available. Books once hand-copied were now mass-produced. Under Cosimo de Medici forty-five copyists working feverishly for two years had produced just 200 volumes; by the year 1500 some 1,000 printers had produced over 9 million books.

Erasmus and Machiavelli

Two of the most important philosophers of the humanistic period of the Renaissance were Desiderius Erasmus (1466–1536) and Niccolò Machiavelli (1469–1527). Erasmus combined an enthusiasm for the classics with a populist, entertaining style. A Christian, Erasmus celebrated the human spirit in his writings and saw no tension between the classics and religious faith. In "the Godly Feast," a dialogue he wrote in 1522, one of his characters says:

Sacred scripture is of course the basic authority for everything; yet I sometimes run across ancient sayings or pagan writings—even the poets—so purely and reverently and admirably expressed that I can't help believing their authors' hearts were moved by some divine power. And perhaps the spirit of Christ is more widespread than we understand, and the company of the saints includes many not in our calendar.

Erasmus had been bolder in an earlier, more famous work, *The Praise of Folly* (1509). This satirical work takes jabs at many targets, most of all the church. Erasmus believed that the church was laden with "folly": the monks could be petty, corrupt, and ignorant. Its officials possessed power and could do greater wrongs because of that power. While his work inspired the Protestant reformers to follow, especially Martin Luther with whom Erasmus feuded, he did not wish to break the church but only to heal it.

FACT

Humanism, a philosophy prevalent during the Renaissance, is the belief in and celebration of the potential and abilities of humans, without dependence on divine intervention to solve humankind's problems.

Machiavelli is undoubtedly the most important political philosopher of the era and is best known for *The Prince*. During his political career (1494–1512) he served as secretary of the chancellery of the Council of Ten at Florence. The book attests to the corrupt practices among leaders in Renaissance Italy. Not only does the book justify the amoral political standards of the time, but more importantly it is a practical guide to unscrupulous rulers—in his own time and ages to come—who wished to gain or retain power over the masses.

The author's justification of "might is right" politics gave rise to a word that lives on. *Machiavellianism* is now a pejorative term stating that in politics the "end justifies the means." It condones the attainment of political power, without questioning *how* such power is attained. Power is praiseworthy in itself, regardless of what moral standards are used to achieve it, according to Machiavelli.

Machiavellianism, named for the Renaissance political philosopher Niccolò Machiavelli, has come to mean any form of political ruthlessness wherein the end justifies the means. It now has a thoroughly negative connotation and is hurled as an epithet to attack one's opponents.

Machiavelli had practical advice for rulers. A wise ruler will eliminate even those who aided him in his rise to power. Such people know too much about the ruler's techniques used to gain power and could threaten his rule. The ruler should have the traits of a fox (in order to outwit his opponents) and a lion (in order to intimidate his enemies). In addition, he is better served by building an appearance of dignity and virility, without a hint of effeminacy.

Protestant Reformation

Erasmus had rebuked the church for its corrupt ways. But his pointed writings created just a fraction of the clamor of those of a young Augustinian monk to follow him. Martin Luther (1483–1546) inveighed against the clergy's attention to self-indulgence and greed. But nothing focused his attention like the sale of papal indulgences by a Dominican friar named Tetzel. Any person could pay a fee and buy off the guilt and penalties for his or her sins. Luther knew that such a practice was theologically corrupt and nailed his famous "Ninety-five Theses" to the door of the Wittenberg Castle church in 1517. In time his bold action would incite a major protest against the church that would be felt across Europe. The revolution was called the Protestant Reformation.

FACT

The Protestant Reformation was in part a response to the rampant corruption that had spread through the papacy. Martin Luther was outraged by the selling of indulgences—in other words, paying a monetary fee for the sacrament of confession.

The issue of selling indulgences was just a symptom of a greater cause. Luther's attack on indulgences led to a battle with the church over issues of fundamental importance concerning theology and church authority. His protest resounded all the way to Rome. Both sides were so entrenched in their positions that Pope Leo X thought it necessary to excommunicate Luther in 1520.

Luther was not the radical antireligionist that many of his opponents made him out to be. In fact, he was close to Augustine on many doctrinal matters, including his views on the authority of Scripture, God's punishment for sin, and other issues. But his excommunication had far-reaching effects throughout Europe. In 1530 England broke away from Rome over the issue of Henry VIII's dispute with the pope about his divorce. John Calvin (1509–64) developed a reform theology that attracted followers in France, Holland, Scotland, and England. Among the major Protestant movements, Calvinism steered furthest away from Catholicism in doctrine and practice.

INSIGHT

An interesting note about Luther and Calvin is their contribution to their respective languages. This was an age when educated people spoke Latin. With the humanist movement and the Reformation, nations came to celebrate their uniqueness and their languages. Luther and Calvin's voluminous writings in their native languages helped contribute to the evolution of modern German and French.

Luther had taught that people could follow their own interpretation of the Bible and individual conscience. In undercutting the religious authority of the Catholic Church, downplaying subservience to tradition, and placing new importance on the individual, the Reformation caused a groundswell against all intellectual authorities and traditions. The upshot of the Protestant Reformation was that more worshipers followed their own personal reflections.

The Copernican Revolution

The Polish astronomer Nicholas Copernicus (1473–1543) provided the first modern theory of planetary motion that was heliocentric—that placed the sun motionless at the center of the solar system with all the planets, including the earth, revolving around it.

His theory ran counter to the Ptolemaic system advanced nearly 1,500 years before. The church embraced the Ptolemaic system, which held that the sun revolved around the earth. As it turned out, Copernicus's system was not published until 1543, the year he died.

After studying astronomy at the University of Krakow, Copernicus spent several years in Italy studying various subjects, including medicine and canon law. Around 1500 he lectured in Rome on mathematics and astronomy. By 1512 he had settled in Frauenburg, East Prussia, where he had been nominated canon of the cathedral. There he performed his canonical duties and also practiced medicine.

The Copernican System

The work that immortalized Copernicus was his *De revolutionibus orbium coelestium* (The Revolution of the Heavenly Bodies), in which he sets forth his beliefs concerning the universe, known as "the Copernican system." The treatise, which was dedicated to Pope Paul III, was probably completed by 1530, but it was not published until Copernicus was on his deathbed. Modern astronomy was built upon the foundation of the Copernican system.

The new astronomy opposed the theological orthodoxy of the day. The church could not relinquish its belief that the earth was at the center of the solar system. If the earth was not at the center, then humankind's importance was symbolically reduced. Fearing controversy and even condemnation by the church, Copernicus held off publishing his book.

It was published a few days before his death. At first it did not engender controversy. In fact, it escaped Catholic condemnation until the time of Galileo. This was due in part to the book being dedicated to the pope. Furthermore, a friend, who was a Lutheran clergyman, had prudently added a preface saying that the Copernican theory was only a hypothesis.

Galileo Galilei

Galileo (1564–1642) rejected the teleological view of nature espoused by Aristotle and embraced by Thomas Aquinas in his fifth argument for God's existence. Galileo didn't think it was the Bible's place to instruct about the astronomical data describing the workings of the universe. Thus his famous remark, the Bible is "to teach us how to go to heaven, not how the heavens go." An empiricist astronomer, philosopher, and mathematician, Galileo thought that the way to understand "the book of nature" is to read it in the language of mathematics.

Galileo was born on February 15, 1564, in Pisa. He and his family moved to Florence in 1572. He nearly became a priest, but after a short period of study he left and enrolled at the University of Pisa to earn a medical degree. He didn't finish that degree either, but instead studied mathematics notably. In 1592 he was appointed, at a much higher salary, to the position of mathematician at the University of Padua.

It was during his Paduan period that Galileo worked out much of his mechanics and began his work with the telescope, which had been invented by the Dutchman Hans Lippershey in 1608. In 1610 Galileo published *The Starry Messenger,* and soon after accepted a position as mathematician *and* philosopher to the Grand Duke of Tuscany (and a nonteaching professorship at Pisa). Late in 1610, the Collegio Romano in Rome certified the results of Galileo's telescopic observations as presented in his book. In 1611 he became a member of the first scientific society, the Academia dei Lincei.

In 1613–14 Galileo entered into discussions of Copernicanism through his student Benedetto Castelli, and wrote a *Letter to Castelli on the Reltionship Between Science and the Bible.* In February 1616, the Sacred Congregation of the Index condemned Copernicus's book *On the Revolution of the*

Heavenly Orbs, pending correction. Galileo then was called to an audience with Cardinal Robert Bellarmine and advised not to teach or defend Copernican theory.

FACT

Legend has it that Galileo offered the pope the opportunity to look through his telescope and see for himself the true nature of the cosmos. The pope refused. Regardless of the scientific data involved, the pope had made up his mind.

In 1623 Galileo published *The Assayer,* in which he dealt with the nature of comets, arguing that they were sublunary phenomena. In this book, he made some of his most famous methodological pronouncements, including the claim that the book of nature is written in the language of mathematics. The same year Maffeo Barberini, Galileo's supporter and friend, was elected Pope Urban VIII. Galileo felt empowered to begin work on his *Dialogues Concerning the Two Great World Systems.* It was published with an authoriztion from Florence (and not Rome) in 1632. Shortly afterward the Inquisition banned its sale, and Galileo was ordered to Rome for trial. In 1633 he was condemned. In 1634, while Galileo was under house arrest, his daughter, Maria Celeste, died. At this time he began work on his final book, *Discourses and Mathematical Demonstrations Concerning Two New Sciences.* This book was smuggled out of Italy and published in Holland. Galileo died early in 1642. Due to his conviction, he was buried obscurely until 1737.

Galileo and the Rejection of Teleology

Galileo was an empiricist, basing his conclusions on the evidence he studied. His guiding principle was to measure and quantify nature. He rejected the Aristotelian assumption that every material body has a place in the order of things and that the motion of objects is to be explained by the natural tendency of each body to seek its own place. Instead, he observed, weighed, measured, and calculated in order to test his mathematical hypotheses. He was convinced that mathematics would reveal the structure and the laws of the universe. In an essay known as "The Assayer" (1623), he wrote:

Philosophy is written in this grand book, the universe, which stands continually open to our gaze. But the book cannot be understood unless one first learns to comprehend the language and read the letters in which it is composed. It is written in the language of mathematics, and its characters are triangles, circles, and other geometric figures without which it is humanly impossible to understand a single word of it: without those one wanders around in the dark labyrinth.

So underlying Galileo's investigation of nature is the presupposition that mathematics was the key to understanding the universe. He is therefore regarded as a scientist rather than a philosopher. His thinking became the basis for the scientific revolution in seventeenth-century Europe.

For many, Galileo will always be associated with two discoveries. With the use of a telescope he supported Copernicus's notion that Ptolemy's hypothesis of an earth-centered solar system was seriously flawed. Despite his work, in 1633 he publicly recanted his views on the matter to save his life. He remained under house arrest until his death.

Galileo cannot merely be pigeonholed as an astronomer. Some of his most important work lay in dynamics and the principles of movement. Galileo was the first to discover the law of falling bodies, or constant acceleration, published after his recantation and while he was still under house arrest. He found that bodies do not fall with velocities proportional to their weights, but he did not arrive at the correct conclusion (that the velocity is proportional to time and independent of both weight and density) until about twenty years later. The famous story about Galileo dropping weights from the Leaning Tower of Pisa is probably fictional.

In addition, what would later become Newton's celebrated first law of motion was directly taken from Galileo's principle of inertia, namely that a body moves in a straight line with uniform velocity unless acted upon. This principle was important in helping to support Copernicus's theory, for critics claimed that if the heliocentric theory were true, that a falling body should not fall in a straight line, but in fact should fall somewhat to the west of the point it was dropped, on account of the eastwise rotation of the earth. It had been proven by experiment that this was not the case, a result that led many to dismiss Copernicus as wrong even if they did not share the religious reasons for rejecting him. It took Galileo's work in dynamics to show why the prediction was not fulfilled. Simply put, the falling stone retains the rotational velocity of Earth.

Galileo changed the language of the way nature was described. He quantified the processes in nature. Whether he was summoned before the Inquisition or not is irrelevant. He was forced to recant his view that Copernicus's theory correctly described the heavens. But his clash with the church pointed the way to a new science.

Evaluation and Significance

The Renaissance is known best for its meaning—the "rebirth" of the classics. But it is also known for its transition to a less scholastic and more modern outlook on culture, religion, art, philosophy, and science. As much as Plato and Aristotle and other things classical were revived, a new methodological outlook on learning was born.

CHAPTER 10

Early Empiricism: Francis Bacon and Thomas Hobbes

Following the Renaissance, two forerunners of a scientific, experienced-based philosophy were Francis Bacon and Thomas Hobbes. Empiricism (which comes from a Greek word *emperia,* meaning "experience"), especially as it developed over the subsequent centuries with major figures like John Locke, David Hume, and Bishop George Berkeley, was a philosophy that stated all philosophy begins with experience. Comparing himself to Christopher Columbus, Francis Bacon felt the excitement of this new philosophy, and talked of "the breath of new hope which blows on us from the new continent."

The Life of Francis Bacon

Francis Bacon (1561–1626) was an English philosopher, essayist, and statesman. He was born in London. His father was a prominent statesman and his uncle, Lord Burghley, was the most powerful man in Britain. Bacon's mother was a well-educated and pious Puritan. At the age of twelve Bacon attended Trinity College at Cambridge, where he studied law. By the age of sixteen he was on the staff of the English ambassador to France. He should have had a distinguished career in public service.

But his father died at eighteen, leaving little money to support him. As a result, he was always in search of opportunities. Bacon entered Parliament in 1584 and his opposition to Queen Elizabeth's tax program hurt his political advancement. Still, she accepted him as an unofficial member of her Learned Council.

With the succession of James I, however, Bacon assumed a series of distinguished posts. He was knighted in 1603, became attorney general in 1613, lord keeper in 1617, and in 1618 lord chancellor, the highest appointed office in the land. His prospects seemed set. But he was then accused of accepting bribes as a judge. He pleaded guilty, admitting that he had accepted gifts from litigants but adding that it had not influenced his judicial decisions. He was fined 40,000 pounds, banished from the court, disqualified from holding office, and sentenced to the Tower of London. The banishment, fine, and imprisonment were remitted, but his career as a public servant was put to an end.

He spent the rest of his life writing in retirement. Bacon spent his last years working on his lifelong project: the reform of learning and the establishment of an intellectual community dedicated to the discovery of scientific knowledge for the "use and benefit of men." It was a quest for scientific knowledge that led him to his sudden death on April 9, 1626. He had become sick with bronchitis after standing out in frigid weather stuffing a chicken with snow while testing his theory of the preservative and insulating properties of snow.

Bacon's Goal: The Reconstruction of All Knowledge

Bacon's main interest for philosophers lay in his philosophy of science. This was to come in two parts. First, a radical criticism of the Scholastic and Renaissance approach to science would be needed to wipe away the confusions of the past. Second, a methodology would be needed to put science back on a sound footing. He called his project to reform the sciences *the Great Instauration,* which meant "restoration" or "renewal." In fact, he completed only the first of three parts, called the *New Organon,* which refers to Aristotle's logical works, known collectively as the *Organon.*

The first part of Bacon's philosophical project focused on sweeping away what he considered to be past errors in philosophy. Bacon's attitude toward what had gone before can be summed up in a set of similes. Bacon took issue with the metaphysicians and the empirics, such as alchemists and scientists. He termed the metaphysicians "spiders." Like spiders, the metaphysicians spun beautiful and ingenious webs, produced purely from within themselves. The empirics were like ants, scrambling about and collecting quantities of material, and piling them up, without making anything new of them. Instead of being spiders and ants, people should be more like bees—working together not only to collect but to *transform* what they've gathered. Scientists should interpret the data that arises from experience, should carry out experiments to collect new data, and so slowly build up humankind's knowledge of the world.

Bacon insisted that progress in science depended upon starting from scratch: "It is idle to expect any great advancement in science from the superinducing and engrafting of new things upon old. We must begin anew from the very foundations, unless we would revolve for ever in a circle with mean and contemptible progress."

These similes point out the culprits that Bacon viewed as stymieing the advance of human knowledge. More specifically, his targets were two philosophers who by Bacon's time had cast enormous shadows for nearly two millennia: Plato and Aristotle. Bacon was critical of two schools of thought that had emerged from Platonism and Aristotelianism, respectively. He was opposed to the rationalist tendency, inherent in Plato, that knowledge could be attained by examining the content and meaning of words.

This tendency was found not only in Plato himself—who was always concerned with finding precise meanings of terms like *justice, goodness,* and *love,* but also in rationalists under Plato's influence, like Anselm. Anselm (as discussed in Chapter 7) thought that by simply defining a supreme being as a "being than that which none greater can be thought" you can know that such a being exists. Bacon descried this as a spidery tendency to spin something from one's own mind.

He also made attacks on Aristotle, the other giant of the classical period. Aristotle was a naturalist, a biologist who studied more than 500 species in order to note their tendencies for change and growth. To Bacon this was a useless enterprise, since Aristotle was intent upon amassing data but could not arrive at any scientific hypotheses. Bacon thought that there must be a new way of collating and organizing data that would help generate inductive hypotheses. Further, Bacon thought that Aristotle was "only strong for disputations and contentions, but barren of the production of works for the benefit of the life of man," according to his biographer, William Rawley.

The Corruption of the Mind: Bacon's Four Idols

In Book I of the *New Organon,* Bacon introduces his famous doctrine of the "idols." These are characteristic errors, natural tendencies, or defects that beset the mind and prevent it from achieving a full and accurate understanding of nature.

The Idols of the Tribe

These are the natural weaknesses and tendencies common to human nature. Because they are innate, they cannot be completely eliminated, but only recognized and compensated for. Some of Bacon's examples are people's tendency to trust their senses, which are inherently dull and easily deceivable. Another idol of the tribe is the tendency to discern (or even impose) more order in phenomena than is actually there. As Bacon points out, people are apt to find similitude where there is actually singularity, regularity where there is actually randomness, and so on. For instance, you might think that if a person wins a game of Lotto in a certain town that other people in that town will have similar luck, when there is actually no connection between the events. In addition people have a tendency toward "wishful thinking." According to Bacon, people have a natural inclination to accept, believe, and even prove what they would prefer to be true. Finally, people possess a tendency to rush to conclusions and make premature judgments (instead of gradually and painstakingly accumulating evidence).

Imagine you are listening to a baseball game on television. The broadcaster notices that the batter, Smith, has hit home runs on the each of the previous two Tuesdays. "Smith has been successful on Tuesday," the broadcaster says. "And today is Tuesday," he continues, implying that the player might hit another homer. Bacon would probably say the broadcaster sees a pattern where there is none, which is an idol of the tribe.

The Idols of the Cave

Unlike the idols of the tribe, which are common to all human beings, those of the cave vary from individual to individual. They reflect the peculiar distortions, prejudices, and beliefs that humans are subject to owing to their different family backgrounds, childhood experiences, education, training, gender, religion, social class, and the like. So a person born in a certain time and place—for example, the United States after September 11, 2001—might have a more aggressive attitude about warfare than someone not from that time period. Also, a person might exhibit a "cookie-cutter" mentality—that is, a tendency to reduce or confine phenomena within the terms of his or her own narrow training or discipline.

The Idols of the Market Place

These are hindrances to clear thinking that arise, Bacon says, from the "intercourse and association of men with each other." The problem here is language, which has less to do with common speech or slang and more to do with the special discourses, vocabularies, and jargons of various academic communities and disciplines. He points out that "the idols imposed by words on the understanding are of two kinds": "they are either names of things that do not exist" (e.g., the crystalline spheres of Aristotelian cosmology, but also ghosts and other phantasms) or faulty, vague, or misleading names for things that do exist (according to Bacon, abstract qualities and value terms—e.g., *moist, useful,* etc.—can be a particular source of confusion).

The Idols of the Theater

Like the idols of the cave, those of the theater are culturally acquired, not innate. By theater he doesn't mean fiction or drama. Rather, these are idols that derive mainly from grand systems of philosophy. He has three types of philosophy in mind: *sophistical philosophy,* which is unempirical, highly speculative, and abstract, like the Scholastic philosophy common in medieval times; *empirical philosophy,* which is based on too few ideas that are then extrapolated into generalities; *superstitious philosophy,* which is unfounded due to its uneasy marriage of theology and philosophy, found for example in Pythagoras, with his religious cults dedicated to the study of numbers, not to mention creationists of our own time, who invest scientific study with tales of God's creation.

People must be free of all of these idols to attain knowledge. The idols are impediments to knowledge. They function like grime on a window that keeps you from having a clear view of reality. You must eliminate the idols in order to know the world better.

The Future Philosophy

Now that you know of Bacon's criticisms of past philosophies, the question arises: what did he do better than his predecessors? In a letter he wrote at the age of thirty-two Francis Bacon said, "I have taken all knowledge to be my province."

For Bacon, the key to all knowledge is induction. Induction is that process of drawing general principles from a number of particular instances. This was not new in the seventeenth century. In fact, Aristotle had talked about inductive reasoning, or probable reasoning, nearly 2,000 years before Bacon. Bacon's conviction was that inductive reasoning would yield certain knowledge through the study of forms of objects in nature and generalizing about those forms.

No short account can do justice to the scope of Bacon's six-part plan elaborated in the *Great Instauration*. Suffice it to say that his notion that induction can yield certain knowledge is on shaky ground. Few if any believe that induction can yield anything more than probable knowledge. If you say that "All swans are white," you have arrived at a generalization based on limited experience; namely, the experience of the past. But there is no certainty that all swans will continue to be white. There are a long line of empiricists—especially David Hume in the eighteenth century and Bertrand Russell in the twentieth century—who have made this point forcefully.

In his strict separation of the study of nature from the study of the divine, Bacon directly opposed the Thomistic doctrine of seeking knowledge of the supernatural through the natural.

The Life of Thomas Hobbes

It was said that Thomas Hobbes (1588–1679) was born in fear. He was born prematurely on April 5, 1588, because his mother was alarmed by the news that the Spanish Armada was approaching England. Whether this fear colored his political view and his dim view of human nature is anyone's guess. What cannot be denied is that Hobbes became one of the great seventeenth-century philosophers. He lived to ninety-one and in the course of his life made contributions to geometry, ballistics, and optics. But he is best known for his work *Leviathan* (1651), meaning "state," which was a systematic explanation of Hobbes's materialism, ethics, and politics. He hoped that the book would please King Charles II. But he was displeased, since the book advocated the replacement of any government unable to provide peace and safety for the citizens.

The Physics of Knowledge

In the first five chapters of *Leviathan* Hobbes develops the Galilean view of nature that everything is fundamentally matter in motion. Hobbes's materialism claims that every event in the world is determined. You may think that future events are the product of chance, but this is because you are ignorant of their causes. All events in nature are strictly determined. Since human activity is similar to other events in nature, it follows that your behavior is absolutely determined.

Human beings are sensory creatures; they feel the glass as warm, the wine as sweet, and a smell as pungent. Hobbes said that these sensations actually originate as physical motions from the objects in the external world impinging on your sense organs. These motions produce the sensations you have. When you see the rich red hues of a sunset, you are really experiencing the motions of light rays. Looking at the moon, you get the appearance of a bright, luminous circle about the size of a bottle cap.

From these considerations it seemed clear to Hobbes that the object itself and what you experience are two different things. All your thoughts are determined, then, for they begin with sensations. According to Hobbes, "There is no conception in a man's mind which hath not first, totally or by parts, been begotten upon the organs of sense. The rest are derived from that original." Here Hobbes's empiricism is on display. There are no innate ideas; rather, all ideas are all gotten from sense. Your ideas of red, pungent, rectangularity, beauty, and the rest all begin with sense.

Hobbes on Human Activity

Hobbes's metaphysical materialism makes it clear that he believed all motions in nature are determined, but he went even further. He maintained that all behavior is absolutely determined. Hobbes distinguished between vital and voluntary motions.

Vital motions are such automatic activities as the circulation of the blood, breathing, digestion, and so on. These events are not consciously chosen motions and so are determined by our nervous system and bodily state.

You might expect Hobbes to say something different about *voluntary motions* since these are chosen by human beings. You believe you are acting freely when you choose this or that car, or select this soft drink instead of that one. But Hobbes thought otherwise.

All voluntary motions begin with a type of motion he calls *endeavor*. Endeavor plays out as either (1) desire, which is motion toward something or (2) aversion, which is motion away from something. So you might desire a cold drink on a summer day. That same day you might leave a car on the train that is not air-conditioned. For each individual, these are correlated with what is experienced as pleasurable or painful. In this way, Hobbes deduces our psychological responses to reality and our activities from physiological responses. This is how your behavior is determined without fail.

But how can Hobbes explain those situations in which you seem undecided and unable to make up your mind? For instance, suppose you are having difficulty deciding whether to have a third drink or not. You may experience this as (1) an alternating succession of the feelings of desire and aversion for the drink, or (2) the motion between two competing desires, or (3) two conflicting aversions (though not in the case of the drink).

Of all your desires and aversions, the strongest one wins out. The last motion, following deliberation, can be called an act of the will. But this "will" has been mechanically determined by all the forces acting on it. The will is not free any more than the movement of a material object like a billiard ball is.

Hobbes's Psychological Egoism and the State of Nature

The determinism found in nature and human activity also applies to human motivation. On this point Hobbes is clear: people are egoistic hedonists, always guided by their own pursuit of pleasure. Hence, you are unfailingly self-interested, psychologically determined to seek your own pleasure. What is good, according to this view? Good is simply what makes you feel good, and that is what you will pursue. This understanding of human nature also affected Hobbes's view of politics.

Egoism

Hobbes embraced the view that human beings are self-interested in their behavior. He does not merely state that people act in their own interest some of the time. Rather, as a psychological egoist he takes it to be true that *all* persons at *all* times pursue what is best for them.

You call the object of a desire good and the object of an aversion evil, which are terms derived from pleasure and pain. Good and evil are thus subjective notions. But how can so many egoists pursuing their own goods ever live together harmoniously in a community? This leads to a discussion of Hobbes's political theory.

To ask whether or not one ought to act in this way is an irrelevant question.

Ethics and the State of Nature

Morality is subjective, not absolute, according to Hobbes. If by "good" you mean what is an object of desire and "evil" is an object of aversion, then you are determined to pursue the first and avoid the second. This has to do with the laws of human psychology. Good and evil are terms derived from pleasure and pain. Since people find different things pleasurable and painful, good and evil are subjective notions. But if we are all seeking our own well-being, even to the detriment of others, what are the chances that people can live peaceably in a society?

To answer the question, Hobbes talks about an imaginary condition called the "state of nature." In essence, he is asking what our situation would be like if there were no government. In this state of nature everyone has a right to everything, even to one another's body. If we are all egoistic hedonists, this state of nature will be a state of war, when "all against all" is the rule for living.

In the state of nature, the law of the jungle rules and only the fittest survive. While Aristotle said that people were "social animals" who needed communion with others, Hobbes would say that having sympathy for others required social conditioning. Altruism is not an innate emotion. The state of nature, then, is a state of fear. The state of nature is a place where there is always "a danger of violent death; and the life of man solitary, poor, nasty, brutish and short."

Politics: The Need for a Social Contract and a Strong Sovereign

Self-interest will compel human beings to create a government. Each person can best look out for his best interests by having a government to protect his basic rights. It is the only cure for the untethered self-interest that most men live with.

Hobbes states in *Leviathan* that when men leave a state of nature and agree to create a government, it is as if individuals sign an agreement, a social contract which says:

I authorize and give up my right of governing myself, to this man, or to this assembly of men, on this condition, that thou give up thy right to him, and authorize all his actions in like manner.

From his own experience of political chaos, Hobbes concluded that the worst tyrant is better than no government at all, or a weak, ineffective government. Hence, his sovereign has absolute power. Men are grasping by nature, which makes everyone in society vulnerable. If this is a proper diagnosis of our natural human illness, then it must be said that Hobbes proposed a cure: a strong ruler.

An authoritarian sovereign is not a choice but a requirement, a necessary counter-weight to what Hobbes called "the natural condition of mankind," which turns all of society into a selfish playground. The ruler reigns above the law. He needn't obey the law, for unlike other citizens he is not subject to the social contract but simply sees to it that his subjects live up to the contract which they have agreed to obey. His duty is to punish those who transgress the laws.

Evaluation and Significance

The story of Francis Bacon's contributions to philosophy is a mixed one. While he was a prime mover in the early empiricist movement in philosophy, he made no important scientific discoveries. Because of his attention given to induction and his rejection of Aristotelian science in its search for "final causes" in nature, he was one of the first thinkers to attempt to systematize the scientific method. Despite this hankering for method, he had no understanding of the role of theory in scientific discovery. In addition, he shows little appreciation for theory, imagination, and speculation in the pursuit of scientific knowledge. As a result, in his discussion of the great scientists he fails to mention Johannes Kepler, Galileo, Copernicus, or William Harvey's work on the blood. In time, the received opinion on Bacon was that his views on scientific method was too naive to produce great science.

Thomas Hobbes's reputation as an important thinker in many areas remains. His materialistic psychology of perception was a model for scientific thinkers to come. Despite his importance in developing a materialistic account of how people perceive and come to know things, Hobbes is no doubt most famous for his political doctrine. He has been referred to as the founder of modern political science. "Hobbes is the father of us all," Karl Marx, the economist and author of the *Communist Manifesto*, said in the nineteenth century.

He was original in seeing the state as an artificial construct, but necessary because of the egoistic nature of human beings. Hobbes's ideas of the state of nature and the social contract influenced political thinkers over the next two centuries. The most prominent of those thinkers include John Locke (1632–1704) and Jean Jacques Rousseau (1712–78).

CHAPTER 11

René Descartes: The Father of Modern Philosophy

René Descartes (1596–1650) laid out the agenda for modern philosophy in several important ways. For one, he claimed to have left behind the "shaky foundations" of knowledge from the time of the medieval schoolmen. He established a quest for certain knowledge about all matters—including nature, God, and the soul—and a deductive geometric method to attain it. In his greatest work, the *Meditations,* he plays out that quest for certainty in the sciences, metaphysics, and epistemology.

The Life of René Descartes

René Descartes was born at La Haye, a small town in Touraine, France. As a young man, Descartes received a good Scholastic education at the Jesuit college of La Flèche, one of the most famous schools in Europe. He admired his teachers greatly but was dissatisfied with the course of instruction, which centered on the received opinions of the ancients. Descartes believed that mathematics alone yielded certain knowledge. After attending La Flèche Descartes went on to attain a law degree and, with a family fortune to back him, began a series of travels. In 1618 he set off for Holland to serve as a soldier under Maurice of Nassau.

Publications

By 1628 he wrote the *Rules for the Direction of the Understanding,* which was unfinished and not published until after his death. The book laid out the rules of his method for science and philosophy. The same year he went again to Holland. In 1633 he had finished *Le Monde* (The World), a book on physics that presented the world as essentially matter in motion. He was eager to publish it but withdrew it when he heard of the condemnation of Galileo by the Inquisition for teaching, as *Le Monde* did, the Copernican system. Descartes sent his treatise away to a friend, to avoid the temptation to publish it. (It was eventually published in 1664, after his death.)

Four years later, in 1637, he rebounded with *Discourse on the Method of Rightly Conducting One's Reason and Seeking Truth in the Sciences.* It was the first great philosophical work written in French, and it created a style that became a model for expression of abstract thought in the language.

FACT

Descartes experienced a life-altering vision on November 10, 1619. Then twenty-three, he was shut in by a harsh winter in Holland and spent a day in intense philosophical reflection. That evening, the intellectual reverie of the day culminated in three vivid dreams. The dreams gave him a vision of his mission in life; to find the key to the mysteries of nature in a new philosophy based on mathematical reason.

In 1641 he published *Meditations on First Philosophy,* together with six sets of *Objections,* from various distinguished persons, including Hobbes and Pierre Gassendi, to whom Descartes had submitted the work, and Descartes's *Replies to the Objections.* Taken together, the text might well be Descartes's most important and famous work. In 1644 he wrote *Principles of Philosophy*, which contains, among other topics, his ideas on cosmology. He dedicated the book to Princess Elizabeth of Bohemia, with whom he was in correspondence.

Death in Sweden

In 1649 Descartes consented to the requests of Queen Christina of Sweden, who had read the *Principles* and the last work published in his lifetime, the *Passions of the Soul,* to instruct her in his philosophy. She had assembled a distinguished circle in Stockholm. Still, he was reluctant to go, writing to a friend that Sweden was the land of "bears, rocks, and ice." Nevertheless, he did go and had the unpleasant task of meeting with her three times a week at five o'clock in the morning. Descartes had always been a late riser because of his frail health, and his constitution could not take the frigid cold and early hours. The climate and schedule wore him down until he caught pneumonia and died on February 11, 1650.

Rationalism

Descartes is recognized as "the Father of Modern Philosophy." This epithet is due to his leaving behind medieval thinking and taking the methodology of the sciences to establish a rational foundation for truth. It is also the case because Descartes doesn't quote other thinkers but is doing philosophy on his own. This is evident from his beginning statements with phrases like "It seems to me that . . ." or "I am convinced that . . ."; it all adds up to an image of the solitary thinker.

In general, rationalism is a philosophic approach that emphasizes reason as the primary source of knowledge. Unlike Hobbes and other empiricists to come who thought that knowledge began with sense perceptions, Descartes thought that knowledge was prior to and independent of sense perceptions. In fact, truth is not tested by sense-verification procedures.

Descartes's Agenda

As stated, Descartes was dissatisfied with his Scholastic education at the Jesuit college of La Flèche. Even though it was one of the most renowned schools in Europe, he thought that the course of instruction bowed too politely in the direction of the ancients.

In his *Discourse on Method* Descartes says of philosophy, "It has been cultivated for many centuries by the most excellent minds and yet there is still no point in it which is not disputed and hence doubtful." Descartes concluded that "nothing solid could have been built upon such shaky foundations." His learning left him with nothing but doubts. His intellectual quest was to find something certain.

In essence, his life's philosophy centered around three goals. The first was to eliminate doubt and find certainty. All he had heard were conflicting opinions from various philosophers. The only certainty in his learning was uncertainty. Opinions in conflict also weakened the foundations of the various sciences.

A second goal, like the first, falls under the theory of knowledge. It was his quest for a set of principles, or starting points, from which he could deduce all answers to scientific questions. Is there some certain proposition that would serve as solid bedrock upon which to build a system of knowledge?

His third goal was a metaphysical one. As a man of science and mathematics, Descartes sought to reconcile his mechanistic view of the universe with his own religious perspective. If the world was a deterministic machine as Hobbes and other materialists had argued, then how would there be room for human freedom? What need was there for God in such a universe? Descartes wanted to be loyal to two important masters: science and spirituality.

Descartes's Meditations on First Philosophy

The full title of Rene Descartes's little book, written in 1640–41, is *Meditations on First Philosophy*. The word *first* is notable. If you sat down to philosophize on several meanings, sitting before the fireplace as Descartes did on separate evenings, what would come first in order? Wouldn't you start with a survey of the things you thought you could know? What could you know with certainty? That might be the place to start. In these six meditations, which constitute Descartes's best-known work, he is searching for what is first—some proposition that cannot be doubted so he can use it as a foundation for knowledge.

René Descartes takes us step by step on this intellectual journey, this quest for certainty. This is the same Descartes who wrote in his *Discourses:*

> *From my childhood I have been nourished upon letters, and because I was persuaded that by their means one could acquire a clear and certain knowledge of all that is useful in life, I was extremely eager to learn them. But as soon as I had completed the course of study at the end of which one is normally admitted to the ranks of the learned, I completely changed my opinion. For I found myself beset by so many doubts and errors that I came to think I had gained nothing from my attempts to become educated but increasing recognition of my ignorance.*

So his starting point is reality and what can be known about it. Here, Descartes uses a metaphysical approach, asking "What is out there? What kinds of things do I know?" As soon as you ask those questions, you're doing epistemology, too. For the following question is, "How do you know the ordinary things you think you know?"

For Descartes, the skeptical knife cuts even deeper than questions in philosophy.

Even sciences—like physics, anatomy, and chemistry, to name just a few—are ultimately founded on observations and more observations, all made by your senses.

"The reports of the senses cannot be trusted," Descartes says, "since they have deceived me in the past." He says in the *Meditations,* "It is prudent to never trust completely those who have deceived us even once." If the existence of material objects like billiard balls, tides, and microscopic organisms are in doubt, the empirical sciences which describe the behavior of those objects must also be in doubt.

But of course it must be different with mathematics. Since Descartes thinks these studies don't depend for their conclusions upon really existent material objects, your doubts about empirical science don't apply to them. So when you read the stock page and it mentions losses, gains, and dividends, you can trust those reliable indexes, no? And when you read about the scores in yesterday's sports pages, aren't they also certain?

But here Descartes uncovers a fresh reason for doubt. Suppose there is a "malicious demon" of the "utmost power and cunning," one who has employed all his energies to deceive you, he says in the first meditation. Could it be that the reality you claim to observe is nothing but a dream that such an all-powerful being has created in your mind? Surely this is a possibility. Thus even sciences like geometry and calculus are cast into doubt.

The Second Meditation: Is There Something That Cannot Be Doubted?

After the thoroughgoing doubt of his first meditation, Descartes set out to renew his search for certain knowledge. It seems that the lesson of that first exercise is that everything can be doubted, with all avenues to knowledge leading to fruitless dead ends. What is left standing? Is there even one starting point that will allow Descartes to emerge from this destructive first meditation and start to construct a body of knowledge? In other words, is there one thing that he cannot doubt? Is it true, sadly, that all he can be certain of is that he's certain of nothing at all?

In the second meditation he first reviews his doubts of the day before and says, "I have convinced myself that there is nothing in the world, no earth, no sky, no minds, no bodies." But from all this does it follow that he does not exist?

The Starting Point: I Think, Therefore I Am

The question that Descartes raises in his second meditation is about mental activity. If he is doubting something, or affirming something, or willing or thinking something, then these actions mean that he exists. Thus. "I think; therefore, I am" is the start of Descartes's first bit of knowledge.

The one thing he knows is that he exists. How? It is the one thing that he cannot doubt. Put another way, it is true every time he tries to doubt it. And about this evil deceiver—let him deceive as much as he will. But even an all-powerful deceiver can never bring it about that he is nothing so long as he thinks he is something. The very act of doubting is self-defeating, since a doubting being must exist in order to doubt. Thus Descartes bellows that the proposition "I am, I exist, is necessarily true whenever it is put forward by me or conceived in my mind."

Descartes uses this truth as a starting point to launch his investigation into knowledge. But what is this "I"? At one time he thought that he was a "rational animal." But what is an animal? And what does it mean to be rational? Originally he thought that part of his identity had to do with bodily nature—the combination of arms and legs and the mechanical way in which his parts operated. But then he raised a legitimate doubt about such bodies. But he still knows that he is a "thing that thinks." That is, he is a being that doubts, affirms, understands, denies, wills, and so forth. This affords a clearer picture of what your thinking nature is.

Comparing This "Thing That Thinks" with the Nature of Bodily Things

But in addition to this idea of an individual as a thinking being are those ideas of corporeal things which the senses observe and which the mind forms images of. These things seem to be known with greater distinctness than this "I" that the mind strains to form an image of. Is it true that such bodies are understood most distinctly of all things?

Consider one kind of body. Take a piece of wax, Descartes suggests. Its color, shape, and size are easy to observe. Its scent is of fresh honeycomb.

Put it close to a fire, however, and all these sensual properties undergo alteration as it slowly melts, expands, grows hot, changes its scent, and ceases to own the same solidity. Is it the "same" wax? (Yes! No one has smuggled in a new chunk of wax to replace it!) But it is not the wax of the individual's imagination or senses. That is, it is not known by the senses, not by vision, touch, or imagination—nor has it ever been—but is known by purely mental scrutiny. Its nature or essence as an extended substance remains. This the individual knows, but he does not know it with his senses.

Descartes's Method

A word about method here is important. Beginning with his rigorous doubt of the first meditation and continuing with the "I think; therefore, I am" intuition of the second, Descartes employed what is known as the geometric method. Recall that geometric proofs proceed from strong starting points, usually functioning as givens and postulates in the proofs, and then deduce further truths based on those starting points. This method appealed to Descartes the mathematician, who had contributed coordinates now known as "Cartesian coordinates." Undoubtedly, his contributions to geometry influenced his philosophical system. Like two other thinkers of the Enlightenment era, Galileo and Sir Isaac Newton, Descartes believed that the world can be mathematically understood. Moreover, he thought that the geometric method of deduction offered the model for certain knowledge. Could the same model be used for philosophy? Descartes set out to test all beliefs by the mathematical criterion of certainty.

In his *Discourse on Method* Descartes states that he would accept only those beliefs that appeared "clearly and distinctly" to be true. For Descartes, that means you know it with intuitive certainty. It's also a visual metaphor—as in "I see" when you mean "I understand." Intuition doesn't require discursive reasoning; it's an immediate apprehension of truth.

"Clearly and distinctly" also applied to the kind of self-evidence found in the propositions of mathematics and logic (like three times three equals nine and "everything is equal to itself," according to the law of identity). Descartes thought that you could "see" or know such propositions by the "natural light of reason." He thought such propositions were "indubitable," meaning not only that they were hard to doubt but were actually incapable of being doubted. Such propositions are known *a priori*.

Descartes's Two Arguments for the Existence of God

In building his edifice of knowledge Descartes uses two arguments for the existence of God. It is something of a paradox that he would attempt proofs of God's existence. After all, he claims that the "school men" and all prior philosophers have served up only doubtful opinions. Yet he undertakes two proofs, the same kind of proofs undertaken by Augustine in the fourth century to Thomas Aquinas in the thirteenth.

The Causal Argument for God's Existence

In the third meditation Descartes offers up an argument that he hopes will show that God is the source of all perfection. It could be labeled the causal argument, and a form of it appears in the Neo-Platonic reason of Augustine. Though Descartes recognizes him as an imperfect being, he is able to entertain the idea of God as a perfect being. Since he is incapable of generating such an idea on his own, there must be some greater cause of the idea. The argument relies on the Scholastic principle that there must be as much reality in the cause in as in the effect. So any ideas of perfection require perfect causes of them. Therefore God, the perfect cause, must exist.

One way of countering the argument would be to deny the premise and say that you do not have a perfect idea of God. Rather, you have only an approximation of that perfect idea. Since our idea of God would then be imperfect, it would not require a perfect cause and the conclusion wouldn't follow.

The Ontological Argument for God's Existence

Descartes's second argument for the existence of God occurs in the fifth meditation. Though the wording is slightly different, it recalls Anselm's ontological argument from late in the eleventh century. Here Descartes considers the idea of a most perfect being and what such an idea contains. If the being is truly perfect, then it would lack nothing. Therefore, it would not lack existence. So God's essence contains his existence. "We can no more think of God without existence than we can think of a mountain without a valley," Descartes says.

The argument about God's existence following necessarily from his essence also has implications for the consideration of the evil deceiver raised in the first meditation. For if God is perfect, he is incapable of being a deceiver. He cannot lead anyone into error, either. Deceit and induced error would be inconsistent with the character of an imperfect being. Since he cannot lead you into error, you can attain knowledge of all those matters he doubted in meditation one, especially the truth about material objects.

The Mind-Body Relationship

Descartes believed that mind and body were two different kinds of substances. Consciousness is the essential property of mind substance. By contrast, extension in length, breadth, and depth is the essential property of bodily or material substance. One of the crucial questions for Descartes is how these two substances interact. How can one kind of substance, which is lacking in physical properties, have any influence on another kind of substance that is physical?

By the time Descartes had reached his sixth and final meditation he had solved all of his first meditation doubts. To recap, he had doubted whether there are material objects, whether God was a deceiver, who would mislead him about what his senses revealed. But having offered up two arguments for the existence of God, Descartes is certain that it would be logically inconsistent for this God—who is a perfect being—to be a deceiver. As such, Descartes feels certain that material objects cause our sensations and that God would not mislead him about this.

Cartesian Dualism and Interaction

Descartes believed that persons are combinations of mental and physical substance. This is known as *dualism.* But he was faced with a problem of explaining how these two substances can interact to form the union that we call a person. "My soul is not in my body as a pilot in a ship," Descartes says in meditation six. "I am most tightly bound to it." Descartes wants to say that when a person acts, a kind of causation is at work. For instance, if you decide to walk across the room, there is a mental act, willing, which then causes you to take the walk. But he must explain the details of this cause-effect relationship.

In his book the *Passions of the Soul,* a work written toward the end of his life, Descartes gives an account of this cause-effect relationship between mind and body. He claims that the interaction occurs in "a certain very small gland," namely the pineal gland, which is situated at the base of the brain. But this doesn't offer a satisfactory explanation of how a material substance can affect a nonmaterial substance.

You can see and understand a material substance affecting another material substance. You see a billiard ball contacting another, or a ship pushing aside water as it moves along in the sea. But you see no examples of something material affecting something immaterial. Nor do you see an example of the reverse. Without an example of such an occurrence, it is unclear how you can ever understand it.

No wonder that Princess Elizabeth of Bohemia, who corresponded frequently with Descartes on the matter, wanted his explanation of the issue. She wrote:

I beg of you to tell me how the human soul can determine the movement of the animal spirits of the body so as to perform voluntary acts—being as it is merely a conscious substance. For the determination of movements seems always to come about from the moving body's being propelled . . . but you utterly exclude extension from your notion of soul, and contact seems to be incompatible with a thing's being immaterial.

For some philosophers, a satisfactory answer to the princess's question has never been provided.

Evaluation and Significance

Descartes's influence on modern philosophy cannot be denied. After all, as a man of science and faith, he set the agenda for epistemology and metaphysics to follow.

Some argue that Descartes's references to God in his works—especially in his *Meditations* in 1641—were insincere and only an attempt to appease the church and escape the wrath that awaited other modern thinkers. But it might be argued that his piety was genuine. This is made clear by his pilgrimage to the shrine in Italy. Besides, the existence of God in his system plays too central a role to be a mere public relations gambit.

CHAPTER 12

Philosopher in Exile: Baruch Spinoza

Baruch Spinoza fits well into the group of seventeenth-century philosophers that includes company like René Descartes, Thomas Hobbes, and Wilhelm Leibniz. Like them, he is systematic, laying out his philosophy as if it were a mathematically deduced proof. Spinoza's metaphysics is unique: he said God was the one substance in the universe. For this claim about God he was criticized as a materialist and an atheist. For people said if everything is God, then God is the material universe. Though widely criticized, and even excommunicated for his thinking, he remains one of philosophy's true original thinkers.

The Life of Baruch Spinoza

Baruch Spinoza (1632–77) was born in Amsterdam of Jewish parents who were refugees from the Spanish Inquisition. They had fled Spain in quest of the religious tolerance of the Netherlands. Spinoza was brought up an orthodox Jew and studied the work of many Jewish philosophers, including Moses Maimonides. Spinoza was well versed in Jewish Arabic philosophy and theology, but he became increasingly influenced by modern rationalism and science, particularly the writings of Hobbes and Descartes.

His thinking moved further and further away from traditional Jewish thought, until in 1656 he was excommunicated from his synagogue for alleged heresies. He was a teacher, but earned his living primarily by being a lens grinder and polisher. He was a man of personal integrity who led a frugal lifestyle. He turned down a professorship at the University of Heidelberg and a pension from the French king, in both cases because he wanted to avoid any risk of losing his intellectual independence. Evidence suggests that he lived a life of simplicity, courage, and personal charm.

He kept company with a group of Protestants known as the "Collegians," a sect without priests. In 1661 he began writing a *Treatise on the Correction of the Understanding,* a work that shows the influence of and also criticizes Descartes. In 1663 he also began to write his major philosophical work, the *Ethics,* but it was not completed until 1675 because he had put it aside in order to write a treatise in defense of liberty, thought, and speech.

FACT

Spinoza's influence has extended beyond the field of philosophy. George Eliot, the nineteenth-century novelist, produced the first known English translation of the *Ethics*. In the twentieth century W. Somerset Maugham alluded to a central concept in Spinoza with the title of his novel *Of Human Bondage.*

The *Ethics* had to wait for publication until after his death, but it was his greatest work. It is presented in the form of Euclid's *Elements,* with numbered definitions, axioms, and propositions, each with a demonstration. Like Descartes, Spinoza had imposed a geometric, thoroughly deductive method in his style of philosophy. He died at the age of forty-five, the victim of a pulmonary condition, probably the result of his years as a lens grinder.

Pantheism: God Is Everywhere

In the first part of Spinoza's *Ethics* he takes up the subject of the divine nature. Spinoza is investigating the ultimate nature of reality, or practicing metaphysics. He calls the first principle of the universe God, sometimes substance.

Since Aristotle had said that only substance is capable of independent existence, Spinoza inferred that only God filled such a bill. No other being possessed such infinite attributes. Since only substance is self-caused, free, and infinite, God must be the only substance. He exists necessarily.

Spinoza argues that the nature of such a substance cannot be divided, nor can a second such substance even be conceived. Then Spinoza turns to a statement about his best-known doctrine: whatever is, is in God, and nothing can either be or be conceived without God.

The Universe: Freedom and Necessity

In Book I of his *Ethics,* Spinoza develops his doctrine of necessity. On the one hand, nothing outside of his own nature restricts God's activity, and in this sense he is free. So God is the only free agent in the universe. Nature on the other hand—whether trees, or stars, or rivers—consists of nothing contingent, but everything is necessarily determined by factors outside its own nature. Nothing could have been produced in any other manner than how it is now or was in the past.

The appendix to Book I includes Spinoza's discussion of the world and God's nature. It also includes his famous refutation of theology. Christian doctrine depicts God as acting purposefully to achieve certain ends. But Spinoza denies this picture of things.

According to the *Ethics*, whatever happens in nature is the necessary outpouring of God's own nature. He is free in terms of being uncaused; but God is unfree in terms of the creation he has made. Nature is what it is necessarily. It could not have been different. The world has emanated from God necessarily.

Put another way, the universe contains nothing that is contingent or that could be other than it is. Spinoza says in *Ethics,* "In the nature of things nothing contingent is admitted, but all things are determined by the necessity of the divine nature to exist and act in a certain way." God is free in the sense of being self-determining—and uncaused—and he determines to produce things in a logically necessary manner.

QUESTION?

What did Einstein say about Spinoza?
Albert Einstein named Spinoza as the philosopher who exerted the most influence on his worldview. Spinoza equated God (infinite substance) with Nature, consistent with Einstein's belief in an impersonal deity. In 1929, Einstein was asked in a telegram by Rabbi Herbert S. Goldstein whether he believed in God. Einstein responded: "I believe in Spinoza's God who reveals himself in the orderly harmony of what exists, not in a God who concerns himself with the fates and actions of human beings."

Besides calling the universe a "necessary" creation, Spinoza is antitraditional in another way. He disagrees that God alone is perfect and the natural order less than perfect, a view traditionally based on the doctrine of original sin. In Book II Spinoza equates reality with perfection. Since it is true that nothing in nature could be otherwise than it is, and all things in nature are a part of God and follow necessarily from his nature, God would not be complete without the whole natural order. It is perfectly logical then that each manifestation of God—each part of the natural order—should be just as perfect as it is real.

Another radical idea follows suit: Spinoza asserted that God is extended and that material things are a part of his nature. This contrasts loudly with Christian views that had made God responsible for the creation of the physical world, but had not made God himself material, even in part.

Spinoza's belief is known as pantheism. Simply put, this is the view that God is identical with the universe. All things are imbued with God's existence, in the sense that all things are in God. God exists necessarily, though only two of his attributes are known to humans: thought and extension.

Freedom and Bondage

Since everything is what it is, not by choice but by necessity, this impacts human beings as well. If God is one substance and all other things "modes" or modifications of that one substance, then necessity applies to human beings, too. Insofar as human beings understand why everything is as it is, the more genuine their knowledge is. A person possesses more happiness and "peace of mind" in proportion as his knowledge is more genuine.

Determinism

Determinism is the doctrine that everything in nature cannot be other than what it is. This applies not only to "objects" in nature—that is, to all sorts of material things—but applies to human nature as well. Human beings do not act freely. In Part I Spinoza wrote:

All things depend on the power of God. That things should be different from what they are would involve a change in the will of God, and the will of God cannot change (as we have most clearly shown from the perfection of God): therefore things could not be otherwise than as they are.
Because of this,
There is no mind absolute or free will, but the mind is determined for willing this or that by a cause which is determined in its turn by another cause, and this one again by another, and so on to infinity.

These passages reveal Spinoza as a thorough-going determinist. Still, Part V of his *Ethics* is entitled "Concerning the Power of the Intellect or Human Freedom." In this section he shows that the use of one's intellect may "lead to liberty."

Escaping Bondage

Once you posseses the highest kind of knowledge, which for Spinoza is intuitive knowledge, you attain the "intellectual love of God." Human beings are only modes of God and thus have only partial understanding. The more knowledge you have of God, the less you suffer from evil emotions. What emotions? The emotions of hatred, anger, envy, to name a few. You act when you are the adequate cause of anything; you suffer when you are the cause only partially. Human freedom is freedom from passivity and suffering.

Spinoza offers up a moving ethic at the end of Book IV of the *Ethics,* saying that "the free man thinks of nothing less than of death; that, living among the ignorant he strives as much as possible to avoid their favors; that he endeavors to unite other men with himself in friendship; that he never acts fraudulently; that he hates no one, envies no one, is angry with no one."

An emotion can be restrained or removed only by an opposed and stronger emotion. So your ability to withstand the pressures around you, to ward off sorrow, to fight excessive desire, depends on you fighting those emotions with equal vigor. The task of overcoming such emotions is never final, but constant. Its task is accomplished with knowledge and virtue. And the highest virtue of the mind is to know God. Knowing God makes your ideas more adequate and your power to act is thereby increased.

Men disagree as far as their ideas are disturbed by emotions; when guided by reason they tend to understand and thus to agree. An emotion that is a passion and is thus destructive of your power ceases to be a passion as soon as you form a clear idea of it. By understanding all the causes that play upon you, you can oppose any threat to your freedom or your power.

Another Rationalist: Wilhelm Leibniz

Like Descartes and Spinoza, Leibniz (1646–1716) was one of the great rationalists. As with his two rationalist predecessors, he believed that reality is knowable by reason. Leibniz's philosophical system is founded on a small number of basic principles, of which the best known are the principle of sufficient reason and the principle of the indiscernibility of identicals (sometimes known as Leibniz's Law).

The first says that there is a reason that every fact is what it is and not otherwise; nothing happens without a reason. For example, Leibniz argued that because there could be no reason for the world to be created at one moment rather than another, the world couldn't have been created at a particular moment. The second says that if two things are identical, they have all their properties in common.

The Life of Wilhelm Leibniz

Leibniz was a polymath almost without peer. He was a mathematician, jurist, historian, scientist, diplomat, poet, inventor, and courtier. His father was a professor of philosophy at Leipzig University, but Leibniz turned down an academic career. He entered into the employ of Baron Boineburg in Frankfurt, while also continuing his study in the law and pursuing his interest in physics, especially of motion.

Leibniz claimed that all monads were connected with one another. "This connection or adaptation of all created things with each, and of each with the rest, means that each simple substance has relations which express all the others, and hence is a perpetual living mirror of the universe."

His best-known works are the *Discourse on Metaphysics* (1686), the *New Essays Concerning the Human Understanding* (1704), the *Theodicy* (1710), and the *Monadology* (1714). Only the *Theodicy* was published in his lifetime. Every bit as famous was the series of letters he exchanged with Antoine Arnaud concerning freedom and the concept of an individual, and with Clarke concerning the Newtonian universe. No listing of his writings, even if it were comprehensive, can indicate the scope of his interests, abilities, inventiveness, sheer intellectual power, and prodigality. The task of compiling a complete edition of his work did not being until 1923 and is not yet finished.

Monads and God

Descartes was a *dualist,* arguing for the existence of two kinds of substance, mind and matter. Spinoza was a *monist,* maintaining that there was just one substance and modes of that substance. Leibniz held that the world is composed of an infinity of simple substances, which he called *monads.* Monads are the simplest units of existence and each monad is a different simple substance which is unextended and without parts.

God is an infinitely perfect being who from an infinite number of possible worlds creates the best possible world. He cannot, however, create a perfect world, for that would be logically impossible. To do so he would have to reproduce himself exactly. God is nonextended spirit; thus, a reproduction of his qualities would be indiscernible and so nonexistent. Thus the best of all possible worlds is the one containing as much existence as possible compatible with the greatest degree of perfection. Everything in the universe unfolds according to a pre-established pattern.

Evaluation and Significance

In the final analysis Spinoza was an original thinker for any number of reasons. This original thinking caused him no small amount of harassment from authorities. When he described nature as necessarily what it is, he attacked the teleological view that says nature has a design or end. "We have shown . . . that nature does nothing for the sake of an end, for that eternal and infinite being whom we call God or Nature acts by the same necessity by which he exists."

Spinoza was not only influenced by Aristotle's thoughts on substance but also by the ethical portion of Aristotle's doctrine. Spinoza maintained that "Each thing, insofar as it can, endeavors to persevere in its being." From this it follows that "Man necessarily endeavors, insofar as he can, to persevere in his being." Like Aristotle, Spinoza begins with the general statement that "according to the laws of his own nature each person aims at which he considers to be good." From a consideration of this end he finds the means to achieve that end.

CHAPTER 13

Enlightenment Empiricism: Sir Isaac Newton and John Locke

Sir Isaac Newton (1642–1727) and John Locke (1632–1704) are Enlightenment philosophers. Thinkers during the European Enlightenment were confident that man could solve his problems—problems of government, morals, and society included—by the use of reason. Even the universe could be mathematically understood. Newton gave mathematical substance to this idea with the discovery of laws of motion and gravitation. John Locke ushered in the Enlightenment with the publication of *An Essay on Human Understanding* in 1690.

The Life of Sir Isaac Newton

Newton was born in Woolsthorpe, Lincolnshire. He attended Cambridge University, receiving his bachelor's degree in 1665. By 1669 he was Lucasian Professor of Mathematics. He was elected fellow of the distinguished Royal Society in 1671 and served as its president from 1703 to his death. In his later years he was involved more in political and governmental affairs rather than in scientific work. Over the course of his life he attained unparalleled scientific achievements. Less known were his sustained interests in ancient chronology, biblical study, theology, and alchemy.

Discoveries and Publications

Newton's genius was manifest by his early twenties. From 1664 to 1667 he discovered the binomial theorem; the "method of fluxions" (calculus); the principle of the composition of light; and fundamentals of his theory of universal gravitation. His masterpiece, *Philosophiae Naturalis Principia Mathematica* (The Mathematical Principles of Natural Philosophy), appeared in 1687. Simply put, this work sets forth the mathematical laws of physics and "the system of the world." Not unlike Spinoza's *Ethics*, Newton's masterpiece followed the model of Euclidean geometry. Starting from mathematical definitions and axioms, Newton deduced propositions. In Newton's view, the world system was comprised of material bodies (masses composed of hard particles) at rest or in motion and interacting according to three axioms or *laws of motion:*

1. Every body continues in its state of rest or of uniform motion in a straight line unless it is compelled to change that state by forces impressed upon it.
2. The change of motion is proportional to the motive force impressed and is made in the direction of the straight line in which that force is impressed. (Here, the impressed forced equals mass times the rate of change of velocity, i.e., acceleration. Thus, the familiar formula, $F = MA$.)
3. To every action there is always opposed an equal reaction; or, the mutual action of two bodies upon each other is always equal and directed to contrary parts.

Newton's general law of gravitation is: every particle of matter attracts every other particle with a force varying directly as the product of their masses and inversely as the square of the distance between them.

To the Enlightenment, Newton was more than a great physicist and mathematician. He was a cultural hero. The poet Alexander Pope voiced the spirit of the age in writing:

Nature and Nature's laws lay hid in night:
God said, Let Newton be! And all was Light.

Newton's Philosophical Standing

Newton's elucidation of the laws of motion was preceded by a "scholium" in which he enunciates the ultimate conditions of his universal system: absolute time, space, place, and motion. He speaks of these as independently existing "quantities" according to which true measurements of bodies and motions can be made as distinct from relative "sensible measures" and apparent observations.

This scholium was the subject of much critical evaluation, however. Newton had always insisted on adherence to experimental observation and induction for advancing scientific knowledge, and he rejected speculative metaphysics. But absolute time and space are not observable.

The Life of John Locke

John Locke, the first great British empiricist, was born in Somerset. His father was an attorney and Parliamentarian who fought against Charles I. Locke attended Oxford, receiving his bachelor's in 1656. He stayed on to take his master's degree in 1664 and was appointed censor of moral philosophy. He lectured in Greek, Latin, rhetoric, and philosophy. But he also studied and performed experiments in chemistry and meteorology.

He embarked on the study of medicine and became well qualified, but never practiced. He was offered diplomatic work but refused and returned to Oxford to concentrate on philosophy in 1665. He found a kindred spirit in the Earl of Shaftesbury, who invited Locke to live in his London house as his personal physician. Lively discussions of politics and philosophy flourished side by side in that household. Locke was politically involved in trying to get William of Orange on the English throne.

Locke's philosophical high watermark was undoubtedly 1690, when his *Essay* and his *Two Treatises of Government* were published. Both works inspired lively debate. His *Two Treatises* argued against the divine right of kings and maintained that men are free and equal in the state of nature and possess certain natural rights. His political doctrines were incorporated into the American constitution and the constitution established in France in 1871.

As his health waned toward the end of his life, he engaged in public service. For the last thirteen years of his life he lived at Oates (the home of Sir Francis and Lady Mesham), some twenty miles outside of London. He was still writing, corresponding, and debating, and enjoying the affection and respect of many. He died at Oates on October 28, 1704, while Lady Mesham was reading the Psalms to him.

Locke's legacy is vast: he was a notable political, economic, and religious thinker. He was a "latitudinarian" and broad churchman in theology and a liberal in politics. He argued against the authority of the Bible and the church. Unlike Hobbes, who had argued for the necessity of an authoritarian sovereign, Locke maintained that political sovereignty depends upon the consent of the governed and ecclesiastical authority upon the consent of reason. He was also an ardent defender of freedom of thought and speech. His main works are *Two Treatises on Government* (1689), *An Essay on Human Understanding* (1690), *Reasonableness in Some Thoughts on Education* (1693), and *Christianity* (1695).

All Knowledge Begins with Sensation

Rationalism and empiricism are distinct epistemologies. A fundamental difference between rationalists and empiricists concerns how each thinks you arrive at knowledge. For one, the two views differ over whether you possess innate (inborn) ideas, prior to your actual experiences. Rationalists maintain that you have knowledge of reality prior to your experiences. Put another way, you don't need sensations to have knowledge. Empiricists like Locke think differently. According to Locke, your ideas of qualities like redness and sweetness and of entities like triangles begin with sensations of those objects. There is no knowledge prior to sensation.

Like other empiricists, Locke said knowledge is imprinted on the mind by sensations. Locke maintained that these sensations *impress* themselves upon the mind as if it were a *tabula rasa,* a blank table or "white paper void of all characters, without any ideas," as he put it. Where do all the ideas— that is, all the materials in reasoning and knowing—come from? In a word, they come from experience; hence the name "empiricism."

There are two kinds of experience, external and internal, and two corresponding paths to knowledge: (1) sensations provide you with ideas emanating from external entities and experiences (from objects outside yourself); (2) inner reflection also provides ideas as part of the world within. Your mind receives ideas in the same way that a blank page receives pen marks on it. Sensation or "sense experience," as Locke refers to it, presents sensible qualities to the mind, such as cold, blueness, and softness. When the mind reflects on these sensations, it receives a second set of ideas pertaining to these sensory operations. These include *perception, thinking, doubting, believing, reasoning, knowing,* and *willing.*

No Innate Ideas

As with other philosophers of the seventeenth and eighteenth centuries, Locke was fascinated with questions about the limits of the human mind. In his "Epistle to the Reader" he introduces the subject matter, saying that the job of the philosopher is that of an "under-laborer" who must clear the ground and remove "some of the rubbish in the way of our knowledge." He thought that rationalism had claimed that the power of reason to know things was greater than it actually was and had actually "meddled in things" that exceed the mind's comprehension.

In his *Essay,* which comprises four large books, Locke began his argument by pointing out that while innate ideas are universally accepted by humankind, such universal agreement does not prove them to be innate. Even manifest principles of logic such as the principle of identity ("Everything is equal to itself"), the principle of contradiction ("It is impossible for the same thing to be and not to be"), and the principle of the excluded middle ("Something either is or it isn't") are not even known to "children and to idiots," Locke says. So how could we have known such principles at birth?

FACT

The school of empiricism rejects Descartes and the rationalist notion of innate ideas. They believe that everything you know must come from sensory experience and observations of the physical world. Prior to such experience the mind is "a blank slate."

Further, when someone maintains that he knows mathematics and logical truths *a priori*—that is by reason and not by experience—this hardly proves that such notions are innate. Even moral principles—such as the Golden Rule or particular moral propositions like "Stealing is wrong"—are not known innately, for they require proof.

Simple and Complex Ideas

After a person has sensations, his mind forms ideas. For instance, you see a red rose that smells sweet and soon are able to form ideas of redness and sweetness. Obviously, you don't need to be looking at a red thing or presently smelling a sweet thing to have the ideas of such things in your mind. Anything of which the mind is aware Locke calls an "idea."

How can ideas be categorized? Locke distinguishes between *simple ideas,* which come from one sense, such as bitter, sour, cold, and hot, which contain no other ideas and which cannot be created by you, and *complex ideas,* which are produced by the mind when it compounds and combines simple ideas. God is one example of a complex idea. To arrive at the idea of God, you can simply enlarge your stock of simple ideas such as existence, time, knowledge, power, goodness, and so on. Complex ideas may also be strange things such as unicorns or satyrs that have no actual existence but will always be analyzable into a medley of simple ideas acquired through experience.

Primary Qualities, Secondary Qualities, and Substance

In his systematic *Essay,* Locke distinguished between ideas, whether simple or complex, and objective reality, or that external world which the ideas designate. Ideas, like those of greenness and hardness, are within you. By contrast, real things are outside of you and possess the powers or qualities that excite your ideas. These powers or qualities include primary and secondary qualities.

The primary qualities of objects are their real qualities. That is, they are measurable and objective. These qualities are in the objects themselves. Such primary qualities include *solidity, extension, figure, motion, rest,* and *number,* all of which excite or produce similar ideas in your mind. Thus, when you say that you experience primary qualities, your ideas are only copies of the qualities themselves, like mental images corresponding to the external things as they really exist.

The objects themselves also produce those sensations that are not in the objects themselves but constitute the *secondary qualities* which you associate with them. Unlike primary qualities, which are objective, these secondary qualities are subjective. Examples of these secondary qualities are color, sound, smell, and taste.

To explain his idea of secondary qualities, Locke uses the example of porphyry, a crystal of reddish color. This red stone does have the primary quality of occupying space, but it only appears to have the secondary quality of redness. In fact, the proof of the redness being secondary and not primary is that the color changes according to the light that shines on it!

Locke also postulated a third quality of objects to explain how they can cause changes in the primary qualities of other objects, just as the sun has the power to "make wax white, and fire to make lead fluid." In other words, any object can so change or affect other things that you will sense them differently from the way you did before.

Besides primary and secondary qualities, Locke believed in the existence of *substance*. Substance means literally "standing under." A thing's substance is a substratum underlying and supporting the primary qualities of it. But believing in a nondescript "substance" provides difficulties for an empiricist.

For one, what is this substance like? Locke confessed that he was unable to answer this question—he called substance an "I-know-not-what" thing. He therefore fits the category of a metaphysical agnostic, asserting that the ultimate nature of reality remains unknown. You know only the primary and secondary qualities belonging to a substance, but the substance itself remains inscrutable.

Degrees of Knowledge

Locke classified knowledge into three degrees, or levels: intuitive, demonstrative, and sensitive. Intuitive knowledge is immediate and is the highest kind of knowledge. Demonstrative knowledge results from a chain of reasoning, as in logic or mathematical proofs. Sensitive knowledge concerns those things you know that originate from your senses.

Intuitive knowledge consists of the immediate awareness of agreement or disagreement between two ideas. For example, you have an immediate, indubitable knowledge that five is greater than three.

Locke is similar to Descartes in thinking that people have an immediate knowledge of their own existence. If you know that you doubt, then you know (as Descartes had asserted) that you must exist in order to doubt. You also know intuitively that a square is not a triangle, that powder blue is different from royal blue, and so forth.

Demonstrative knowledge consists of understanding (by means of reasoning) the logical relationships among ideas. If you know that all men are mortal, and Socrates is a man, then you know demonstrably that Socrates is mortal. This deductive conclusion comes from a chain of reasoning. Other examples are the deductive conclusions of geometry and calculus.

Sensitive knowledge begins with perceptions of particular objects. You accept these perceptions as real, but they represent probable facts and not certain truths about the external world. Cause-effect relationships fall into this category. For instance, if you notice repeatedly that a certain event precedes a given result—like a cue ball contacting an eight ball and sending it into the corner pocket—you conclude that there is probably a cause-effect relationship between them. So your knowledge of such cause-effect relations begins with sensations.

God and Moral Knowledge

True to his empiricism, Locke tries to construct the idea of God—that is, an infinite being—from his finite experiences. Starting with the reflective knowledge of your own mind and your finite experience of human existence—duration, knowledge, power, wisdom, and all other positive qualities—Locke says in his *Essay*, "We enlarge every one of these with our idea of infinity; and so putting them together, make our complex idea of God."

Two things should be noted. One, Locke differs greatly from the rationalists. Rationalists like Anselm and René Descartes use conceptual proofs in their attempts to prove God's existence. They define God as a supreme being whose very essence implies his existence. For Locke this would not do, since for Locke God is a complex idea extrapolated from an individual's own ideas of finitude. To begin to assert God's existence by using an idea of perfection is, as he states in *Essay*, "an ill way of establishing his truth and silencing atheists." He reasons that (a) some people lack an idea of God altogether, and (b) among those who possess ideas of God, their ideas are at variance.

Cosmological Argument

In one respect, Locke is hardly different from several medieval philosophers. For instance, he is similar to Thomas Aquinas in the manner that he argues for the existence of God. Locke's argument is mainly "cosmological" and fits the definition of what he calls "demonstrative knowledge."

Locke believed that you could prove the existence of God with the same degree of certainty that you can deduce conclusions in geometry.

That is, he believed that since you know that nature is a system of causes and powers, you must conclude that there is an original, supreme source of this system, namely, God.

On the one hand, nature could not have existed eternally; on the other hand, it could not have come from nothing, for then it would be uncaused. Therefore, it must have been brought into existence by a supremely intelligent being.

His conclusion combines premises found in Aquinas, especially his second "casual" argument and his fifth "design" argument, with rational intuitions found in Descartes. He used Descartes's intuitions that:

1. Something cannot come from nothing.
2. The cause must have all the perfections that it imparts to its effect.

From these considerations he deduces the existence of an eternal, powerful, and intelligent cause.

Locke subscribed to deism as opposed to theism. Deism is a system of thought based on reason—not on belief—which acknowledges the existence of God and his creation of the world, but denies the theistic idea that God intervenes in the world, either in the forms of miracles or revelation. This was a popular view in the seventeenth century.

Morality

There are no innate moral principles "written on the heart," Locke said. Since Locke rejected the notion of innate ideas, moral, political, and religious ideas must be regarded as arising from experiences. Since you have no direct sensations corresponding to good and evil, you must find other sensations from which these notions are derived.

As might be expected with an empiricist philosopher, Locke begins with the experiences of pleasure and pain. Simply put, you call "good" whatever tends to cause pleasure and "evil" anything that tends to produce pain. In this manner, he is not unlike Epicurus and Hobbes before him.

Locke, however, goes beyond the standards of the individual in assessing morality and turns to the standards of society. In fact, moral good and evil must be in conformity with or opposed to the law of the land. There are three kinds of laws:

1. The divine law
2. The civil law
3. The law of opinion or reputation

Because the last two have their origin in human values, they will be of relative value, depending on the time and place being considered. The laws of one land will allow for practices that are prohibited elsewhere.

That said, Locke believed, perhaps naively, that conformity to God's law tends to advance the general good of humankind. Further, he argued, there is at least a core of agreement among civil law, divine law, and the law of opinion or reputation. All three would no doubt agree that stealing and killing are evil and that generosity and consideration for others are good. Locke claimed in Book II of the *Essay* that God's law may be discovered either through "the light of nature" or "the voice of revelation."

FACT

The founding fathers of the United States were deeply influenced by the philosophy of John Locke, especially his notion of social contract and his belief that humankind is endowed with certain inalienable rights, including life, liberty, and the pursuit of happiness.

Locke ventures on to shaky ground, however, when he displays his rationalist colors. He concludes in his *Essay* that "morality is capable of demonstration as well as mathematics." Among his candidates for rationally demonstrable principles, he includes "Where there is no property there is no injustice." He claims, amusingly, that this is as certain as any demonstration in Euclidean geometry. But, obviously, there are many injustices that don't involve property.

When he returns to his empiricist foundation, he seems to occupy sturdier ground. Though the moral codes of societies differ, he says, there is a high degree of uniformity among them. Why is this so? Locke's answer is that *experience* teaches which kinds of behavior are beneficial and which are not. Thus, the law of opinion or reputation carries its own wisdom, since it is based on the collective experience of citizens. Indeed, societies know well that killing, stealing, and other practices fail to advance the satisfaction of the community.

Locke's optimism about human motives in a state of nature is diametrically opposed to Thomas Hobbes's idea. (Hobbes had said that life in a presocietal state of nature would be "nasty, brutish, and short.") According to Locke, people, even without government, are peaceful, happy, and basically benevolent. Despite occasional differences, people on the whole will get on quite well together.

Natural Law and Natural Rights

Locke's political theory (set forth in 1690 in his *Two Treatises of Government*) defended the doctrine of human liberty and human rights against absolutism. Men are born free and equal, since in a state of nature only natural laws obtained and they knew of legal standards. When a society developed, the members entered into a social contract in which they granted to selected officials certain powers set forth in their constitution. Government is therefore collective by nature; it is founded on and hence always subject to the mutual consent and joint decisions of the citizens.

In *Two Treatises* he argues against the divine right of kings and maintains that all men are free and equal in the state of nature and possess certain natural rights. Locke's political doctrines were incorporated into the American Constitution and into the constitution in France in 1871. It was Thomas Jefferson who said of Locke's *Second Treatise*, "It is perfect as far as it goes," meaning that it was a blueprint for a working constitution.

During his lifetime Locke published most of his political writings anonymously, preferring to keep them separate from the *Essay,* which he regarded as his most important work.

QUESTION?

What is the difference between Hobbes's and Locke's social contract?
Thomas Hobbes believed that a social contract existed between the ruler and the masses in an effort, by any means necessary, to keep civilization from reverting to its natural state, which Hobbes believed was savage anarchy. Locke believed that the contract is there for the greater good of society and to uphold the inherent rights of the individuals.

Evaluation and Significance

Locke's main philosophical concern, like many of the philosophers of the seventeenth and eighteenth centuries, was epistemological. Specifically, his questions were about the capabilities of the human mind. His theory of knowledge is of major importance to the empirical philosophy that succeeded the continental rationalism founded by Descartes. The *Essay,* he maintains in the opening sentences of Book I, is a critical inquiry "into the original, certainty, and extent of human knowledge, together with the grounds and degrees of belief, option and assent."

He was an original, the first philosopher who set out to explore the limits of knowledge starting from an empirical base. It took David Hume to expose his vulnerable flanks. For David Hume—who alongside Locke appeared like a radical skeptic—thought that Locke was inconsistent in his empirical principles. In particular, he maintained that Locke's ideas of substance, the self, and God cannot be known from experience.

As Locke had maintained that all knowledge begins with sensations, so too did Newton embrace empiricism as the basis for all scientific laws. Take any one of his laws, such as the law of gravitation, and you will find that it describes the observable behavior of natural bodies and justifies your calculations about the future.

CHAPTER 14

David Hume:
The Radical Skeptic

David Hume (1711–76) cannot be omitted from a list of the greatest philosophers. Hume took empirical philosophy further than Locke did. He applied it relentlessly to issues of how people attain knowledge, to beliefs about God and miracles, and to moral philosophy. When he was finished wielding empiricist principles like a scalpel, nothing that could not be known by experience remained standing.

The Life of David Hume

Born in Edinburgh in 1711, David Hume's father died when he was two. His mother, who came from a family of lawyers, dedicated herself to her children's education. He was steered toward the law and admitted to Edinburgh University at the age of twelve. There he discovered he had "an insurmountable aversion to everything but the pursuits of philosophy and general learning."

Hume left the university without taking a degree but carried on a life of study at home. When he was just twenty-eight, he published his first—and as it turned out his greatest—philosophical work, the *Treatise of Human Nature* (1739). His reputation as a philosopher was for attacking orthodoxies. As a result, he failed to land an academic position at the University of Glasgow in 1752. His iconoclastic reputation grew with the publication of his *Natural History of Religion* in 1757. The volume took an unkind look at the origin of our religious impulses. He then claimed to "live quietly and keep remote from all clamor," and so he withheld publication of *Dialogues Concerning Natural Religion* until after his death. It would become a classic in the philosophy of religion. He also wrote a six-volume *History of England*.

Today, *A Treatise of Human Nature* is considered one of the most important works in the history of philosophy. But the British public in 1739 didn't share that view. It hardly sold. In Hume's words, it "fell dead-born from the press, without reaching such distinction as even to excite a murmur among the zealots."

He lived the last years of his life in his hometown of Edinburgh, where he was quite prominent in intellectual and literary circles. Two years of constant illness preceded his death in 1776. It is nearly impossible to capture the importance of Hume's contribution to philosophy and the extent of his influence over the two centuries since his death.

Knowledge Begins with Sense Impressions

David Hume allows that the human mind possesses the freedom to roam across all sorts of territory. But, he adds, the mind is "really confined within very narrow limits." After all is said and done, the contents of the mind can all be reduced to the materials given by the senses and experience, materials that Hume calls perceptions. The perceptions of the mind take two forms, which Hume distinguishes as impressions and ideas.

The Logic of Impressions and Ideas

Hume opens his *Treatise* by considering the ways in which a human being perceives the world around him. He says that perceptions are of two kinds: *impressions,* which are "all our sensations, passions, and emotions as they make their first appearance in the soul," and *ideas,* which are the "faint images of these impressions in thinking and reasoning." The impression of the Beethoven sonata comes as you are listening to the music. The idea of the sonata comes to you in the hours, days, and months afterward. Impressions or ideas may be either simple or complex.

All simple ideas come from simple impressions. Impressions and ideas make up the total content of the mind. The original stuff of thought, however, is called an *impression,* which is similar to John Locke's "sensation." When you look at a cup of coffee, the shape of that cup, as well as the color and other qualities of it, and the aroma of the beverage "impress" themselves upon your organs of sense. So impressions are the first building blocks of knowledge.

From impressions come ideas. Ideas, in Hume's words, are copies of impressions. If you turn your eyes away from that cup of coffee, you can still have an *idea* of the cylinder-shape of the cup, the steam rising from the container, even though you are not presently having an impression of it. Without impressions, which are vivid when you first have them, there can be no ideas.

Matters of Fact and Relations of Ideas

Of the many philosophical insights contributed by Hume, perhaps none is greater than his division of knowledge into "matters of fact" and "relations of ideas." According to Hume, if some object of reason is neither a matter of fact nor a relation of ideas, then it cannot count as knowledge at all. Because he thinks that all genuine knowledge is of one or the other kind, his revelation is known as "Hume's Fork."

One of Hume's major objectives in the treatise is to show that:

All the objects of human reason or enquiry may naturally be divided into two kinds, to wit, Relations of Ideas and Matters of Fact. Of the first kind are the sciences of Geometry, Algebra, and Arithmetic; and in short, every affirmation which is either intuitively or demonstratively certain. . . . Propositions of this kind are discoverable by the mere operation of thought, without dependence on what is anywhere existent in the universe.

Matters of Fact, which are the second object of human reason, are not ascertained in the same manner; nor is our evidence of their truth, however great, of a like nature with the foregoing. The contrary of every matter of fact is still possible; because it can never imply a contradiction. . . . That the sun will not rise tomorrow is no less intelligible a proposition and implies no more contradiction than the affirmation that it will rise.

You know propositions like $3 \times 5 = 15$ or that the sum of the interior angles of parallel lines cut by a transversal equal 360 degrees "by the mere operation of thought." Put another way, you know the truth of these claims *a priori,* or prior to experience. They are certainties and cannot be contradicted. You know matters of fact differently.

FACT

Hume was eighteen when he made a philosophical discovery that opened him up to "a new scene of thought." This led him to throw over "every other Pleasure or Business to apply entirely to it." He didn't recount what this insight was, but it was likely his theory of causality: that our beliefs about causes and effect depend on sentiment, custom, and habit, and not upon reason, not upon abstract, general laws of nature.

You can never be sure of matters of fact. To follow Hume's example, you can have impressions of the sun rising on seven consecutive days. Further investigation will tell you that it has always risen. So you may think you are entitled to say "I know for certain that the sun will rise tomorrow." But you cannot know this. All that you know—and all that anyone knows—is that it has always risen. You cannot know that it will continue to rise. You only have impressions *to* this point in time, not *beyond* this point. In addition, there is no logical contradiction in your asserting that the sun will not rise tomorrow.

As Hume says, "The contrary of every mater of fact is still possible; because it can never imply a contradiction." It is unlikely that the sun will not rise tomorrow, but it is still a possibility. Few philosophers have stated a truth as clearly, forcefully, or profoundly. As opposed to relations of ideas, which are known *a priori,* you know matters of fact *a posteriori,* or after experience.

Hume Versus Locke: All Metaphysics Is "Illusion"

If, as Hume contends, the only objects of human knowledge are matters of fact and relations of ideas, then many entities thought to be real will have been cut out by Hume's scalpel. If you have no impression of metaphysical entities like Gods, souls, selves, substances, and other nonperceptible entities, then these things are not objects of human knowledge.

Nowhere is Hume's disagreement with Locke more apparent than on the matter of the existence of metaphysical entities. As you saw, Locke argued for the existence of God, substance, and the soul despite not having a sensation of either of them. He *inferred* the existence of a supreme being from his experience of an orderly universe. Locke also assumed the existence of substance, though he had no experience. He accepted Locke's "I think; therefore, I am" argument for the self.

But Hume rejects the existence of all these metaphysical entities. You cannot have ideas of them, he argues, for without impressions there are no ideas and impressions of them do not exist.

The Self

What does Hume's empiricist razor do to the self? He is very clear. "From what impression could my idea of self be derived?" he asks. Do we have any impression that is invariably associated with our idea of the self? "When I enter most intimately into what I call myself," says Hume, "I always stumble on some particular perception or other, of heat or cold, love or hatred, pain or pleasure. I can never catch *myself* at any time without a perception and can never observe anything but the perception." Minds are "nothing but a bundle or collection of different perceptions." Your memory gives you the impression of your continuous identity. Hume compares the mind to "a kind of theatre where several perceptions successively make their appearance," but adds that "we have not the most distant notion of the place where these scenes are represented." In short, there is no self over and above the bundle of perceptions we have in the course of a lifetime.

Hume says that when you see a cue ball about to strike another pool ball, you have nothing like a sensory perception of a cause. All that you really see is that "a movement of the cue is followed by the movement of the ball." You see such a "succession" of events. This is "all that appears to the outward senses." But no one has any perception of an occult cause.

God

Hume was a skeptic about God's existence. He was inclined to deny the traditional design arguments philosophers used to demonstrate the existence of God (see Thomas Aquinas's "fifth way" argument on page 101). Hume thought that the argument breaks down. For one, the inference from an orderly universe to a maker of the universe "is uncertain, because the subject lies entirely beyond the reach of human experience." The whole argument from design rests upon the proposition "that the cause or causes of order in the universe probably bear some remote analogy to human intelligence." But how can you assign a cause to the universe when you have never experienced the cause? The existence of the universe is surely an empirical fact, but you cannot infer from it the existence of God, since you have neither impressions of God nor of the alleged act of creation.

FACT

Hume's early essay "Of Superstition and Bondage" made for much secular thinking about the history of religion. At the time, philosophers had to be circumspect in their critiques of religion. In fact, less than fifteen years before Hume was born, eighteen-year-old college student Thomas Aikenhead was put on trial for saying openly that he thought that Christianity was nonsense; he was later convicted and hanged for blasphemy.

In sum, such metaphysical substances don't exist on either prong of Hume's fork. At the end of the *Enquiry Concerning Human Understanding* Hume writes:

If we take in our hand any volume of divinity or school metaphysics, for instance, let us ask, Does it contain any abstract reasoning concerning quantity or number? No. Does it contain any experimental reasoning concerning matter of fact and existence? No. Commit it then to the flames: for it can contain nothing but sophistry and illusion.

Burn all texts that mention metaphysical entities that can never be proven. Considering how many philosophers have written about souls, substances, and Gods, that would make for one enormous bonfire! As strongly as Hume argues, he cannot be considered an atheist, for atheists say without hesitation that there is no God. But Hume has not said that. He argues that you cannot know of the existence or nonexistence of God since you have no impression of him.

Skepticism about Causality

Commonsense thinking tells you that there are cause-effect relationships in the world. You are apt to accept statements like "Every event must have a cause." But Hume goes beyond common sense and asks, "What is the origin of the idea of causality?" Since ideas are copies of impressions, he asks, what impression gives you the idea of causality? His answer is that there is no impression corresponding to that idea.

The games of billiards can be used to illustrate this principle. If you see event A, a seven ball struck by a cue and then event B, the seven ball contacting a six ball, you have witnessed two events. You have an impression of each event. But Hume says there is no third event or relationship like causality.

FACT

David Hume was also skeptical about miracles. He said that when it comes down to considering uniform, consistent laws of nature, like gravity, and you measure those against the testimony of miracles, one must always go with the laws of nature, which far outweigh any testimony about miracles.

How then does the idea of causality arise in the mind? It arises in two ways. Experience furnishes you with two relations: first, there is the relation of *contiguity,* for A and B are always close together; second, there is *priority in time,* for A, the "cause" always precedes B, "the effect." But there is still another relation that the idea of causality suggests to commonsense observers. You think that between A and B there is a "necessary connection." But neither contiguity nor priority implies "necessary" connection between objects.

All that this necessary connection boils down to is the *habit* of mind of expecting event B whenever you have seen event A. "It is by experience only that we infer the existence of one object from another," he says. You have seen one event *constantly conjoined* with a second. But this constant conjunction of objects is not a quality in the objects you observe but is rather a "habit of association" in the mind produced by the repetition of instances of A and B.

Hume's answer is that you are continually observing pairs of events, such as cues striking balls, flames producing heat, penicillin curing strep throat, and so on. One part of the pair makes you think of the other: you come to expect heat when you see flames. In the end you come to say that a flame *must* produce heat and you call the flame the cause of the heat.

This is where the idea of cause and effect comes from. What you call cause and effect is not "in the world" but "in us"; it is psychological predisposition to expect a second event to occur after seeing the first. What Hume has provided is a description of the way in which the belief about cause and effect arises.

Morality

Hume's views on morality are distinctly empirical. You are not born knowing moral ideas. But Hume does recognize in humanity an instinctive capacity for empathy. That is just the beginning.

No matter what culture a person is a part of or what time he was born into, Hume thought that there were universal ethical feelings that cut across differences in culture, time, and place. Imagine a person witnessing a heroic act. In 2006 a New York man dove into the path of an oncoming train to help a man who had fallen onto the subway tracks. People who learned of his action called it "heroic" and "altruistic." Hume would say that the man's action aroused a feeling of approval in observers. "A generous, a brave, a noble deed, performed by an adversary, commands our approbation; while in its consequences it may be acknowledged to be prejudicial to our particular interest," Hume says.

According to Hume, your sense of morality includes an instinctive capacity to "bestow praise on virtuous actions, performed in distant ages and remote countries; where the utmost subtlety of imagination would not discover any appearances of self-interest, or had any connection of our present happiness and security with events so widely separated from us."

The Moral Sense School

Hume is recognized as being a member of the "moral sense school" of philosophers, so-called because they thought the moral sense was like a sixth sense. Your sense of sympathy and antipathy, which is responsible for your feelings of approval and disapproval, is the sense Hume refers to most. "Reason is and ought to be the slave of the passions," Hume wrote. It is emotions like sympathy, which better than reason alone, lead you to the correct assessments of human behavior.

The sympathetic feelings that you experience are not restricted to events that you see before your eyes. When you learn of heinous actions—such as accounts of genocide and slavery in history—your sense of disapproval is aroused. Feelings of approval and disapproval are built into the human frame.

Utilitarianism

According to Hume's critics, Hume's ethics was grounded too shakily on feelings of approval and disapproval. Morality, his critics continued, needs to be based on something fixed, permanent, and absolute. How can the entire plan of morality be based in unstable faculties and emotions? Further, critics argue, you find the role of God completely absent from Hume's account. Thus, his whole approach is both flimsy and atheistic, according to some.

But not according to Jeremy Bentham. Bentham, a British philosopher known as "the Father of Utilitarianism," was attracted to Hume's account. Bentham was in search of a nonreligious approach to morality that was based on empirical fact and not in mysterious rational intuitions. Bentham honed in on Hume's contention that you assess actions based on their usefulness—or, as Hume expressed it, their "utility." This became the basis of the ethical thought of utilitarianism, championed by Bentham and others throughout the nineteenth century.

Utility connects his moral sense idea. This is because you approve of actions that are "useful" or have utility and disapprove of those without utility.

FACT

Hume once told a friend about his "conversion" to Christianity. He was passing along the Nor Loch in Edinburgh and he slipped and fell into the mud. Being heavyset, he could not regain his feet. Some passing fishwives refused to help the well-known atheist until he recited the Lord's Prayer and the Apostle's Creed. He did so and was helped up by the brawny women. Hume later said that Edinburgh fishwives were the "most acute theologians he had ever met."

Another Empiricist: George Berkeley

Locke's theory of knowledge might be labeled commonsense realism or representative realism. This is because he believed that a person's sensation of objects—and her ideas about them—faithfully represent the way the world is. Bishop Berkeley did something far more radical: he denied the existence of matter.

George Berkeley (1685–1753) was Irish by birth though of British descent. When he was fifteen he attended Trinity College, Dublin, where his studies included Locke's philosophy. Before he turned thirty and in a space of three years he wrote *A Treatise Concerning the Principles of Human Knowledge* in 1710 and *Three Dialogues Between Hylas and Philonous* in 1713.

"To Be Is to Be Perceived"

Many philosophers will forever be associated with a single statement. For René Descartes "I think; therefore, I am" (or *cogito ergo sum*) is a starting point for metaphysics and epistemology. John Locke said that each of us is a "blank slate" (or *tabula rasa*) prior to sensation. For Berkeley that phrase is, "To be is to be perceived" (or *esse es percipi).* His philosophy is called *idealism,* for he argues that, strictly speaking, only ideas have existence.

His philosophy and other philosophies that take the view that the external world is somehow produced by the mind is known as *idealism.* There are only two kinds of things that exist: spirits and ideas. Spirits perceive and ideas are perceived. Ideas are passive, but spirits are active and able to cause ideas. Human beings are finite spirits, but God is an infinite spirit who causes many of their ideas.

For example, if you perceive a rose, your idea of the rose has existence. But the rose has no existence separate from your idea of it. Berkeley's startling and provocative formula—"To be is to be perceived"—means that things exist only if they are being perceived or can be perceived. It follows from this that if something were not being perceived, it would not exist. The only sense that can be made of the word *existence* is connected with the perception of that thing. He wrote:

All the choir of heaven and furniture of the earth, in a word all the mighty frame of the world, have not any subsistence without a mind, that their being

*is to be perceived or known; that consequently so long as they are not actu-
ally perceived by me, or do not exist in my mind or that of any other created
spirit, they must either have no existence at all, or else subsist in the mind of
some eternal spirit.*

Thus, to those who argue that material things have some kind of absolute existence without any relation to their being perceived, Berkeley replies,
"that is unintelligible." He explains: "The absolute existence of unthinking
matter are words without meaning." This says that sensible things exist only
insofar as they are perceived. "The only thing whose existence we deny is
what the philosophers call matter or corporeal substance."

The upshot is that when philosophers such as Locke label things *substance* and others use terms like *matter,* they are using words that denote
nothing. If you mean by matter or substance some independently existing
thing out in the world, then you are referring to something that does not
exist. Also, Locke's distinction between primary and secondary qualities
(between such structural properties as figure, motion, and shape, on the
one hand, and color, odor, and sound, on the other) on the ground that the
former are objective, the latter subjective, cannot be maintained; the primary qualities depend on the secondary; they are equally subjective.

Berkeley also denied the existence of what are called abstract objects—
or what the medievals called "universals" and what Plato called "forms" or
"ideas." For instance, if someone said that redness exists apart from any
red thing or that goodness exists apart from any good action or person,
then he is saying that redness and goodness exist as independent entities.
For Berkeley this is impossible, since nothing that is not being perceived
can exist. The idea of redness without a red thing or goodness without a
good action is a nonsense idea, every bit as much as matter without a sensation of it.

God and the Existence of Things

Is Berkeley saying that when you leave your room and cease to perceive your furniture and computer that these objects cease to exist? No. For
another mind is still perceiving these objects, even when you have left the

building. For even if you are not perceiving these objects, God is perceiving them. Berkley explains:

> *When I deny sensible things an existence out of my mind, I do not mean my mind in particular, but all minds. Now it is plain that things have an existence exterior to my mind, since I find them by experience to be independent of it. There is therefore some other mind wherein they exist, during the intervals between the time of my perceiving them. . . . There is an omnipresent eternal mind, which knows and comprehends all things, and exhibits them to our view in such a manner and according to such rules as he himself has ordained, and are termed by us The Laws of Nature.*

The existence of things, therefore, depends upon the existence of God, and God is the cause of the orderliness of things in nature.

The order in nature is created and maintained by God, who secures the reality of all things by his perception.

Evaluation and Significance

More than any philosopher in history, David Hume laid the groundwork for the skepticism and strict empiricism of the twentieth century. One only has to look ahead to the analytic philosophy of Bertrand Russell, especially in his essay "On Induction," and the logical positivism of A. J. Ayer in his book *Language, Truth, and Logic* with its attack on all metaphysics and theology. The reach of David Hume's radical skepticism extended for centuries.

It is not merely that Hume laid the groundwork for empiricisms and skeptical schools of thought to come. His influence is larger. For Hume gave to philosophy an impetus to question any and all statements that could not be substantiated with reason or by exacting tests of experience. He spared no target, be it morality or the follies of organized religion, including statements about God, the soul, and claims about the same.

Berkeley took empiricism in the direction of immaterialism, denying the existance of matter and indeed all objects said to exist independently of thought.

CHAPTER 15

Immanuel Kant: Combining Empiricism and Rationalism

Kant goes down in the history of thought as a giant. Kant declared himself neither empiricist nor rationalist but achieved a synthesis of the two in his greatest work *The Critique of Pure Reason* (1781), which marked the end of the period of the Enlightenment and began a new period of philosophy, German idealism. Kant claimed that knowledge was impossible without accepting truths from both rationalist and empiricist schools of thought. He based his ethics on reason and said that moral duties could be deduced by all rational beings.

The Life of Immanuel Kant

Immanuel Kant (1724–1904) was born in Konigsberg (now Kaliningrad), East Prussia. He was also educated at Konigsberg University, which became famous as a center of philosophy through his long tenure on its faculty. Kant was brought up a pietist. This sect of Protestants were known to lead puritanical lives and were devoted to religious duties. Kant also taught an incredible variety of courses at the University of Konigsberg, including metaphysics, logic, philosophical theology, ethics, aesthetics, as well as nonphilosophical topics such as geography, mathematics, physics, and anthropology.

Aside from Kant's teaching and publishing, he lived a largely uneventful life, hardly traveling from his native Konigsberg. Despite such limited travel, Kant achieved universal fame in philosophy.

Kant's "Copernican Revolution"

Kant noticed a problem with the empiricist manner of coming to knowledge. If all you come to know and collect are particular sensations or particular impressions, as the empiricists said, how can you arrive at necessary and universal knowledge? Put another way, how can you explain the possibility of scientific knowledge, or, more precisely, the relationship between causes and effect, which enables the mind to grasp scientific truths? Kant had an answer to the question that bridges the gap between two schools of thought—rationalism and empiricism.

QUESTION?

What personal traits did Kant exhibit?
Immanuel Kant lived a quiet, orderly life, but he enjoyed the company of others. He hardly traveled and he earned a legendary reputation for punctuality. It was said that people could set their clocks by him as he took his early morning walk past their windows.

Kant's own theory of knowledge reconfigures the way humans know things. Rather than saying that people are all passive perceivers observing the world, Kant believed that humans are active in knowing the world. In agreeing with his empiricist predecessors he says, "There can be no doubt that all our knowledge begins with experience. But though all our knowledge begins with experience, it does not follow that it all arises out of experience."

Instead of an outside-in approach to knowledge of the empiricists, in which objects cause passive perceivers to have "sensations" (Locke) or "impressions" (Hume), Kant said that the categories of space and time—which he called "forms of intuition"—were imposed on experiences by the human mind in order to make sense of it. This Kant proudly called his "Copernican Revolution." Just as Copernicus rejected the idea that the sun revolved around the earth, Kant had solved the problem of how the mind acquires knowledge from experience by arguing that the mind imposes principles upon experience to generate knowledge.

FACT

Kant proposed that the mind has "categories of understanding," which catalogue, codify, and make sense of the world. The mind cannot experience anything that is not filtered through the mind's eye. Therefore, you can never know the true nature of reality. In this sense, Kant claims that indeed "perception is reality."

Kant is saying that in order to have any knowledge, the mind needs to have a set of further organizing principles. These principles are found in the faculty of the understanding. Just as a cookie is the product of a certain content (the dough) being processed by a form (the cookie press), so knowledge is the product of content (what you sense) and understanding (space and time as forms of intuition) working together.

In other words, both *a priori* and *a posteriori* elements are essential. Without sensation, no object would be perceptible. Without understanding, no object could be conceived. As Kant said in his *Critique of Pure Reason*, "Thoughts without contents are empty, perceptions without conceptions are blind. . . . Understanding can perceive nothing, the senses can think nothing. Knowledge arises only from their united action."

Hume Versus Kant on the Possibilities of Knowledge

Despite Kant's "Copernican Revolution," the issue between Kant and empiricism comes down to what kinds of things are known. Kant confessed that the skeptical challenge set forth by Hume "awakened me from my dogmatic slumbers." One way of capturing the issue between them is to ask what kinds of propositions or judgments can be known.

Hume had said that all knowledge fit one of two categories. True propositions were either matters of fact or relations of ideas. The first kind includes contingent statements, such as "Cadillacs are long-lasting cars." These statements are truths of observation or fact, but are contingently true only. The second kind includes statements such as "Triangles have three angles." These are necessarily true, but empty, since they tell you nothing about the world. Statements that fall into neither category—like metaphysical statements—are pure "sophistry and illusion," Hume claimed.

But Kant thought that Hume's two categories were inadequate. For one, statements like "Every effect had a cause" would be unjustified on Hume's system, since he reduced causality to the "habit" of expectation that the future will always resemble the past. So Kant's remedy was to introduce a third class of propositions—what he called synthetic *a priori* propositions.

Kant spoke succinctly about the limits of knowledge. For Kant, the only world that one can know is the world of objects that appear within experience. He refers to the things in the world as they appear to you as phenomena. What one cannot have knowledge of are things-in-themselves, i.e., noumena.

Types of Judgments

Hume and Kant agree on the existence of these first three types of statements.

- **Analytic *a priori:*** In analytic judgments the subject of the sentence implies the predicate. "Squares have four sides" is an example. The subject "square" implies the predicate "four sides." We also know this *a priori*—or before experience—not after experience.
- **Analytic *a posteriori:*** There are none, since any analytic judgment is known prior to any experience.
- **Synthetic *a posteriori:*** In a sentence like "Japanese cars are more reliable than French cars" the subject "Japanese cars" does not imply the truth of the predicate "more reliable than French cars." It is called a synthetic proposition, since it brings together two different ideas. It can be established as true, but true empirically.

However, a disagreement would arise over a fourth category, synthetic *a priori.*

From 1770 through 1781 Kant went into isolation to write his masterwork, the *Critique of Pure Reason.* His preoccupation was to explain his quest to understand the connection between sensible and intellectual faculties. Though fond of conversation and the company of others, Kant isolated himself, despite friends' attempts to bring him out.

Synthetic a priori

Hume, who was skeptical about any claims that go beyond a person's experience as a perceiver, claims that there are no synthetic statements known *a priori.* Metaphysical statements about Gods, souls, substance, and causality are included. Kant disagreed, arguing that "Every event has a cause" is one example of a synthetic *a priori* statement. It is synthetic, since it cannot be established by an analysis of its terms, and it is *a priori* and necessary because the concept of causality is a pure concept of understanding—like space and time—and is part of the intellectual structure. It is an *a priori* and necessary condition of the manner in which people experience the world.

What Appears and What Is: Phenomena and Noumena

Contrary to Hume, Kant argued that synthetic *a priori* judgments are possible in mathematics and physics. But are they possible in metaphysics? Kant was pessimistic about the ability of human reason to acquire theoretical knowledge of any reality lying beyond the boundaries of human experience. According to Kant, one cannot know things-in-themselves.

Kant maintained that one could have knowledge of causality in the realm of appearances. In fact, the rationalist and empiricist traditions begun by both René Descartes and John Locke had both assumed there was a dichotomy between ideas about reality and the real world itself. How could one be sure that the ideas in one's mind correspond to the real world? One cannot. Locke adopts the "representative realist" position, since he thinks ideas represent primary qualities.

God's Existence Cannot Be Proven

From what has been said already, Kant argues that you cannot know of any reality beyond the appearances of things. So though Kant thought that you have knowledge of synthetic *a priori* truths, you only know of these in the world of mathematics and physics. Because you can only know the phenomena and not the noumena, this rules out a host of metaphysical propositions. Included among these are statements like "God exists," "Humans have immortal souls," and so forth. This is because concepts like "God" and "soul" are not revealed in actual experience. Kant said that you can think of such concepts. In fact, they can be inspiring to people and profoundly important in their lives. But you can never know them, for neither Gods nor souls are objects of actual experience.

Neither sense experience (perception) nor the understanding provides information about God, the soul, or the ultimate nature of reality (noumena). Because these three "ideals of reason," as Kant labeled them, transcend the bounds of experience, they are unknowable by the human mind, and you must be forever agnostic as to their existence and nature. Just as you cannot prove these ideals of reason, no one can disprove them either. Kant stated that he had "limited all that we can know to mere phenomena." Despite Kant's disagreement with Hume on the matter of synthetic *a priori* knowledge, he agreed that all knowledge about the world is limited to what can be perceived in actual experience. In *Critique of Pure Reason* Kant, like Hume, calls traditional metaphysics "transcendent illusions." In this way, he says, he "found it necessary to deny knowledge of God, freedom, immortality, in order to find a place for faith."

Ethical Doctrine

If Kant's reputation as a philosopher owed solely to his *Critique of Pure Reason,* with its Copernican Revolution and sundry revelations, he would be held in high esteem. But in addition to his mighty contributions in metaphysics and epistemology, Kant made landmark contributions to ethics. His approach in moral philosophy is the same as with epistemology: since moral principles cannot be established from experience, the mind must contribute its own rational principles to experience. Acting morally is grounded in acting rationally.

To understand Kant's ethics, you must attend to several matters. For one, you must understand what he means by a good will and how he argues that the morality of an action has nothing to do with what is attained by the action. Second, to possess a good will means to act from a motive of duty. Third, an agent acting from duty acts in accord with the moral law or the categorical imperative.

FACT

Kant was raised in a strict pietist household, a then-popular Pentecostal reform movement that stressed intense religious devotion, personal humility, and a literal reading of the Bible. He thus received a stern education that was strict, punitive, and disciplinary and favored Latin and religious instruction over mathematics and science.

A Good Will

Kant begins his little book *The Groundwork of the Metaphysics of Morals* by praising a good will: "Nothing in the world can possibly be conceived which could be called good without qualification except a good will." He proceeds to argue that power, health, wealth, intelligence, wit, judgment, and other qualities are only conditionally good. What is needed to complete these qualities is a good will. For even a villain can have intelligence, sound judgment, and the rest. Osama bin Laden and Adolf Hitler could be described as intelligent; they cannot be described as having the requisite good will or character needed to make proper use of such gifts.

A will is good, Kant says, not because of what it achieves. It is good solely because of its willing. In other words, it must be "good in itself" without regard for consequences. To illustrate his notion of a good will, he compares the morality of two merchants.

The merchants in question perform the same action by giving the correct change to their customers. Suppose you find out that one gave the correct change because he didn't want to suffer a bad reputation by cheating customers. Suppose further that the other gave the correct change because he thought it was his moral duty to do so. Which merchant's action had moral worth? Only the action done from a motive of duty had moral worth. The other action revealed a selfish concern with one's own business reputation and thus possesses no moral worth. Thus, for Kant actions leading to identical consequences do not have the same moral worth. The goodness of an action has everything to do with its motive (Kant calls it a "maxim") and nothing to go with what the action produces.

Acting from Duty: The Categorical Imperative

An agent acting from duty acts with respect for the moral law, according to Kant. This is the only attribute of a good will. Kant's basic moral principle is "Act according to that maxim which you can at the same time will to become a universal law." This is his famed categorical imperative.

It has also been called his universality principle. It requires that we act in a manner that we would will everyone to act. He gives four illustrations of duties to show how the imperative applies.

FACT

It is widely believed that Kant lived only a strict and predictable life, which includes the oft-repeated story that neighbors would set their clocks by his daily walks. This is true only in part. As a young man Kant was a gregarious socialite and he remained fond of attending and hosting dinner parties for most of his life.

Perfect and Imperfect Duties

Kant's first illustration concerns self-preservation: the duty not to commit suicide. Kant instances "a man reduced to despair by a series of misfortunes" but enough in possession of his reason to ask whether it would be "contrary to duty to take his own life." Could the maxim of his action become a universal law of nature? No, for agents possess self-love and must use this self-love to improve life. It would be a contradiction to use self-love to end one's life. With this example you can see that Kant permits no exceptions. No agent, no matter how dire his circumstances, is permitted to end his life. Kant calls such obligations without exception "perfect duties."

Kant's second illustration concerns a person who intends to borrow money and make a false promise to repay it. It might be prudent to make such a promise; that is, it may benefit the agent. But the real question is whether the false promise would be consistent with duty. Here one may inquire whether the maxim of making a false promise should become a universal law. The answer must be "no," since no one would then put any trust in promises, but instead would ridicule all statements beginning with "I promise" as vain pretences. The obligation to keep promises—and to tell the truth generally—is another perfect duty. Unlike the duty to self-preservation, which is a "duty to oneself," the obligation to keep promises is a duty to others.

The third illustration concerns the duty to develop one's talents. If a person possesses a faculty or talent that would be useful, would it be contrary to duty to neglect such a talent? Yes, for ethics are grounded in rationality and rational beings will that their faculties should be developed, since "they serve him and have been given him for all sorts of possible purposes. The duty to develop one's talents is an "imperfect" duty to oneself. An "imperfect" duty is one with exceptions. Which of two talents an agent develops—and when and how the agent develops it—is up to him.

Finally, just as agents are not obligated to develop every faculty and talent they possess, so too they are not obligated to give to others in every instance. There is some leeway for the agent to pick and choose who he will benefit. But he cannot will to live a life where he benefits no one. "It is impossible that such a principle should have the universal validity of a law of nature," Kant says. "Such a will would contradict itself, since many cases might occur in which one would have need of the love and sympathy of others, and in which, by such a law of nature, sprung from his own will, we would deprive himself of all hope of the aid he desires." No man is an island; it is inconsistent for you to will to help no one, since you would then be cutting yourself off from the aid of others, should you ever need it.

Evaluation and Significance

Immanuel Kant was arguably the most important philosopher since the time of Plato and Aristotle. The breadth and depth of his thought is one reason for this reputation. No topic escaped his view. He wrote most famously on metaphysics, epistemology, and ethics, but he also explored aesthetics (*Critique of Judgment,* 1790) and applied ethics in his writings on peace.

No philosopher is immune from criticism, however, and Immanuel Kant was not exempt from counterargument. His ethical arguments have been subject to criticisms. One criticism is that Kant is too unyielding and unable to tolerate exceptions. Thus his universal prohibitions of suicide and keeping promises fail to acknowledge any exceptions at all. If a person had full-blown AIDS or metastasized cancer he would have no better excuse for ending his life than a person suffering some temporary emotional duress. Each is misusing his self-love, according to Kant. But that same premise can be turned back on him. It is arguable that a person wants to end his life because of self-love.

One can also see exceptions to his prohibition on lying. After all, there are lies employed for larger purposes. If a man who appears mad comes to your front door and asks you to return the gun that you promised you would hold for him, you might lie and tell him you put it in storage. Your motive is to save a life, since you fear what he would do with the gun in an agitated state. Both the suicide case and the lying point up the difficulty of conducting ethics without a consideration of consequences, as Kant did.

CHAPTER 16

Utilitarianism: A Philosophy of Pleasure and Happiness

Immanuel Kant's "deontological," or duty-based, approach to ethics put little stock in the results of actions. Utilitarianism puts all stock in such results. The word utility means "useful." All normative moral theories (those that provide norms of human behavior) define what goodness is, so utilitarianism defines a good action as one that is productive of good consequences. For Jeremy Bentham good consequences mean increasing one's own quantity of happiness, which amounts to pleasure. For John Stuart Mill, good consequences include qualitative pleasures, not just quantitative ones.

The Life of Jeremy Bentham

The first proponent of utilitarianism was Jeremy Bentham (1748–1832), who was born in London to a wealthy family. To be sure, Bentham was something of a child prodigy. He was studying Latin at the age of three, and his father sent him to Queens College, Oxford, by the age of twelve. He earned a bachelor's degree at the age of fifteen and a master's degree at the age of eighteen. He trained as a lawyer, and his father had decided that Bentham would follow him into the law; he felt quite sure that his son would one day be Lord Chancellor of England (one of the most important functionaries in the government in the United Kingdom).

But Bentham soon grew disillusioned with British law—a layered, complex legal code benefiting the few more than the many—and so decided to write about the law and spent the rest of his life criticizing the existing law and suggesting ways for its improvement. In 1780 he wrote his major work *Introduction of the Principles of Morals and Legislation*.

Bentham might be termed the greatest of the "philosophical radicals," since he proposed many legal and social reforms, but also devised principles on which they should be based. So his *Principles* was written with such reform in mind. The philosophy expressed in this book—utilitarianism—argues that the right act or policy is that which results in "the greatest happiness for the greatest number." He later dropped "for the greatest number" portion of his principle since "the greatest happiness" could be in conflict with "the greatest number." (For example, you could produce ten units of happiness for two people, which is a greater sum—twenty—than producing three units in five people—fifteen.)

Psychological Hedonism: Pleasure, Pain, and Value

Bentham's *Principles* can be divided into three parts: (1) his view on what motivated human beings; (2) an explanation of the principle of utility; (3) and an account of his felicific, or happiness, calculus.

Bentham found pleasure and pain to be the sole motivators and only absolutes in the world. He opens his *Principles* thus:

Nature has put man under the governance of two sovereign masters: pain and pleasure. It is for them alone to point out what we ought to do, as well as to determine what we shall do. On the one hand, the standard of right and wrong, on the other the chain of causes and effects, are fastened to their throne. They govern us in all we do, in all we say, in all we think: every effort we can make to throw off our subjection, will serve but to demonstrate and confirm it. In words a man may pretend to abjure their empire: but in reality he will remain subject to it all the while.

Bentham gives his account of what motivates human beings. As with previous psychological hedonists like Epicurus, Bentham claims that human beings are under the spell of the twin "sovereign masters" pleasure and pain. People will move toward objects and activities they find pleasurable and shun those they find painful. There is possibility for reform, however. If a person finds study to be painful, he will need to have his behavior reformed so that he can take pleasure in it. Perhaps the reward of learning new things or the satisfaction of getting an A on a test will lead him to find learning pleasurable.

QUESTION?

Would Bentham say that it is a higher pleasure to read poetry or play a game?
Bentham said that "the quantity of pleasure being equal, pushpin is as good as poetry" (pushpin was the British name for bowling). Bentham differed from Mill in thinking that quantity of pleasure was more important than quality.

Utility and Value

From Bentham's view of pleasure and pain he derived his rule of utility: that the good is whatever brings about the greatest happiness. Utilitarianism, then, is a teleological moral theory, the goal of which is to produce the greatest amount of net utility (pleasure minus pain) where utility is defined in terms of happiness or pleasure. Thus, if it is within your power to bring about equal amounts of happiness in three people or in two people, you should bring about that happiness in three rather than two.

In general, goodness or value is defined in terms of utility. Utility, in turn, is defined in terms of how much pleasure is produced. With Bentham's philosophy you could analyze topics as diverse as the ethics of warfare, mercy killing, abortion, and other matters of applied ethics. A war could be judged by whether it produced more long-term pleasure or pain. The principle of utility analyzes results but overlooks motives, for as John Stuart Mill, Bentham's successor in utilitarianism said, "He who saves as a fellow creature from drowning does what is morally right, whether his motive be duty or the hope of being paid for his trouble." So in the *motive-act-consequence* schema, it is the last that counts the most.

The Happiness Calculus

For utilitarians an action is right *if and only if* there is no other act the agent could have done instead that has higher utility than it has. But how is this higher utility calculated? Bentham actually had a way of calculating pleasures and pains. In fact, he asserted that there are seven factors that help you measure pleasures and enable you to make the calculation.

Since he had social reform at heart, Bentham thought that legislators ought to improve society by increasing general pleasure and decreasing the pain of its citizens. "Pleasures and the avoidance of pains are the ends which the legislator has in view," Bentham wrote in the *Principles*. The seven "pleasure" factors are intensity, duration, certainty or uncertainty, propinquity or remoteness, fecundity, purity, and extent.

Intensity refers to how strong the pleasure is. *Duration* refers to how long it lasts. *Certainty* or *uncertainty* refers to whether the pleasure will occur or not. *Propinquity* or *remoteness* refers to whether the pleasure is near at hand or far away. *Fecundity* refers to whether the pleasure or pain will be followed by similar sensations. *Purity* (the opposite of fecundity) is the chance of its *not* being followed by sensations of the opposite kind. Finally, *extent* refers to the number of persons affected by the action.

These are the components that make up the "hedonic calculus." How does it apply to actual practice? Bentham offered an answer. Suppose you are contemplating which action to do—study for a final exam that is two days away or attend a campus party on one of the nights before the exam. How would you analyze what to do? "Sum up all the values of the pleasures on one side, and those of all the pains on the other side," Bentham says. A person reviewing these choices finds the *intensity* of the pleasures promised by the party alluring. Meanwhile, studying for a final exam promises only a low-intensity pleasure. The person now adds the factor of *duration* and sees that the pleasures of eating and drinking and socializing at the party are relatively brief. By contrast, studying may produce long-term pleasurable consequences, especially if the student is able to perform well on the test, improve his grade point average, increase his chances of getting the job he wants, or getting into law school, med school, graduate school, and so on. He also sees that the purity of the party pleasure is low, since if he drinks excessively he may have a hangover the following day. So pleasure is followed by pain, whereas studying produces no such pain—aside perhaps from possible minor discomfort to one's eyes or backaches from sitting up straight.

FACT

Jeremy Bentham was a bit eccentric. Bentham's mummified body is present at every Board of Trustees meeting at the University College of London. He bequeathed his fortune to the school with the proviso that he attend every such meeting indefinitely.

The person may include in his calculation certainty and uncertainty, propinquity and remoteness, fecundity, and extent. But the result of Bentham's "hedonic calculus" in this and other cases is clear. The lasting pleasures all fall on the side of the mental pleasure of studying; partying, by contrast, includes only short-term pleasures. One might reply, however, that the person attending the party will meet the love of her life and so the party pleasure may turn out to have greater duration. Following Bentham, our student would sacrifice going to the party to put in the necessary hours studying.

Bentham: The First Philosopher for Animal Rights

Two major philosophers prior to Bentham—René Descartes and Immanuel Kant—had little regard for the rights or even well-being of animals. But Bentham thought that pleasure and pain were primary considerations in the well-being of all sentient beings (beings possessing sensations), not only humans.

Early Indifference to Animals

It is hard to imagine a philosopher being more indifferent to the well-being of animals than René Descartes. According to Descartes, human beings possess the distinguishing feature of being *res cogitans,* or "thinking stuff." That is, humans possess a substantial mind or soul. This mind is the locus of feelings, thought, rationality, and is the basis for free will and moral values. By contrast, Descartes thought that animals have no mind or soul and are therefore ultimately only *res extensa,* or "extended, physical, stuff." Animals are essentially just fleshy machines or automata merely. No "soul" was reflected in their eyes and similarly no real pain was reflected in their apparent pain behavior.

As a consequence of lacking souls they also lack consciousness and cannot feel pleasure or pain. Descartes's teaching is also Christian doctrine, and Descartes accepted the teaching that humans have souls created by God but animals do not. And since soul is identical to mind, if animals have no soul, they are also lacking in mind. And if they have no mind, they cannot feel pain. In order to feel pain a mind is needed.

Jeremy Bentham's philosophy of social hedonism did not mean that everyone was entitled to live out a nonstop pleasure principle. His philosophy resembled the Epicurean philosophy. He asserted that social hedonism meant maximizing pleasure and minimizing pain, which is not the same as saying that you should attend restaurants, bars, and houses of ill repute.

After Descartes, there were mixed views about the rights and well-being of animals during the Enlightenment. In his *Lectures on Ethics* Kant told his students:

So far as animals are concerned, we have no direct duties. Animals are not self-conscious, and are there merely as a means to an end. Their end is man.

Here Kant adopts the same view that Descartes does in asserting that animals are lacking in consciousness. Even the second version of Kant's categorical imperative enjoins people to "treat other persons (or rational beings) as ends but never as means." But Kant allows humans to treat non-humans as they will.

The First Champion of Animal Rights

In 1780, the same year that Kant's *Lectures* were published, Bentham completed his *Introduction to the Principles of Morals and Legislation*. Speaking of animals, Bentham answered Kant definitively:

The question is not, Can they reason? *nor, Can they* talk? *but, Can they* suffer?

Here Bentham the utilitarian shows that rationality is secondary to well-being and value. Pleasures and pains form the foundation of a person's treatment toward sentient beings. Bentham implies that if you cause pain to sentient beings, then you have acted immorally. So in this way utilitarianism comes across as a more compassionate philosophy than Kant's deontology.

In the Old Testament it is stated that man shall have "dominion" over the animals. Bentham may have been the first to denounce that dominion and call it tyranny.

Animal Rights: Bentham's Legacy

Some animal rights detractors claim that nonhumans cannot possess rights. Even if this is true, it doesn't erase your duty not to harm them. You may have a duty, for example, not to destroy a famous building or religious statue, but not because the items have *rights to exist*. Few philosophers, if any, have carried on the spirit of Bentham's defense of animals more than Peter Singer. A philosophy professor at Princeton, Singer has made a strong case for the view that animals' interests are the basis for their having rights—rights that are equal to humans. According to Singer, not to respect the interests of animals is "speciesism." He believes this is an objectionable attitude similar to racism or sexism—objectionable because it treats animals badly simply because they are members of a different species and gives preference to our own species just because we are human beings. But on what grounds is this objectionable?

According to Singer, having interests is connected to the ability to feel pleasure and pain, because the pleasure is derived from the satisfaction of an interest. Animals are different from plants in this regard. Plants have things that are *in their interest* even though they *do not have interests*. Because the interests of animals are similar to ours, they ought to be given equal weight according to Singer. On the one hand, it would make no sense to say that a pig or a horse has a right to vote, because it has no interest in voting. However, according to Singer, it would make sense to say that they have a right not to suffer or not to suffer needlessly or not to be used for no good purpose.

Others argue that animals need not be treated as equal to humans and that their interests ought not to be given equal weight with ours. It is because of the difference in species' *abilities* and *potentialities* that animals are a lesser form of being, according to this view. This does not mean, however, that interests ought to be disregarded.

Whether or not something is cruel to an animal might be determined by the extent of the pain it experiences, as when you speak of cruelty in terms of "unnecessary" pain. But Singer found that many experiments that made use of animals as guinea pigs to test products ranging from vaccines to shampoos to antifreeze were cruel and immoral. No doubt Bentham would have drawn the same conclusion.

The Life of John Stuart Mill

John Stuart Mill (1806–73) was born in London. He was the son of James Mill, a philosopher, economist, and historian. James Mill educated his son with the advice and assistance of Jeremy Bentham. Because of his father's friendship with Bentham, the younger Mill was exposed to the ideas of utilitarianism early on.

Mill learned Greek at the age of three, Latin a little later, and by the age of twelve he was a competent logician, having read Aristotle's books on logic. By sixteen he was a well-trained economist. At twenty he suffered a nervous breakdown, which persuaded him that more was needed in life than devotion to the public good and the cultivation of a sharp intellect. He took up a study of the poets Coleridge, Wordsworth, and Goethe, thinking he needed to develop his aesthetic sensibilities.

In 1843 he wrote a *System of Logic* and in 1848 the *Principles of Political Economy*. But his books on politics and morals remain fresh among all his work. In 1859 he wrote *On Liberty* and in 1861 *Utilitarianism*, which remains the classic defense of the view that humans ought to aim at maximizing the welfare or happiness of all sentient beings.

On Liberty was the most controversial work he wrote in his lifetime. The book was inspired by letters he and his wife Harriet Taylor wrote, in which they expressed how adventurous individuals were becoming all too rare and that societies like America and Great Britain cared more for conformity than individual liberty. In *On Liberty* he writes that there is but one justification for society to interfere in the lives of its citizens—to defend others from harm. This has come to be known as Mill's "harm principle."

FACT

Harriet Taylor was the joint author with Mill of important works such as *The Principles of Political Economy* and *On Liberty.* In Mill's *Autobiography* he wrote that during their marriage as well as the twenty-one years of their confidential friendship "All my published writings were as much my wife's work as mine."

Mill's Version of Utilitarianism

J. S. Mill agreed with Bentham on the basic principle of utility, namely that "Actions are right in proportion as they tend to promote happiness, wrong as they tend to promote the reverse of happiness. By happiness is intended pleasure and the absence of pain; by unhappiness, pain, and the privation of pleasure." But Mill made a distinction that Bentham did not: Mill distinguished between the "quality" of pleasures, not just the "quantity" as Bentham had done in his hedonic calculus.

Mill wrote *Utilitarianism* in response to criticisms abut Jeremy Bentham's hedonistic version of utilitarianism, which failed to differentiate between the kinds and quality of different pleasures and—because of its talk of pleasures—had received the name of a "pig philosophy."

John Stuart Mill's utilitarianism emphasized quality of pleasure rather than the quantity. "It is better to be a human being dissatisfied than a pig satisfied; better to be Socrates dissatisfied than a fool satisfied. And if the fool, or the pig, is of a different opinion, it is because they know only their side of the question. The other party to the comparison knows both sides."

Mill responded by describing a different theory of happiness. Human beings have faculties more elevated than the animal appetites. You cannot measure pleasures on quantity alone, but must include quality.

Of two pleasures, if there be one to which all or almost all who have experience of both give a decided preference, . . . that is the more desirable pleasure. . . . Now, it is an unquestionable fact that those who are equally acquainted with, and equally capable of appreciating and enjoying, both, do give a most marked preference to the manner of existence which employs their higher faculties. Few human beings would consent to be changed into any of the lower animals, for a promise of the fullest allowance of a beast's pleasures; no intelligent being would consent to be a fool, no instructed person would be an ignoramus, no person of feeling and conscience would be selfish and base, even though they should be persuaded that the fool, the dunce, or the rascal is better satisfied with his lot than they are with theirs."

Since Mill has come down on the side of Socrates instead of the fool, he has separated mental pleasures, which he called "higher" pleasures, from physical pleasures, which he implies are "lower" pleasures.

Mill's On Liberty

Mill worked with his wife Harriet Taylor on *On Liberty* (1859). Mill wrote, "The object of this Essay is to assert one very simple principle. . . . That principle is, that the sole end for which mankind are warranted, individually or collectively, in interfering with the liberty of action of any of their number, is self-protection." In short, individuals have the freedom to express what they want in speech or writing, to adopt their own tastes and pursuits, and to shape the lifestyle they desire, as long as they do not harm others.

Mill's discussion of freedom first takes up the issue of the right to free expression and discussion of ideas. He maintains that society is harmed by the suppression of free speech regardless of whether the ideas in question are true or false. For one, even unpopular ideas that are censored might in fact be true.

Finally, dissenters from any viewpoint will bring forth fresh challenges to ideas and force people to re-examine grounds for their convictions. Without this exercise, our "true opinion will become a dead dogma, not a living truth."

When it comes to free speech, Mill would say that the case of Galileo showed that the majority is often wrong and that a lone individual is often right. Humans are fallible and need to be exposed to ideas that will force them to compare the accuracy of their own beliefs against the new idea.

Free speech that caused immediate harm could be restricted. You cannot shout "fire" in a crowded theater. Mill's defense of personal liberty is rooted in utility, being based on what will promote the social good and prevent harm. His example is:

An opinion that corn-dealers are starvers of poor ought to be accommodated when simply circulated through the press, but may justly incur punishment when delivered orally to an excited mob assembled before the house of a corn-dealer.

Mill is pointing out that when it comes to free speech, context matters. This principle is similar to the "clear and present danger" criterion that the U.S. Supreme Court uses to determine when free speech may be limited.

FACT

Mill's other famous book is *The Subjection of Women,* which was a passionate call for equal rights for women, long before the modern feminist movement. It was highly unusual for a man to write such a feminist treatise in the nineteenth century.

The Public and Private Spheres

The example of the corn-dealers and shouting fire in the crowded theater show that Mill recognized a difference between public and private behavior. What you do in the "public sphere" is subject to censure. What you do in private is your own business. About this private sphere Mill writes:

There is a sphere of action in which society, as distinguished from the individual, has, if any, only an indirect interest; comprehending all that portion of a person's life and conduct which affects only himself, or, if it also affects others, only with their free, voluntary, and undeceived consent and participation. . . . This, then, is the appropriate region of human liberty. It comprises, first, the inward domain of consciousness; demanding liberty of conscience, in the most comprehensive sense; liberty of thought and feeling; absolute freedom of opinion and sentiment on all subjects, practical or speculative, scientific, moral, or theological. The liberty of expressing and publishing opinions may seem to fall under a different principle, since it belongs to that part of the conduct of an individual which concerns other people; but, being almost of as much importance as the liberty of thought itself, and resting in great part on the same reasons, is practically inseparable from it.

Added to this freedom of expression is "the liberty of tastes and pursuits; of framing the plan of our life to suit our own character; of doing as we like." In addition, "There is the liberty for individuals to unite, for any purpose not involving harm to others." In sum, "No society in which these liberties are not, on the whole, respected, is free, whatever may be the form of government; and none if completely free in which they do not exist absolute and unqualified." A century and a half after Mill wrote, his thoughts still hold true: namely that censorship, intolerance, and imposed conformity are some of the greatest dangers that a society can face.

Evaluation and Significance

The utilitarian principle was a breath of fresh air in Victorian England, where many people were seeking a nonreligious, clear, independent approach to morality. It was left for succeeding centuries to respond critically to utilitarianism. One of the problems with utilitarianism is that it is not always possible or easy to predict the consequences of your actions. You give a homeless person $5, believing that he will use it to buy a sandwich as he says. But he may well purchase liquor with the money five minutes later. Moreover, there are actions, like war, whose long-term consequences you cannot know for sure.

A second criticism of the utilitarian doctrine is that is seems to be one where the "ends justify the means." If the consequences of your actions are what make those actions right or wrong, then can't you justify any action by saying it is likely to produce good consequences? You might lynch an innocent man because an angry mob of one hundred demands it, reasoning that the interests of the many should take precedence over the interests of the few.

Utilitarianists could respond that you can never foretell consequences, but that no moral theory can ignore consequences all together. Regarding the lynching of an innocent man, the utilitarian philosophy doesn't need to accept the conclusion that the majority must always be appeased, for in the long-term such a practice would not benefit society.

CHAPTER 17

Karl Marx:
Philosopher of Alienation

"The philosophers have only interpreted the world, in various ways; the point is to change it," Karl Marx said in 1845. This sentiment certainly captures the social, political, and economic philosophy of Karl Marx. Marx did not merely stand by playing subject to the world's object. He was intent upon describing the world and prescribing what changes would make the world better.

The Life of Karl Marx

Karl Marx (1818–83) was born to a middle-class Jewish family in the Prussian city of Trier. Marx was first educated at the University of Bonn and later at the University of Berlin. There he discovered philosophy and became a member of a dynamic, socially conscious and active group of thinkers known as "the Young Hegelians." The Young Hegelians included theologians, philosophers who used Hegel's theories and belief that society as they knew it was imperfect and in need of improvement. They launched unrelenting attacks on the Prussian church and government.

When Marx wrote his doctoral thesis on the Greek atomists in 1840 he thought he would avoid submitting it at the University of Berlin and try the University of Jena instead. His views were too radical for academia, however, and he turned to journalism for a career. He moved to Paris and lived as a freelance journalist. There he met Friedrich Engels (1820–95), who alerted Marx to the plight of the working classes. Engels turned Marx toward the study of economics. The two worked and wrote together for the rest of Marx's life.

When he settled in London he became involved in the International Working Men's Association. The last period of his life saw the production of some of his most important writing. Above all, he wrote *Das Kapital* (Capital: A Critique of Political Economy). The first volume was published in 1867 and the second two were edited by Engels and published posthumously in 1885 and 1894.

As his health declined precipitously over the last years of his life, he sought spas around Europe (and one in North Africa), but his health didn't improve. The deaths of his wife and eldest daughter damaged him further, and he died in 1883.

Historical Materialism

"A spectre is haunting Europe—the spectre of Communism. All the powers of old Europe have entered into a holy alliance to exorcise this spectre: Pope and Tsar, Metternich and Guizot, French Radical and German police spies." So opens Karl Marx's *Communist Manifesto*. These bold words certainly captured the times. Written in 1848, his *Manifesto* proclaimed that

Communists would "forcibly overthrow" the existing power structure of society. They would also be fighting history itself, since Marx thought that "historical materialism" was the doctrine that best described how history unfolded.

What is historical materialism? According to Marx, the only correct interpretation of history is an economic one. Historical materialism is the idea that a society's economic structure—whether it be feudalism, capitalism, or Communism—determines the nature of its cultural and social structure. So historical materialism leads to a kind of economic determinism.

Marx believed that people lack the free will to decide their lives because society decides for them. "It is not the consciousness of men that determines their being, but, on the contrary, their social being that determines their consciousness," he wrote.

Those who control the means of production control the culture, including all moral and religious ideas. It is the capitalists who own the means of production or control the mode of production and thereby control the ideas of humankind. Imagine a capitalist who runs or directs a publishing company. This person is in a position to control the ideas to which people are exposed and hence to influence and direct social and cultural developments. To use another example, the class in power can tolerate the speech and protests of members of the lower classes or they can choose to ignore them.

Marx on God and Religion

Most people have mistaken Marx's view on religion by quoting just a single line of it: "Religion is the opium of the people." But this may be the most famous misquotation of his time, for he said so much more than this.

Marx did not dismiss religion as merely some stupid, inane preoccupation of the masses. After all, Marx was the son of a rabbinical family. In his *Contribution to the Critique of Hegel's Philosophy of Right* he wrote:

Religious distress is at the same time the expression of real distress and the protest against real distress. Religion is the sigh of the oppressed creature, the heart of a heartless world, just as it is the spirit of a spiritless situation. It is the opium of the people.

The abolition of religion as the illusory happiness of the people is required for their real happiness. The demand to give up the illusions about its condition is the demand to give up a condition that needs illusions. The criticism of religion is therefore in embryo the criticism of the value of woe, the halo of which is religion. Criticism has plucked the imaginary flowers from the chain, not so that man will wear the chain without any fantasy or consolation but so that he will shake off the chain and cull the living flower.

Karl Marx was not philosophically opposed to religion. In fact, he thought that religious belief is important to an oppressed people who need illusions. At the same time, Marx did not believe that God creates man. Rather man creates religion and a mythical God.

Religion functions as a controlling device of the bourgeoisie. Religion promises the masses a happier existence after death, in the next life, thereby allowing them a better life than their earthy one.

Ending Alienation: Seeking a Humane Society

In this life humans find themselves in what Marx calls a condition of alienation. For Marx the history of humankind is a history of the increasing development of man, and at the same time of increasing alienation. Since historical materialism determines man's will, alienation is the consequence. Another word for alienation is "estrangement," which means that man does not experience himself as the acting agent in the grasp of his own world, but the world remains alien to him.

This sort of alienation exists more in industrial societies. It is expressed in the work and in the division of labor. As private property and the division of labor develop, labor loses its power of being an expression of a man's powers. So men working in a factory, working eighty-four hours a week as men did in the Manchester, England, during Marx's life, are just cogs in a larger machine, engaging in alienating labor that involves no human intelligence or creativity.

INSIGHT

Karl Marx's idea of alienation was based on the distinction between man's existence and his essence. In certain kinds of industrial labor man is alienated from his humanity, his essence, which involves creativity. He is not engaged in the activity that he ought to be doing.

So "workers feel at home only during his leisure time, whereas at work he feels homeless," Marx said in his *Economic and Philosophical Manuscripts of 1844*. In the act of producing for his employer the relationship to his own activity is experienced "as something alien and not belonging to him, activity as suffering (passivity), strength as powerlessness, creation as emasculation."

A more humane society would emancipate man from his servitude. But a new society would be required for a man to attain his essence.

Communism and the New Society

According to Marx, after capitalism has fallen, as it must, there will be a period of transition to a new society called a "dictatorship of the proletariat." Following this will come the first stage of Communism, now called "socialism." Socialism will emancipate man from alienation, and he will then achieve his self-realization.

The history of civilizations until this time is the history of class conflicts, according to Marx. This continual succession of conflicts will no longer exist under Communism. Since there is no more private ownership of the means of production, society will no longer have the tensions and contradictions produced by class divisions. As Marx's friend Friedrich Engels describes it, "It is the assent of man from the kingdom of necessity to the kingdom of freedom."

A famous catch phrase associated with Marx's *Communist Manifesto* concerns the distribution of goods. Marx said that in a Communist society with a just distribution of goods the rule of thumb would be "From each according to his ability, to each according to his means."

Workers in the new society will no longer be separated from the products of their labor and so alienation will cease. Competitive classes will fall away, since there will be no workers/slaves beholden to masters. Persons will no longer be reduced to commodities, like things, but will be able to discover their true selves and their dignity. A dog-eat-dog struggle for goods will give way to a family of humanity.

The new banner of Communism will read: "From each according to his ability, to each according to his means." People will readily accept this change. They will accept it because one change will go deeper than the change in the work environment. You will learn that character traits like greed and selfishness are not intrinsic to human nature, but were only relics of the capitalist world. That competitive environment molded those traits. If you change society, however, according to Marx, you change human nature as you know it.

FACT

Marx's friend Friedrich Engels spoke at his funeral in 1883: "On the fourteenth of March, at a quarter to three in the afternoon, the greatest living thinker ceased to think. He had been left alone for scarcely two minutes, and when we came back we found him in his armchair, peacefully gone to sleep—but forever."

Marx provided but an outline of this new society, with precious few details of it. This is because details of policies would only be decided as the society arose. In general terms, Marx thought the dawn of Communism would restore man to his true essence, where he would thrive: "Communism represents the general resolution of the conflict between man and nature and between man and man. . . . Communism is the riddle of human history solved, and it knows itself to be this solution," Marx said in the *Economic and Philosophic Manuscripts of 1844*.

Evaluation and Significance

Some of Marx's historical predictions hit the mark. The devaluation of workers continues apace, some 150 years since he wrote of alienation on the job. One can even look at the recent American trend of corporate downsizing in information technology (IT) and other departments as reducing human beings to exchangeable commodities. Marx said that industrialists had to achieve "surplus value" and one manner of doing this is to force experienced, higher-paid workers out on the pavement when their continuation is no longer "cost effective." The scenario ends with their jobs being moved abroad to hire cheap labor.

On the other hand, two Marxian views fell wide of the mark. Marx insisted that the collapse of capitalism was inevitable. He was wrong in his view that the collapse was imminent; capitalism persists, more than a century and a half since he wrote *The Communist Manifesto* and nearly that long since he wrote *Das Capital*.

In addition, many professional philosophers and lay readers think that Marx idealized human nature. Unlike Thomas Hobbes, Marx insisted that excessive self-interest, over-weaning greed, and lust for power were manifest only in capitalist societies. But some of the same tendencies were observed in the upper-class members of the Communist Party in the Soviet Union. On the other hand, not all capitalists are driven exclusively by greed. In short, one can say that some features of human nature can be the same in any economic system.

CHAPTER 18

Soren Kierkegaard:
The Father of Existentialism

Soren Kierkegaard practiced philosophy in a new key. Since the time of Plato and Aristotle philosophers had constructed grand systems of thought, built up from observation, reason, and speculation. Kierkegaard, by contrast, stressed the existing individual and how he lives in the world day to day. Kierkegaard lived a short but passionate life and in his philosophy can be found all his personal struggles with belief, choice, love, and a search for meaning.

The Life of Soren Kierkegaard

Soren Kierkegaard (1813–55) was born in Copenhagen, Denmark, into a deeply religious Lutheran family. He was one of seven children brought up in strict fashion by an oppressively religious and gloomy father, Michael, a man burdened by a deep religious guilt and melancholy. Kierkegaard would later claim that he had been born old. By the time he was twenty-one, five of his siblings and his mother had died.

He was schooled in theology, philosophy, and literature at the University of Copenhagen. But he was a dilettante and lived a wandering, debauched life. Then in 1838, at the age of twenty-five, he experienced a reawakening and recommitted to the Christian faith. He spent ten years before finishing his doctoral dissertation *On the Concept of Irony with Constant Reference to Socrates* (1841).

FACT

Events in Kierkegaard's personal life affected his philosophy. He had planned to become a Lutheran pastor, but before he enrolled at a seminary he became engaged to Regina Olsen in 1840. But writing was a poor means of support for a family, even with an inheritance from his father. For this reason he broke off the engagement in 1841, but this precipitated his move to philosophy.

To escape the controversy over a broken engagement, he left for Berlin and wrote his first book, a two-volume work called *Either-Or* (1843), which contrasted the aesthetic (Epicurean) way of life with the ethical (Stoic-Kantian) way of life. He ended up publishing some thirty books, all at his own expense, since only his first book made a profit. Most of them were published under pseudonyms. In fact, he would use one pseudonym to attack his own writings under another. The estrangement from Regina was a topic he returned to in his writings. Philosophically, he found himself in constant opposition to the systematic philosophy of Wilhelm Hegel (1770–1831) that was so popular in Copenhagen at the time.

Kierkegaard was in constant, intense suffering due a back ailment that caused him to tilt backward awkwardly as he walked. He was frustrated in love and frustrated in his vocational aspirations—he was unable to get a teaching post but was still a prolific writer. He was always surrounded with controversy, attacking writers, the Lutheran Church, and contemporary society in general. His own physical suffering and the stress of his writing schedule diminished his health. He collapsed and died at the age of forty-two.

Yet he found solace in a deeply religious life. But he found organized religion tepid, not deeply felt, and unfulfilling.

Pascal's Influence on Kierkegaard

The work of Blaise Pascal (1623–62) was a curious blend of several philosophical tendencies, which influenced the thinking of Kierkegaard. Writing at the time of Descartes, Pascal was a skeptic. In particular, he was skeptical of the Cartesian system and thought that reason alone cannot prove immortality or the existence of God, nor can science or philosophy produce mathematical certainty or proof. Kierkegaard was similarly skeptical of Hegel's philosophy in his lifetime.

Blaise Pascal's greatest work was *Pensées* (or "thoughts") that was unfinished in his lifetime and published posthumously in 1670. In it he discusses how reason takes one only so far in knowledge about God. Since reason cannot show either the nature or existence of God, one must follow the dictates of the heart, for "the heart has its reasons the mind does not know."

QUESTION?

What did Kierkegaard mean by a "leap of faith"?
The leap of faith is his conception of how an individual should believe in God, or how a person would act in love. The leap of faith is not a rational decision. It is transcending rationality in favor of faith.

God's existence cannot be proved, but proof is not desirable either. What is needed is an exercise of faith, the faith that God exists. Thus, Pascal's argument is called "the Wager." Pascal thought it was a reasonable wager to stake everything on God's existence, for there are only two possibilities: "God is or he is not." The agnostic can argue that since reason is unable to decide the issue, a choice either way is unnecessary. But deciding not to choose is a choice. Pascal thought that man must wager. Humans must choose.

"It is not optional; you are committed to it," he argues. Men own two things as stakes in such a wager: their reason and their will (blessedness). There are two things to avoid: error and misery. Since reason alone is unable to make the decision, how can the matter be decided?

If God is, then the man who wagers on his existence by believing in him wins everything and loses nothing, according to Pascal. Thus, he has set it up that the man who wagers for God's existence risks the possibility of finite loss (if God does not exist) or infinite gain (if God does exist). Therefore, anyone seeking to make an intelligent wager would want the greater reward and wager that God exists.

So what Pascal set out to prove was not that God exists but that men *ought to believe* in God's existence. The possibility of infinite gain—including a life of eternal blessedness in the afterlife—far supersedes any sacrifice of material gain or a "eat, drink, and be merry" lifestyle in our present finite existence. Pascal, a philosopher and a mathematician, found one choice to be greater than the other.

Truth and Subjectivity

In Pascal, Kierkegaard discovered a kindred spirit. Pascal's emphasis on the necessity of deciding, choosing, and believing resonated with Kierkegaard. He thought that the history of philosophy since the Greeks had used reason and experience solely to make sense of the world. But choice is the real starting point, since you must make decisions at every turn.

FACT

Kierkegaard was known for his attacks on organized religion, especially of the Danish State Church, of which most Danes were members in the nineteenth century. He attacked the notion of a state church, since such an institution's main objective was to increase membership in the religion. This had the effect of taking the initiative from Christians, who ought to be taking responsibility for their own relationship to God.

Truth is subjectivity, Kierkegaard said. By this strange notion he meant that there is no prefabricated truth "out there" for people who make choices. Rather, as William James would later say, "Truth is made" by an act of will. Choice is your constant companion, though it is a burdensome companion. In his *Journals* Kierkegaard writes, "What I really lack is to be clear in my mind what I am to do, not what I am to know . . . the thing is to find a truth that is true for me, to find the ideas for which I can live and die."

In his book *Concluding Unscientific Postscript* (1844), Kierkegaard sets forth a version of fideism is which faith is said to be higher than reason. Faith, not reason, is the highest virtue a human can reach; faith is necessary for the deepest fulfillment.

The phrase "true for me" means that Kierkegaard has a higher regard for *subjective* truth than *objective* truth. It is the factor that makes Kierkegaard the "Father of Existentialism." Truth is subjectivity. Truth is that on which the individual acts, a way of existing. He exists in his truth and lives in it. The highest expression of subjectivity is passionate belief. This is what it means to think "existentially."

The "Stages on Life's Way"

The essence of Kierkegaard's philosophy can be seen in his doctrine that there are three stages of life experience: aesthetic, ethical, and religious. The three stages are like outlooks or attitudes toward life.

The Aesthetic Stage

In the first stage of life experience, the individual may be either a hedonist in search of pleasure or romance, or an intellectual interested mainly in abstract philosophical speculation. At this stage it is typical to escape boredom and life's pains by sampling an entire smorgasbord of pleasures. The aesthetic stage is a stage of fulfillment of desires, of living for the moment. Here the individual can't get enough. Someone engaging in philosophical abstractions loses himself in speculation, aloft in an ivory tower, remote from events in the real world. The abstract intellectual merely observes the world in a detached and objective manner, without risking involvement.

Kierkegaard saw profoundly how man seeks to escape from himself through diversions that provide him a kind of momentary distraction. This continual search for diversion is described in his "rotation method": Man is bored with life in the country, so he seeks fulfillment in the village; he becomes bored in the village, so he takes on the city. He soon tires of his homeland and travels abroad. He is overcome by boredom in a foreign land and so entertains the possibility of an endless journeying to alleviate his boredom. So the melancholy individual engages in a self-defeating and dizzying hunt for the perfect diversion. But his venture is bound to end in frustration: the search for diversions can never be fulfilled. The aesthetic existence ends in futility.

Kierkegaard had a knack for philosophical aphorisms. One of these showed his distaste for abstract, intellectual philosophy that didn't appeal to emotional and intellectual beings. "The thing is to find a truth which is true for me, to find the idea for which I can live and die."

The aestheticist finally realizes that he cannot find himself outside of himself. There is no fulfillment; neither in his nonstop hedonistic and sensual pursuits nor in the abstractions of his speculative thought. Plato was right: the pleasure seeker is like a leaky sieve. He can never get enough. To discover what is meaningful the agent must turn inward. He will discover earnestness, passions, decision, commitment, and freedom. The result of the pursuits at this stage is a despair that may eventually motivate a person to a commitment of ethical values. In fact, in choosing despair, the self gives birth to itself and passes from the aesthetical stage of indecision to the ethical stage of decisive commitment.

The Ethical Stage

The ethical stage is the stage of decision and resolute commitment. The ethical person accepts limits and follows rules of conduct that the aesthetic person does not. An aesthetic person succumbs to impulse when food or drink or sexual attraction beckons. But the ethical person doesn't give in. Fulfillment at the ethical stage is sought by means of a dedication to duty and obedience to the dictates of an objective morality.

Through decision and commitment the self becomes integrated and anchored. The ethical man, by virtue of having shouldered his responsibility in decision, has his center within himself. His life is centralized and unified. But once again the experience lacks personal meaning and fails to validate one's individual existence. The commitment to the ethical stage can be achieved by an act of faith. You are aware of your guilt and sin.

It is by decision and commitment at this state that the self discovers its integrity and unity. Socrates said "Know thyself." But at the ethical stage this is rendered "choose thyself."

The Religious Stage

The aesthetic stage is characterized by hedonistic pursuits, the ethical stage by regard for duty, and the religious stage by obedience and commitment to God. The religious stage represents the culmination of the first two. In *Stages on Life's Way* (1845), which Kierkegaard wrote two years after *Either-Or*, he gave proper due to the religious stage.

Faith at this stage is the opposite of despair at the first stage. Despair is the unwillingness to be oneself; Christian despair is the "sickness unto death" (the title of his book written in 1849) for the wish to die is the result of despair.

QUESTION?

Did Kierkegaard think that faith existed at the same time as doubt?
Kierkegaard thought that faith existed side by side with doubt in the same individual. Doubt was required, since faith without doubt is lacking in substance. To believe in God's existence without having any doubt would not be faith worth having.

At the religious stage you will to have a personal, subjective experience of God. Only this act can assure you of a relationship with God. A transformation occurs only if one progresses to the religious stage, by choosing to acknowledge one's mortality and sinfulness and the inadequacy of objective ethics to furnish a meaning for oneself and the emptiness that the first two stages lead to.

The Leap of Faith

At the religious stage, you attempt to attain a personal relationship with God. "Man only begins to exist in faith," Kierkegaard thought. So both the aesthetic and ethical stages of life are inadequate. To know God you follow Kierkegaard's famous phrase: you make "a leap of faith."

Kierkegaard brings up the biblical story of Abraham and Isaac. God commands Abraham to kill his son Isaac. In choosing to obey God's command, Abraham is in the position of not being able to understand the command, much less justify it. What difference does it make for Abraham if the action is objectively right? He must choose and therein defines his values. The only way the action can be justified is that it's the surrender to God's will.

FACT

Kierkegaard hid behind pseudonyms in half of his works. He did this so that his works would not be regarded as part of some larger philosophical system. He hoped that readers would read his works at face value without attributing them to some detail of his life.

So Abraham must make a "leap of faith." This leap involves willing and belief more than reason and knowledge. It involves what Kierkegaard calls "the suspension of the ethical."

There would be no need for this leap of faith if God's existence were simply a matter of commonsense or rational reflection.

Kierkegaard's later works frequently attack the institutions of the Christian Church. He believed that going through the motions of a Christian life—like attending church, reciting prayers, following commanded ethical precepts, reading Scripture and so on—is the very antithesis of a Christian life. The importance of the "leap of faith" is that one should have a personal and direct confrontation with the divine. Yet he found solace in a deeply religious life. But he found organized religion tepid, not deeply felt, and unfulfilling.

Evaluation and Significance

Kierkegaard was fresh air in his own century and he remains such nearly 200 years since his birth. His original, antisystematic stress on individual existence, especially the importance of willing and acting, led him to be labeled an existentialist. Other existentialists would follow his path.

His most identifiable doctrine is about the three stages of life. These are stages to attaining selfhood or what people now call "finding oneself." But since one must exist before one can achieve selfhood, existence is prior to humanity. Or, as Jean-Paul Sartre later expressed the idea (see Chapter 21), existence is prior to essence.

Kierkegaard's life and philosophy were centered on existential questions: "How shall I live my life?" "What kinds of life are worth living—the aesthetic, ethical, or religious?" "What does it mean to have faith?" "What does it mean to love?" "What does it mean to accept one's suffering and how can one do this?" His discussions of these questions reveal his unfailing and uncanny philosophical acumen and literary brilliance.

CHAPTER 19

American Philosophy: William James and Pragmatism

Pragmatism is an antisystematic, anti-empirical, anti-rationalist philosophy that grew up in America in the nineteenth century. The word pragmatism fits the American pragmatists Charles Peirce, John Dewey, and William James to a tee. The practical consequences and meaning of ideas in the real world were more important to them than the theoretical coherence of some of the systematic philosophies of the past.

The Meaning of Pragmatism

Although Charles Peirce was "the Father of Pragmatism," William James gave the term its clearest expression. "Pragmatism asks its usual question," said James. "'Grant an idea or belief to be true,' it says, 'what concrete difference will its being true make in one's actual life? . . . What experiences will be different from those which would obtain if the belief were false? What in short is the truth's cash-value in experiential terms?'"

In short, pragmatism asks: What difference will this truth (or belief or concept, etc.) make in your life? If you believe in God, freedom of the will, and moral responsibility, say, will this impact your life for the better? William James did more to popularize pragmatism than the two other American pragmatists Charles Sanders Peirce and John Dewey. Worth quoting is James's most famous dictum describing pragmatism: "There can be no difference anywhere that doesn't make a difference elsewhere." Translation: Things are not true or right because of some theoretical meaning. They must have an application and impact in the real world.

James insisted that all knowledge is pragmatic. It is difficult if not impossible to settle some philosophical questions—like whether there is a God or an afterlife. Neither reason nor empirical evidence seems to settle these matters. Where does that leave you? James thought that the best theory to believe is the one that brings about the best consequences in your life. Ask yourself: "If I believe in God, will it contribute to a successful or meaningful life for me?" If the answer is yes, then it makes sense—that is, it is *pragmatic*—for you to believe in God.

Charles Sanders Peirce

Charles Pierce (1839–1914) is arguably the least famous of the three American pragmatists, but he was the first to use the term. Peirce reasoned that thoughts must have the job of producing beliefs. "Our beliefs guide our desires and shape our actions," he wrote. Underlying every action is a series of beliefs. In contrast, a belief that does not have consequences for action is empty and dead. For instance, you might believe that it is better to buy a new Rambler than a new Gremlin. For fun, you might even debate me on my choice of cars. But the belief that either is better has no practical application when you consider that neither Ramblers nor Gremlins are made anymore.

Peirce's Father, Benjamin Peirce, was a professor of astronomy and mathematics at Harvard University. Charles went on to study chemistry at Harvard in 1855, graduating with a bachelor's degree. He then worked for the United States Coast and Geodetic Survey and earned a master's degree and Sc.B. in chemistry. Despite his education, he could only obtain nontenured teaching posts. He lectured on the philosophy of science while continuing to work for the Coastal Survey. This pattern of full-time work with part-time lecturing in philosophy became the pattern of his life.

FACT

Peirce founded an organization known as "the Metaphysical Club." The club first met in 1870 in Cambridge, Massachusetts, to read and debate philosophical papers. The better-known members of this group included Pierce, William James, and Oliver Wendell Holmes, who would become the chief justice of the Supreme Court.

A Theory of Meaning

Peirce coined the word *pragmatism* from the Greek word *pragma* meaning "work," "act," or "deed." He did this to make a point: to show that words derive their meanings from actions of some sort. Ideas are clear if they can be translated into some kind of operation. For example, the adjectives *hard* and *heavy* have meaning only because you are able to conceive of effects associated with the words. Thus the word hard tends to mean that which cannot be scratched by other substances, as with diamonds. Heavy could mean whatever falls if you let go of it. There would be no difference between hard and heavy things if they did not test differently. From such simple examples Peirce generalized about the nature of meaning and knowledge in general. His basic point was that our idea of anything was our idea of its sensible *effects*.

The Role of Belief

Belief is important in pragmatism, since belief occupies a middle position between thought and action. Beliefs shape your actions. But beliefs are "unfixed" or undercut by doubts, Peirce said. It is when the "irritation of doubt" arises that you must try to justify your beliefs. Faced with doubt, you can try to "fix" your beliefs so that you have a guide for action.

Doubt is an "uneasy and dissatisfied state from which we struggle to free ourselves," Peirce said. You desire to eliminate doubt, but doubt must be genuine, not like Descartes's "make-believe" doubt. When Descartes got up to stoke the fire, he still avoided touching the flames. The goal is to have beliefs that are free from all actual doubt.

You can fix your beliefs by several methods—most of them incorrect—according to Peirce. First, there is the *method of tenacity,* whereby people cling tightly to their beliefs, refusing to even entertain doubts about them or to consider arguments or evidence for another point of view. In this method you pile up all the evidence you can for a belief and shun all evidence to the contrary. You turn "with contempt and hatred from anything that might disturb" your belief. This is the mindset of someone who says, "I know what I believe; don't confuse me with the facts."

A second way of fixing beliefs is the *method of authority.* Here a community of believers follows the beliefs of an authority or an entire institution. A culture based on the principle of authority cannot tolerate diverse opinions or even have contact with other belief systems. You often find the principle of authority at work in people dedicated to a political party or extreme forms of religious thinking. Peirce said that it might be wise to remember the counsel of Montaigne (1532–1592). Montaigne thought that skepticism was an antidote to the intolerance born of excessive religious zeal. Doubt is a good thing, Montaigne thought, it stops fanaticism.

A third method is the *a priori method.* Here one embraces beliefs because they are "agreeable to reason." However, what is agreeable to reason is subjective. Pierce thought that no fixed opinion existed in metaphysics. Plato's idealism was sensible to Platonists; Descartes's dualism was agreeable to *his* sense of reason; Kant's pietism made a sense of duty sound reasonable, even thought it was founded on religion as much as reason. Here one's belief system is a kind of creature comfort, a cozy pet theory or hobbyhorse; a well-entrenched intellectual prejudice.

Peirce disagreed with all of these methods because they failed to fix or settle belief. What they lacked was some connection with experience and behavior. He then offered a fourth method, the *method of science.* This method Peirce praised because of its realistic basis in experience. As a means of resolving conflicts between alternative beliefs, Peirce recommended the scientific method, which he felt was a means to combat personal prejudice.

FACT

Peirce said that all truths need to be revised, a position he called "fallibilism." The one infallible statement is that "All statements are fallible." The end result of Peirce's epistemology is not full-blown certainty, but at any given moment the reassurance that you can find (1) provisional beliefs that work in practice and (2) a method to find better beliefs.

In his works Peirce praises the method of science for three reasons: (1) The method of science requires that you state the truth you believe and how you arrived at it. In this way, your procedures will be known to anyone who wishes to retrace the same steps to test whether the same results occur. Peirce continually emphasizes the public or community character of the method of science. (2) The method of science is self-examining and self-critical. It subjects your cherished conclusions to severe tests. Peirce says this ought also to be your attitude toward all of your beliefs, scientific and otherwise. (3) Peirce thought that science requires cooperation among all members of the scientific community. Such cooperation prevents any individual or group from shaping truth to fit its own interests. Similarly, in questions of belief and truth, it should be possible for anyone to come to the same conclusions.

All told, the method of science is empirical. It is a method rooted in observation and discovers things as they actually are. The method of science highlights errors and is self-corrective. It can be tested independent of our pet beliefs or dearest wishes.

John Dewey

In his lengthy *History of Western Philosophy,* Bertrand Russell wrote, John Dewey (1859–1952) is "generally admitted to be the leading living philosopher in America." Russell's epithet tells you two things: it speaks to the importance of Dewey as a thinker and to the influence of pragmatic thought on American philosophy.

Charles Peirce's emphasis had been on scientific inquiry and the manner of establishing beliefs. William James would broaden pragmatism's outlook to include ideas in psychology, morality, metaphysics, and religion. Dewey's own pragmatism consisted in developing an "instrumental" theory of truth. All three philosophers have in common that they were less interested in the origins of ideas than they were in the consequences of those ideas for the lives of individuals and the future in general.

The Life of John Dewey

John Dewey began his education inauspiciously. Then he opted for a college preparatory program at his local high school in Vermont. He completed the course so rapidly that he attended the University of Vermont at the age of sixteen. He pursued a classical education and was influenced by studying philosophy and the theory of evolution. After graduating he taught at a high school in Pennsylvania for two years before enrolling for a doctoral degree at Johns Hopkins University.

He finished his doctorate in 1884, then taught for ten years at the University of Michigan before heading for the University of Chicago in 1894. He had married Alice Chapman, who inspired his interest in social issues. His social consciousness was also raised by sociologist George Herbert Mead (1863–1931) and social philosopher James Hayden Tufts (1862–1942).

At the University of Chicago he met people who would influence his own philosophy of education, such as educator Ella Flagg Young (1845–1918), whose Ph.D. he supervised and who was deeply involved in the University Laboratory School that Dewey founded. He also befriended social reformer—and eventual winner of the Nobel Peace Prize—Jane Adams (1860–1935).

Dewey moved to Columbia University in 1904, where his academic output in books and journal articles skyrocketed. His work also appeared in popular periodicals, such as the *Nation* and *New Republic*. His reputation outside academia grew. He traversed the globe, lecturing, observing schools, and writing reports on the educational institutions he studied. His biggest influence was undoubtedly in China, where his educational theories are still influential today.

Dewey retired in 1930 but continued his broad travel and work until his death in New York in 1952.

FACT

Toward the end of his life John Dewey wrote that his ideas owed more to the people he'd known than the books he'd read. While studying for his Ph.D. at Johns Hopkins his three main influences were psychologist G. Stanley Hall, Hegelian idealist George Sylvester Morris, and pragmatist Charles Peirce.

Instrumentalism

Dewey's own version of pragmatism was called *instrumentalism*. He wished to replace the correspondence theory of truth—where true statements are defined as those that "correspond to reality"—to a new idea of "the truth is what works."

Under the correspondence theory, if you say Force equals Mass times Acceleration, your statement is true if it corresponds to reality. But Dewey thought this was a "metaphysical" claim—for how can you know what "reality" is, beyond how it appears to you? You should agree or disagree with the hypothesis $F = MA$ because it works or doesn't work. The hypothesis must have predictable consequences. The proof of an idea consists in it being subject to predictable results. In other words, in Dewey's cumbersome expression: "According to experimental inquiry, the validity of the object of thought depends upon the consequences of the operations which define the object of thought." Ideas that measure up to the criterion of truth possess "warranted assertibility," which is a term Dewey substitutes for belief, knowledge, or proof.

Dewey accepted Peirce's idea that the object of scientific inquiry is belief. Inquiry originates in doubt and there are methods for overcoming that doubt, as Peirce said. But Dewey goes further in saying that the problem must be defined before you can reach a solution. You can only reach a solution by accepting observable facts. In his book *How We Think*, Dewey lays out five steps for solving problems:

- Step one is to observe the main components of a problem.
- In step two you think further about the problem to assess its complete difficulty and appreciate the larger context it is part of.
- In step three you make hypotheses that move toward a possible solution of it.
- The fourth step includes an analysis of your hypothesis in terms of past experience, choosing other potentially feasible solutions.
- The fifth step involves putting these possible solutions into practice experimentally or inductively and checking the results against your actual experiences.

You might picture Copernicus testing the heliocentric hypothesis in this fashion, checking it against his mathematical calculations and past hypotheses in order to confirm it. The five steps combined make up our reflective thinking.

Now his definition of truth shows its fuller meaning. Truth is a means of satisfying human needs. Truth is many things: useful, public, and objective; that is, it benefits society, not just the individual who discovers it. Pragmatists were united in the belief that practical consequences are the only valid test of truth, but it was Dewey who worked out these step-by-step procedures, starting with formulating the problem and moving toward a practical solution.

William James

William James (1842–1910) simplified and popularized pragmatic thought like no other thinker. "The whole function of philosophy ought to be to find out what definite difference it will make to you and to me, at definite times of our life, if this world-formula or that world-formula be the true one," he said. What "difference" beliefs made was more obvious—and in some ways more important—than whether those beliefs are true. James was especially concerned with all of philosophy's "open" questions. This included the issues of morality, God's existence, free will and determinism, and immortality. He answered all of these in a pragmatic and personal way. He may not have answered them for everyone, but he answered them for himself in a manner that other found profitable.

Life

Williams James earned his medical degree from Harvard at the age of twenty-seven. But medicine's loss would become philosophy's gain. When he published *Principles of Psychology* in 1890, the field was still in its infancy. He made philosophy his full-time occupation and taught with Josiah Royce, George Santayana, and C. S. Pierce. "Pierce wrote as a logician and James as a humanist," Dewey said. James looked at the value of philosophy in terms of its contribution to his life. For James, the consequences of a belief were to be understood in terms of the personal and practical impact it has in the life of an individual.

Of belief in God, he wrote: "On pragmatist principles, if the hypothesis of God works satisfactorily in the widest sense of the word, it is 'true.'"

Similar to Dewey, truth for James is not correspondence, but involves asking, "What concrete difference will it make in anyone's actual life?" James says that true beliefs have the characteristic that "they pay" or have practical "cash value." He defines truth in terms of "what works," or "gives satisfaction," or the "practical consequences" of a person's beliefs. "The true is whatever proves itself to be good in the way of belief" and "Truth happens to an idea. It becomes true, is made true by events."

In response to his critics that his view is too subjective, he tries to provide criteria for truth: "True ideas are those that we can assimilate, validate, corroborate, and verify. False ideas are those we cannot. . . . . In addition, as humans are constituted in point of fact, we find that to believe in other men's minds, in independent physical realities, in past events, in eternal logical relations, is satisfactory."

Options

When you wonder what side of an important issue to take we have options. Options are of several kinds: (1) they are living or dead, (2) forced or avoidable, and (3) momentous or trivial. An option is genuine when it is of the forced, living, and momentous kind.

- **Living or Dead:** A living option is only when both options are in play. If someone says to you, "Be a Tory or a member of the Green Party," at least one of these is dead (there are no Tories anymore) and the other is near dead, since more than 99 percent of the population are not members of the Green Party. If he says, "Be a believer in God or a nonbeliever," then this is a living option, since both choices are open.
- **Forced or Avoidable:** If someone says, "Choose between buying a Cadillac or buying a Chrysler," she doesn't offer you a genuine option for it is not forced. You might ride a motorcycle and not buy a car at all or you may buy a Chevrolet or a Ford. Also, if she says "Love me or hate me," or "Call my theory true or false," you have avoidable options in both cases, since you may decline loving her or hating her and may make no judgment about her theory. But if she says, "Either believe in a supreme being or don't believe," that is a forced option, for there is no standing outside the alternatives (agnosticism, which lies between belief and nonbelief, is a choice). "Either believe in free will or determinism" is another metaphysical dilemma. Every dilemma based on a complete logical disjunction, with no possibility of not choosing, is an option of this forced kind.
- **Momentous or Trivial:** The beliefs about God and free will are momentous. Similarly, if you are a scientist and someone from the Centers for Disease Control says, "You have an opportunity to work on this cure for AIDS," your decision about what to do is momentous, not trivial. It is more momentous if the chance will not come along again.

As a further illustration of his pragmatic idea of options being live, forced, and momentous, James considers Pascal and his celebrated

"Wager" argument. As stated in Chapter 18, Pascal said you cannot know but you must either believe or not believe that God is. Which will you do? Your human reason cannot say for sure. So you weigh what your gains and losses would be if you wager all you have on God's existence. If you win the wager, you gain eternal beatitude; if you lose, you lose nothing at all. James agreed: Pascal's choice was forced, living, and momentous, and that belief or disbelief was not merely a matter for debate. Rather, how you choose makes a profound difference in our lives.

In general, James argued that you have a right to believe what is subjectively and pragmatically appealing concerning a genuine option when the evidence is insufficient. Religious beliefs are forced, living, and momentous and our "passional nature not only lawfully may, but must, decide an option between propositions, whenever it is a genuine option which cannot be decided on intellectual grounds."

Free Will and Morality

Likewise, William James said that you could not rationally prove that human will is either free or determined. To solve the problem, according to James, you simply ask the pragmatic question, "What does a deterministic world imply?" That is, what kind of universe are you are living in if all events without exception are rigorously determined from the beginning of time so that they could not have happened in any other way? We could only answer that such a universe is like a machine, where each part fits tightly and all the other gears are interlocked. But James thinks that you are different from gears in a machine.

What sets us apart is consciousness. For one thing, you are capable of judgments of regret. For instance, you might regret your treatment of another person or regret your shabby effort in school or on a job. But could you have had such regrets if events in the universe were as rigidly fixed as the determinist says and could not have been otherwise?

Besides judgments of regret, you can also make judgments of moral approval and disapproval. You judge people and yourself to be wrong on certain occasions. When people steal or kill, you judge them, but you would probably not make such judgments if you thought that determinism was true, since determinism says all such actions are determined or inevitable.

THE EVERYTHING GUIDE TO UNDERSTANDING PHILOSOPHY

From the standpoint of free will, however, you believe the agents could have done otherwise. In conclusion, James says the problem is a very "personal" one and that he cannot personally conceive of the universe as a place where murder must happen. Instead, it is a place where murder can happen and ought not.

In *The Varieties of Religious Experience* James spoke of the role that religion plays in contemporary society. Since he had said that something is true if it works, you can apply this to prayer by saying it works for the individual psyche to think that prayers are heard, but the person will not necessarily get what he prays for.

So for James the free will option is pragmatically truer because it better accommodates judgments of regret and morality. In *Meaning and Truth* (1909), he says, "Of two competing views of the universe which in all other respects are equal, but of which the first denies some vital human need while the second satisfies it, the second will be favored by sane men for the simple reason that it makes the world seem more rational."

Evaluation and Significance

Though the philosophical movement known as pragmatism originated in New England about 150 years ago, it is as different and refreshing in the twenty-first century as it was in the mid-nineteenth century. For one, it offers up an altogether relaxed attitude about what is true, meaningful, and significant in people's lives.

Peirce first used the word *pragmatism* to emphasize a kind of experiential approach to arriving at true beliefs, as opposed to the metaphysical concerns of Hegel and Kant and of the rationalists and empiricists that dominated philosophical conversation in his time. He argued that both approaches left something to be desired with their insistence that truths were eternal and necessary on the one hand and derived from sense impressions on the other.

All one needs to do to understand pragmatism's continual appeal is to review three moments in its history. Charles Peirce stated that metaphysical certainty is a luxurious commodity rarely found, acknowledging that all truths need to be revised. He named his position "fallibilism." Is there an infallible statement anywhere? Yes, the one infallible statement is that "All statements are fallible." With full-blown certainty nowhere in sight, we can still find provisional beliefs that work in practice.

Dewey's own version of pragmatism sounded a similar note. He wished to replace the correspondence theory of truth with a modified idea of "truth is what works." These truths would be instrumental in finding further truths. He called his doctrine "instrumentalism."

William James countered the ominous view of a contemporary, W. K. Clifford, who claimed, "It is wrong always and everywhere to believe anything upon insufficient evidence." James responded to Clifford's mortal fear of being wrong by saying that on some issues we lack sufficient evidence one way or another. To not take a stand on issues like the existence of God and freedom of the will is to live in fear of being duped, according to James. Yet, since these are open questions it is quite reasonable to "will to believe" what you choose.

CHAPTER 20

Analytic Philosophy: A New Look at Old Philosophical Problems

Analytic philosophy hasn't just poured old wine into new bottles. It has shown that the utmost importance must be put on analyzing the wine itself. Analytic philosophy has been preoccupied with unpacking the meaning of statements and assessing the overall cogency of arguments. Philosophy in the analytic period has been less given to grandiose systems with bold statements about metaphysics and morals, and more given to dissecting claims piecemeal.

20

The Analytic Turn

Analytic philosophy was a philosophical movement that was especially strong in England and the United States in the twentieth century. Analytic philosophy concentrated on language and the attempt to analyze statements in order to get clear about philosophical problems.

It was once said that "Philosophers raise a dust and then they complain that they cannot see." Analytic philosophers tried to solve the problem and clear the dust by getting clear about the language they use. They sought to break down statements and concepts into their clearest logical forms.

In the twenty-first century the analytic approach to philosophy continues to be the dominant trend in philosophy in the English-speaking world. In the early part of the twentieth century and continuing on through today, a number of philosophers have held the conviction that clarifying language—and making it unambiguous and concise—is the most pressing and important task of philosophy. This movement is known as *analytic* or *linguistic* philosophy. Philosophers within this movement believe that analysis is the correct approach to philosophy. There are at least two reasons for this "linguistic turn" in philosophy.

One, the philosophers thought science had taken over much of the territory formerly occupied by philosophy. If various special sciences had taken over the acquisition of knowledge about the world, then the only task that remained for philosophy was to clarify linguistic meaning. As Mortiz Schlick, an early member of the analytic movement, put it, "Science should be defined as the pursuit of truth" and philosophy as "the pursuit of meaning."

Even if Schlick's conclusion contains a kernel of truth, there are still many questions that philosophy considers and these questions have not been subsumed by the special sciences. These include but are not limited to: questions in normative and applied ethics; arguments about the nature and existence of God; the issue of free will versus determinism; issues in the philosophy of mind, including mind-body interaction. These issues are still the special province of philosophy.

A second reason for the linguistic turn in philosophy is the new and more powerful methods of logic that had been developed in the twentieth century. These methods promised to shed new light on some of the old philosophical stalemates. With these logical techniques, expressions that appeared to be meaningful propositions, but that were actually vague, equivocal, misleading, or nonsensical, could be exposed and eliminated by careful analysis.

One striking example of this tendency is the philosophy of A. J. Ayer and the movement known as *logical positivism.*

A. J. Ayer and Logical Positivism

Perhaps there is no more striking and unmistakable example of how language and issues of meaning can be wielded on philosophical problems than that of logical positivism. A. J. Ayer (1910–89), in his influential book *Language, Truth, and Logic,* applied the scalpel of positivism, also called logical empiricism, to issues in ethics, theology, and metaphysics.

The Verification Principle

A. J. Ayer applied a principle called "the verification principle" to statements to see if they were meaningful statements. "To test whether a sentence expresses a genuine empirical hypothesis, I adopt a modified verification principle," Ayer wrote. "I require of an empirical hypothesis not that it should be conclusively verifiable, but that some possible sense experience should be relevant to the determination of its truth or falsehood. If a putative proposition fails to satisfy this principle, and is not a tautology, then I hold that it is metaphysical and that it is neither true nor false but literally senseless."

The positivists were not trying to decide whether some statement was true or false. They thought that was the job of science. Philosophy's task was to decide what it means to say that a statement has meaning. A meaningful statement is one that provides information about the world. Ayer's verifiability principle can be illustrated by seeing what he would say about the following statements:

1. The cat is on the mat.
2. The stock market crashed in October 1931.
3. The Chicago Cubs last won the World Series in 1908.
4. Michael Jordan owns the highest p.p.g. of all-time (30.1).
5. My soul will go to heaven or hell after stopping off in purgatory.
6. Krishna is an avatar of Vishnu.

If you are sitting in a room in which there is a cat on the mat, then the first statement is true. Even if there was no cat on the mat, the statement is not meaningless, only false. For at least some "possible sense experience," in Ayer's words, that would make it true. Statement 2 is false (the market crashed in 1929), but it too is not meaningless. Statements 3 and 4 are true, since they satisfy the empirical demands of the verification principle. But statements 5 and 6 are the kinds that are exposed by Ayer's verification principle. They mention entities like "soul," "heaven," "purgatory," "Krishna," and "Vishnu." These entities are metaphysical and cannot be sensed. Thus, the statements are not true or false but "nonsense"—in a very literal way. In fact, you cannot even imagine the kinds of experiences that would verify such entities.

QUESTION?

Is "God is almighty" a meaningful statement, according to Ayer?
Hardly. Have you ever seen God on Main Street, walking or buying groceries in town? If not, has he been part of some other sense experience? Probably not. Do you expect him to be part of some future sense experience? If not, then the statement is not meaningful.

Theological and Moral Statements

A. J. Ayer quotes F. H. Bradley as saying, "The absolute enters into, but is itself incapable of evolution and progress." But such theological statements cannot be verified or proven false. Similarly, statements such as "All reality is material" or "All reality is immaterial" are beyond the bounds of experience and therefore are neither true nor false, but are pseudo-propositions.

British philosopher Antony Flew makes a point similar to Ayer's about other theological statements. Flew claims that the statement "God loves his children as a father loves his son" is not really falsifiable. In fact, religious people will maintain there is a loving God even when their lives are filled with suffering. Ayer suggests then that such grandiose theological claims are not falsifiable and so are really meaningless.

According to Antony Flew, one of the conditions of meaningful statements is that they are falsifiable. The statement "Water freezes at 32° Fahrenheit" is meaningful because one can imagine conditions under which it could be falsified; namely, if water froze at some other temperature. Since it has been empirically shown that it freezes at 32°F, it has passed the test of falsifiability.

It is not just the statements themselves but the denial of such statements that are meaningless. So the atheist's assertion that "There is no God" is just as unverifiable and meaningless as the positive claim that there is. At best, metaphysical and theological statements express our feelings about the world.

Even moral statements such as "Abortion is wrong" are senseless, since "wrongness," unlike "redness," cannot be sensed. In sum, statements containing value terms, as well as theological and metaphysical terms, make about as much sense as "Turquoise water is virtuous" or "Prufroths blick schoochingly."

According to positivists, when someone says "You acted wrongly in stealing that money" this does not make a verifiable factual claim about stealing. Instead, when a person morally condemns an act of stealing, what they are actually doing is stating a fact plus expressing an emotion or attitude toward it such as "You stole the money!—Ugh, Boo, Hiss!" This thought was developed further in the "emotivist" philosophy of Charles Stevenson.

According to Ayer, statements in which value terms like *good, evil, right,* and *just* appear are not empirical statements, for they do not describe the world. As such, value statements—like theological and metaphysical statements—are nonsensical.

INSIGHT

According to Ayer, claims containing value terms are not genuine propositions but pseudo-propositions. "Murder is morally bad" may express several things, but none of those things is empirical. "The bottle is green" makes sense, since you can verify that you see green. But can you see "badness" or "goodness"? If not, claims containing such terms are nonsense.

Positivism and the Legacy of David Hume

You may recall from the chapter on empiricism David Hume's thoughts that you should pick up any volume of divinity or school metaphysics and ask, "Does it contain any abstract reasoning concerning quantity or number? No. Does it contain any experimental reasoning concerning matters of fact and existence? No. Commit it to the flames: for it can contain nothing but sophistry and illusion."

Much Like Hume, the logical positivists believed all genuine knowledge falls within the two realms of science:

1. The formal sciences of logic and mathematics
2. The empirical sciences

The first kind of knowledge is expressed in what are called *analytic propositions*. The truth or falsity of these sorts of statements is based on the logical form of language or on the definition of words. Thus "2 + 2 = 4" and "all bachelors are unmarried" are examples of true analytic statements. Wittgenstein called all such statements tautologies.

False analytic statements, such as "A square has three sides," or "3 × 3 = 8," are identified by the fact that they contain a contradiction. Since tautologies are always true and contradictions are always false, no matter what is the case, analytic statements do not give you any factual knowledge about the way the world is.

The second class of statements consists of empirical statements. Unlike analytic statements, both true and false empirical statements do make claims about the world. Since analytic and empirical statements are the only sorts of meaningful statements there are, any proposition that does not fall into either category is not simply false, nor is it merely unknowable, it is meaningless.

Plato's metaphysical assertion that "Forms exist in a world of ideas" cannot be verified. So Ayer would agree with Hume that all pages on which such metaphysical propositions are written should be cast into the flames.

Bertrand Russell and Analysis

Bertrand Russell (1872–1970) lived to the age of ninety-eight and touched almost every area of philosophy. Born in Wales and educated at Cambridge, Russell would make major contributions to mathematics and logical analysis, for which he received much acclaim. From 1910 to 1949 he was occupied with moral, political, and social issues. One illustration of his analytical acumen was his theory of definite descriptions.

Definite Descriptions

Russell had a different approach than the logical positivists on the meaning of sentences. This is especially true of his treatment of sentences that fail to refer to reality. For instance, consider a statement like "The present king of France is bald." Since there is no present king of France, do sentences of this sort count as false or meaningless? You end up with a problem no matter which way you decide.

To say it is meaningless goes against a person's ability to understand what the sentence is trying to convey. To say that it is false, on the other hand, implies that its contradiction—"The present king of France is not bald"—is true. But this statement about the king not being bald is no truer than the first. So how can one deal with sentences such as these that fail to refer to anything?

Russell's answer was original. He maintained that such sentences were descriptions consisting of a conjunction of separate claims. First, that there is some person who is the king of France; second, that there is just one person who is the king of France; third, that any person who is the king of France is bald. Each of these parts can be tested as true or false. But the first is false, since there is no king of France. Logically, any statement that is a conjunction of propositions is false if any one of the conjuncts is false. The conjunction is false, then.

FACT

Bertrand Russell was denied a professorial appointment at City College in the City University of New York. He was denied because it was learned that he had written *Marriage and Morals,* which discussed the feasibility of having an open marriage. A parent of one college student was offended and the Board of Education rejected Russell's appointment.

The German philosopher Gottlob Frege did more to originate analytic philosophy with his predicate logic. Bertrand Russell used predicate logic to reveal philosophical problems more clearly. To take one example, Russell showed how the English word *is* can be expressed in three different ways:

In 'the ball is blue: the is of predication says that 'x is P': P (x)
In 'there is a ball': the is of existence says that there is an x: ∃ *(x)*
In 'twelve is half of twenty-four' the is of identity says that x is the same as y: x = Y

But Russell's theory of definite descriptions shows that it is possible to speak sensibly of things that do not exist. Since Russell, it has become a standard tool of logical analysis.

Bertrand Russell and the Problem of Induction

Bertrand Russell wrote an important essay called "On Induction" in his little book *The Problems of Philosophy.* His treatment of induction harkens back to the skeptic David Hume, who maintained that there was no "necessary connection" between the occurrence of two events A and B, but only a "habit" of expecting that the occurrence of A, say the movement of one billiard ball, will lead to B, the movement of another ball that A contacts. Hume was talking about causality in nature.

Using careful analysis and re-exploring the problem in new language, Russell showed that Hume was right: induction could never be justified. As Russell puts it:

> *The problem we have to discuss is whether there is any reason for believing in what is called 'the uniformity of nature.' The belief in the uniformity of nature is the belief that everything that has happened or will happen is an instance of some general law to which there are no exceptions.*

But can you establish that there is a "uniformity of nature?" In answering, Russell the empiricist comes out looking very much like David Hume the empiricist. There are enough examples that show that the uniformity of nature is difficult to show. Russell notes that domestic animals expect food when they see the person who usually feeds them. But the man who feeds the chicken every day throughout its life at last "wrings its neck instead, showing that more refined views as to the uniformity of nature would have been useful to the chicken."

Also, Russell says, "Food that has a certain appearance generally has a certain taste, and it is a severe shock to our expectations when the familiar appearance is found to be associated with an unusual taste." So you expected the green apple to taste as it did the last five times you had one or that the penicillin that cured your strep throat a dozen times will do so again. But all you are doing here is expecting that the future will resemble the past. The problem is, Russell says, that you can have experience of "past futures," but you have not yet sampled those "future futures."

Russell allows that the principle we have been examining is called "the principle of induction," which runs as follows:

> *When a thing of a certain sort A has been found to be associated with a thing of a certain other sort B, and has never been found dissociated from a thing of the sort B, the greater the number of cases in which A and B have been associated, the greater is the probability that they will be associated in a fresh case in which one of them is known to be present.*

Even though you believe that probabilities are reliable, you really don't know those either. For even if the sun has always risen and so you expect to see it rise tomorrow, what can you use for your justification? That it has always risen in the past? But you cannot assume the past in predicting the future. To do so would be "begging the question," that is, assuming the very thing to be proven.

Does God Exist?

In 1948 Bertrand Russell debated Father Frederick C. Copleston, a Jesuit Roman Catholic priest. An agnostic, Russell made for a dramatic contrast with Fr. Copleston, who wrote the nineteen-volume work *A History of Philosophy*. The debate broke down into three separate arguments for the existence of God: the argument from contingency, the moral argument, and the religious argument.

The Argument from Contingency

Copleston supports the argument from contingency—essentially, that the world is contingent or non-necessary and depends on some necessary being for its existence. Half of the transcript of their debate is taken up with this issue. Copleston proposes a four-part definition of God: we mean by God a supreme personal being distinct from the world and creator of the world. Russell accepts the definition but explains that he does not think that the "non-existence of God can be proved."

From the outset the debate reveals Russell's analytic tendencies, working on breaking down Copleston's claims about God. Copleston argues that in order to explain objects that exist you must "come to a being which contains within itself the reason for its own existence." This is what he means by a "necessary being."

But Russell, an empiricist, replies in a very Humean fashion: "I would only admit a necessary being if there were a being whose existence it is self-contradictory to deny." The word *necessary* then applies to no one thing, since all things are contingent. So the word *necessary* is a useless word, except when it is being applied to analytic propositions like "A bachelor is an unmarried man" or "Irrational animals are animals."

Copleston presses the point, arguing that "an infinite series of contingent beings will be, to my way of thinking, as unable to cause itself as one contingent being." But Russell again applies his analytical scalpel: you get your concept of a cause from your observation of particular things; but the concept of cause doesn't apply to the total series of causes. The universe, Russell says, "is just there."

INSIGHT

Various arguments for God's existence fail to work on empirical grounds, according to Russell. Since Russell is an empiricist, he believes that the truth of any claims about God creating the world will depend in large part on their being observed. But who has observed the creation of the world or of any other things in it?

The Religious Experience and Moral Arguments for God's Existence

After employing his argument from contingency, Copleston tries a familiar argument grounded in religious experience. Normal citizens and saints throughout history have heard voices or felt touched in some way by the presence of something outside of themselves. People have had experiences of "something transcending the self, something transcending all the normal objects of experience, something which cannot be pictured or conceptualized, but of the reality of which doubt is impossible . . . at least during the experience."

The best way to explain the experience, Copleston continues, is that there is actually "some objective cause of that experience. I don't regard religious experience as a strict proof of the existence of God . . . but I think it is true to say that the *best explanation* of it is the existence of God." (Italics added.) Here Copleston borrowed the scientific term "best explanation" to account for religious experiences. In short, if person X is having a religious experience of a God, there must be a cause for that experience, namely God himself.

Russell disagrees. People can all experience the same thing, like a clock, which tells them that the clock is not a hallucination. But religious experiences, by their nature, are experiences of individuals that "tend to be very private." Moreover, if you assume whatever people report as being true, "including demons and devils—does the experience of them prove that they exist?" In short, some experience of X, something outside myself, "doesn't prove the existence of something outside of me," according to Russell.

Copleston's "moral argument" for the existence of God claims that if there is a universal moral law, there must be "an author" of that law. But Russell contends that if there is a moral law, it is not absolute but always changing. For people have at various times thought cannibalism was a duty, not to mention segregation, slavery, the oppression of women, and so forth. This would seem to indicate that people's consciences are "amazingly different in different times and places." The fact of variety seems to indicate that the conclusion does not follow: there is no one transcendent author of the moral law, but lots of different "terrestrial law" givers, like parents, teachers, and leaders.

Evaluation and Significance

There is little question that analytic philosophy changed the manner in which philosophy was done. Using newer methods of logical and linguistic analysis illuminated old philosophical queries in ethics, metaphysics, and epistemology. Looking to the future, analytic philosophy's reach will be long and wide. We know this by its influence to this point, which has included ethics (including the work of philosophers such as Charles Stevenson, R. M. Hare, and Phillipa Foot), philosophy of religion (for instance, the work of William Alston, John Mackie, and Alvin Plantinga), and political philosophy (including John Rawls and Robert Nozick).

CHAPTER 21

Twentieth-Century Existentialism: Existence Precedes Essence

Man is alone, forlorn, and without excuses in being utterly responsible for his life. Life itself is absurd. Only we can bring meaning to it. Thinkers like Sartre and Albert Camus took on themes that were intensely personal, such as dread, boredom, alienation, the absurd, freedom, commitment, and nothingness. All of this was wildly different from traditional philosophies like rationalism and empiricism.

Jean-Paul Sartre

Jean-Paul Sartre (1905–80) would become the leading voice of atheistic existentialism. He was a novelist, critic, political activist, and philosopher. Later in his life he moved away from existentialism and developed his own style of Marxist ideology.

During World War II Sartre was a soldier and for nine months was a prisoner of war in Germany. After he was released he worked in the Resistance Movement. With his long-time mate Simone de Beauvoir, he edited *Les Temps Moderns,* a wildly popular and *au currant* monthly review devoted to socialist and existentialist concerns.

Humanity: "Existence Precedes Essence"

After World War II, Sartre wrote a small, popular book explaining the tenets of existentialism. In *Existentialism and Human Emotions* (1947) Sartre sets forth the novel and exciting idea of human freedom that identified him as one of the most renowned postwar philosophers of the twentieth century. The phrase "existence precedes essence" says that there is no such thing as a given human nature. On the contrary, it is your own choices and acts that make up your identity. Man first exists and his choices then define his essence.

FACT

In 1964, Jean-Paul Sartre was awarded the Nobel Prize for literature for his novel *Nausea.* He refused to accept the $53,000 prize money because he did not want to become a tool of the establishment. Sartre lived on the income of the sales of his philosophy and fiction.

Sartre's dictum that "existence precedes essence" separates him from several major classical philosophers, beginning with Plato and Aristotle. For Plato, truth is eternal, unchangeable, and absolute, and knowing it is the central goal of philosophy. According to Plato, there are eternally existing forms and your job is to discover them through philosophical contemplation, through reason. Human beings have a common eternal "essentialist" nature defined by reason.

Aristotle, too, said that humans are rational animals. He said:

Reason is the true self of every person, since it is the supreme and better part. It will be strange, then, if he should choose not his own life, but some other's. . . . What is naturally proper to every creature is the highest and pleasantest for him. And so, to man, this will be the life of reason, since reason is, in the highest sense, a man's self.

In one way or another, all the major philosophical systems from Plato through the Middle Ages down to Descartes, Leibniz, Kant, and Hegel carried on this essentialist tradition. Truth is outside of you, and your job is to use reason to discover it.

But Sartre says, "There is no human nature. . . . Man is nothing but what he makes of himself." Sartre expressed nature in the formula, "man's existence precedes essence." By this he means that you have no fixed nature and have not been created for any particular purpose. Things like paper cutters and hammers have set natures, since they have been created to fulfill a set purpose. But mankind is not created by God or evolution or anything else; you simply find yourself existing by no choice of your own and have to decide what to make of yourself. Each person must create her own essence.

Freedom and Atheism

Sartre rejects the existence of God in a tidy argument. If a sovereign God existed, then persons would not be free agents. Persons are free agents, however. So a sovereign God does not exist. Further, if persons are not divinely created beings, then there was no plan and no blueprint for what they are intended to be.

"Man first of all exists, encounters himself, surges up in the world—and defines himself afterward," Sartre says. He faults previous atheists for supposing they could remove the concept of God from their systems and still go on talking about human nature and objective values. Instead, "There is no human nature, because there is no God to have a conception of it."

Without a human nature to appeal to, you are condemned to be free. Sartre says you do not *have* freedom, you *are* freedom. Freedom is not one property among many, but is intrinsic to the sort of beings you are, for at each moment of your existence you are creating yourself anew. "We are condemned to be free," he says, because freedom is a great human burden. For with freedom comes responsibility for your life. Blame cannot be placed on your environment or on God.

During his time in a German prison camp after 1940 and later in the French Resistance, Sartre decided to write on behalf of democracy. A major preoccupation from that time on is his attempt to link the freedom inherent in human nature with political freedom. He may own the most radical view of human freedom in the history of thought.

You are born into a situation. Those features of your existence that you cannot change Sartre calls "facticity." So, you were born into this environment, not another, born to these parents, not some others. Therefore, you might look at these facts as impositions on your freedom caused by past events over which you had no control. But these facts don't have a meaning until you assign them a meaning. Your true freedom comes to the fore in the ways in which you respond to your facticity.

If you were born into affluence, you can continue to pursue that life as you grow older, or you can shun that life and join the priesthood, or you can fight for the rights of the poor. So it is with gender. Gender is a biological fact, but this bit of facticity tells nothing about what it means to be this or that gender. Hence, scientific facts tell you very little about how to live your life. You still have significant freedom in determining the outcome of your life.

Sartre quotes Dostoyevsky's pronouncement "If God does not exist, every thing would be permitted." There are no objective values or religious commandments to appeal to. "We have neither behind us, no before us in a luminous realm of values, any means of justification or excuse," Sartre says. "We are left alone, without excuse."

He tells the story of a poor, orphaned man who had a disastrous love affair and was denied a military career because he failed an exam. He believes his terrible situation is a sign he should serve God and becomes a Jesuit priest. Sartre says this is the meaning that this individual chose to assign to these experiences. However, he could just as easily decide that they mean he should become a revolutionary. There is no moral almanac to tell the individual what to do. The gist of Sartre's philosophy is that individuals give these facts meaning by deciding how to act.

INSIGHT

In his *Essays in Existentialism* Sartre talks about man being "thrown into existence" without having chosen it: "If man, as the existentialist conceives him, is indefinable, it is because at first he is nothing. Only afterward will he be something, and he himself will have made what he will be."

Freedom and the Two Modes of Being

One of the reasons that you possess freedom is that you possess what objects do not—consciousness. Being the Cartesian that he was, Sartre followed Descartes in distinguishing between extended substance and mental substance. One characteristic of mental substance is freedom.

Sartre said that when you analyze what appears to you, you discover two modes of being. First, there is the sort of being manifested in objects. This is called the in-itself (*l'en-soi*). The term *in-itself* signifies that objects are self-contained or self-identical. Sartre considers a manufactured object like a paper cutter. It is a man-made object designed for a purpose. Nothing in this object—or any objects—transcends what it currently is. A bottle, a mountain, or a house simply exists.

The second sort of being is what characterizes human consciousness. Sartre calls this sort of being the for-itself (*le pour-soi*). The term *for-itself* signifies that such beings are conscious and self-aware. Rather than being determined by external causes, as objects are bound by gravity, you are capable of spontaneous freedom and living your life in terms of future possibilities. You are "subjectivity," Sartre wrote in *Existentialism and Human*

Emotions, "Man first of all is the being who hurls himself toward the future and who is conscious of imagining himself as being in the future."

Sartre's greatest work was *Being and Nothingness* (1943). The title captures the two modes of being. Being in-itself is simply there, without possibilities. When consciousness is present, however, "nothingness" is introduced into the world. Only the for-itself can become separate from the bare existence of things in the causal order in this way. Consciousness has the ability to separate itself from things and to live in the "what-is-not" (the realm of possibilities). You become aware of your own consciousness by being aware of the gap between yourself and the world of causally determined objects.

Bad Faith and Authenticity

You inauthentically identify yourself with any number of roles and think you are unfree to be anything else. A security guard may try a little too hard to be a security guard and he thereby eliminates his possibility of being anything else. Sartre criticizes an obsequious waiter who is trying too hard to identify with his role as a waiter.

In his own life, Sartre refused to identify with the public's attempt to lock him into the identity of being a famous writer. So Jean-Paul Sartre the famous writer, philosopher, and activist refused to identify his free spontaneous self with the public's attempt to lock him into the identity of being a famous writer. In response to an interviewer's question, Sartre said:

> *You know, the fame seems to go on in someone else's life, it has happened to someone else. There is me and then there is the other person. The other person has written books and is read. . . . He exists, I know, but he doesn't bother me; I use him . . . but I do not think of him as being me.*

Sartre uses the term *bad faith* to refer to the attempt to deny your freedom, to see yourself as a product of your "facticity," limited by your circumstances, or the attempt to identify yourself with your past choices while choosing all of your future possibilities. You feel a need to be an "in-itself," a being that is limited by its nature, defined, that has an identity.

When a young man came to Sartre seeking ethical advice—whether to fight for his country or stay home to aid his sick mother—the only advice Sartre would give him was "You are free, therefore choose—that is to say, invent." Only when you take responsibility for the meaning of your past and present, and self-consciously choose your future, will you achieve authenticity, the one value Sartre seems to embrace in an otherwise valueless universe.

Albert Camus: The Myth of Sisyphus *and the Absurd*

Born in Mondovi, Algeria, to a French family, Albert Camus (1913–60) would make his mark as a philosophical novelist and essayist. At the age of seventeen he contracted tuberculosis, which effectively ended his playing goalkeeper for the football team at the University of Algiers. It also caused him to pursue his studies part-time, and he took odd jobs including working as a private tutor.

He joined the anti-German resistance in Paris during World War II. His most well-known writings include the novel *The Stranger* (written in 1940, published in 1942) and a book-length essay *The Myth of Sisyphus* (written in 1941, published in 1943). Both explore the theme of the "absurd."

FACT

Sisyphus was a figure from Greek mythology who was condemned by the gods to push a rock up a mountain for all eternity. As he gets the rock to the top it rolls down again, and he must start over. Albert Camus saw the parallels between Sisyphus and the workman of his day spending time at the "same tasks" every day.

As part of his involvement with the resistance during the war, Camus edited an underground newspaper, *Combat*. In fact, Camus became the paper's editor in 1943, and when the Allies liberated Paris, Camus reported on the last of the fighting. Few French editors besides Camus publicly expressed opposition to America's dropping the atom bomb on Hiroshima on August 8, 1945. He resigned from the paper when he thought it was becoming too commercial two years later.

At that time he made the acquaintance of Jean-Paul Sartre. The two became habitués of the Café de Flore on the Boulevard Saint-Germain in Paris, where talk of politics and existentialism flowed freely. Camus made frequent stops in the United States, where he lectured on French thinking. He also voiced strong criticisms of Communist ideology, which led him to separate from Sartre.

Human rights became his focus in the 1950s. He protested Soviet oppression in Eastern Europe. He was also a vigilant pacifist and voiced his opposition to capital punishment around the globe. He was awarded the Nobel Prize for literature in 1957, not for his novel *The Fall,* published that year, but for his writings against capital punishment in the essay "Reflexions Sur La Guillotine."

Camus died suddenly in a car accident on January 4, 1960. The train ticket found in his pocket might suggest that he had planned to travel by train but changed his mind. Oddly, Camus had uttered a remark earlier in his life that the most absurd way to die would be in a car accident.

The Absurd

Camus describes the absurd both as the human condition and as "a widespread sensitivity of our times." While several of Camus's works deal with the absurdity of human existence, *The Myth of Sisyphus* may use the absurd in the most direct way. The absurd can be defined as the confrontation between yourself—with your longing for meaning, rationality, and justice—and an "indifferent silent universe." Condemned by the Gods to the endless, futile task of rolling a rock up a mountain (which would roll back down before he could get it to the peak), Sisyphus was a kind of metaphor for the human condition: he is trying to fulfill a task, but his effort is laborious and hopeless.

In an essay entitled "An Absurd Reasoning," Camus wrote: "This divorce between man and his life, the actor and his setting, is properly the feeling of absurdity." But it's what Camus does with the absurd that makes up the most interesting part of his philosophy. It would be one thing to recognize our human condition but suggest nothing to do in response to that condition. Camus does both.

QUESTION?

Does existentialism in the twentieth century extend beyond France?
Yes, in the twentieth century existentialism infiltrated American art forms. For one, Herman Hesse's 1928 novel *Steppenwolf,* based on an idea in Kierkegaard's *Either- Or* (1843), was a popular work. Also, Jack Kerouac and the Beat poets of the 1950s adopted existentialist themes.

He does advise that you not run from your human condition. You should not commit suicide. Instead you must embrace the absurd. He calls keeping the absurd alive an "attitude of permanent revolution." He writes:

Living is keeping the absurd alive. Keeping it alive is, above all, contemplating it. The absurd dies only when we turn away from it. One of the only coherent philosophical positions is thus revolt. It is a constant confrontation between man and his own obscurity. . . . It challenges the world anew every second.

Like the heroic doctor in his novel *The Plague,* one must persist in the face of absurdity. One must live on with persistence and valor, for this is all there is.

Martin Heidegger: The Quest for Being

"The Quest for Being" is how Heidegger described the direction of his philosophy. His contributions are at once those of a metaphysician and an existentialist, though he denied any connection to existentialism. Preoccupied as he was with being as such, he claimed his concerns were not those of existentialism, a philosophy concerned primarily with personal existence.

Martin Heidegger (1889–1976) was born at Baden in Germany. He studied philosophy at Freiburg University, where Edmund Husserl, the phenomenologist who influenced Heidegger greatly, taught from 1916 to 1929.

Heidegger was a professor at Marburg in 1923 before returning to Freiburg in 1928. By 1933 he was rector of the university.

In his inaugural address he lauded National Socialism and aligned himself with the Nazi movement. For a time, he advocated a fusion of philosophical thought and Nazi politics. He resigned his post as a rector ten months later, but his brief association with Nazism followed him for the rest of his life. In an interview with the German magazine *Der Spiegel* in 1966, Heidegger responded to his critics but prohibited the interview from being published until after his death.

FACT

Heidegger's interview with *Der Spiegel* was published on May 31, 1976, five days after his death. He declared he saw in National Socialism the promise of a "new dawn." He had even warned his students in 1933, "Do not let doctrines and ideas be the rules of your Being. The Fuhrer and he alone is the present and the future German reality and its rule."

Heidegger disavowed the Nazis in the interview that was published posthumously. He chided his own ignorance: "I would today no longer write the sentences which you cite. Even by 1934 I no longer said such things."

What Is Being?

Despite the political controversy that enveloped his life, Heidegger was better known for his metaphysics. Heidegger tried to reorient philosophy. He thought that philosophy since the Greeks had been preoccupied with an off-key question: what exists and what you can know about what exists. Heidegger thought that the question made an unwarranted assumption.

The Platonic way of putting the question about being—as well as Descartes's way of putting it—presupposes a dualism of subject and object. Heidegger rejects this dualism since he rejects the notion of a world external to us as conscious spectators.

Heidegger instead focuses on the question "What is being?" The question derives from a more fundamental one: "Why is there something rather than nothing?" Before Heidegger, few had addressed the question. For Heidegger, however, an answer is essential before any other philosophical questions commence.

Heidegger's answer to the question "What is Being?" reverts to what kind of being one is oneself. He attributes to Being the name *Dasein*—"being there." This means that Dasein is a perspective from which action originates. Above all, Dasein knows that it is finite and mortal. From this insight arises angst or dread. But a complete awareness of our own mortality is required for us to have a direction or meaning. Self-awareness will result in a life created out of this dread and sense of finitude. In fact, an authentic life depends on realizing that you must make a meaning by your own actions. With his concepts of dread and authenticity, he is not far afield from Camus and Sartre, who had a concept of an authentic life.

The question of why there is something rather than nothing comes back to Dasein. Without Dasein choosing to make something out of nothing, there would be nothing. It sounds like Camus urging us to keep the absurd with us.

Evaluation and Significance

The existentialism of the twentieth century continued some of the themes of Soren Kierkegaard, the Danish "Father of Existentialism" from the century before. Kierkegaard had stressed the importance of the individual and "truth as subjectivity." Sartre and Camus took up the individual's relentless burden of making life meaningful, even in the presence of a godless, meaningless universe.

Existentialism is not without its critics. British philosopher Roger Scruton criticized Sartre's existentialist ethics for lacking any objective force. Thus, any individual's "authentic" lifestyle, which Sartre recommends, is a "purely self-made morality." Sartre urges that each individual chooses not only for himself, but for all mankind. But it is not clear that five individuals, each seeking his own kind of authenticity, will end up choosing a moral life.

CHAPTER 22

The Legacy of Darwinism and the God Question

Scientific reasoning is offering up new challenges to religion in the present century. Religious views of the world have been challenged strongly since Darwin's publication of *The Origin of Species* in 1859. Now scientific problems like global warming and regimes that mix politics with religion have led many to doubt the global utility of religion. As a consequence, several bestselling books that undermine religion have come to the forefront.

The Present Social Context

It is a time of religious ferment in the United States. This may be true of any time period, but it seems especially true now. The battle over whether to teach Charles Darwin's theory of evolution in the schools or whether to teach creationism—now called "Intelligent design"—continues, even though that battle was fought in Dayton, Tennessee, in "the Scopes Monkey Trial" some eighty years ago. The Ten Commandments have often been removed from public places by court order.

Carl Sagan and The Varieties of Scientific Experience

Carl Sagan (1934–96) was professor of astronomy and space sciences and director of the Laboratory for Planetary Studies at Cornell University. For many, however, Sagan will forever be associated with astronomy because of the public television series *Cosmos,* based on a book of the same name. Sagan appeared regularly on the Tonight Show with Johnny Carson, explaining to his host the story of the "billions and billions" of galaxies in space. Toward the end of his life Sagan taught critical thinking at Cornell, which led him to appreciate rational arguments even more.

Science and Religion

Sagan wrote frequently on issues of religion and science. He began one lecture with a quote from Leonardo da Vinci. In his notebooks da Vinci wrote: "Whoever in discussion adduces authority uses not intellect but memory." Sagan respected the inquiring intellect of his scientific predecessor, but also his courage in the early sixteenth century, when most knowledge was derived from authority and not intellect.

Leonardo da Vinci had his own encounters with religion and science. During a trip to the Apennine mountaintop, he discovered the fossilized remains of shellfish that ordinarily lived on the ocean floor. How could such a thing have happened? The current theological wisdom explained that the Great Flood of Noah had lifted the clams and oysters to such a height. But according to the Bible the flood lasted only forty days. Would this be suffi-cient time to carry the shellfish to the mountaintops? During what stage in the life cycle of the shellfish had they been deposited?—and so on.

Da Vinci concluded that the biblical interpretation could not work. He proposed another alternative: over great periods of time the mountaintops had pushed up through the oceans. While his hypothesis was inconsistent with the prevailing theological one, it turned out to be the correct answer, as science would establish.

Sagan talked about three kinds of Gods. There is the God of the Judeo-Christian-Islamic tradition who is omnipotent, omniscient, compassion-ate, creator of the universe, is responsive to prayer, performs miracles, and intervenes in history in other ways. A second sort of God—and one worse from a human standpoint—would be a god who was oblivious to humans. Such was Aristotle's god, whose activity was spent thinking about his own thinking. A third kind of God would be the one of Baruch Spinoza and Albert Einstein.

Einstein and Spinoza meant by "God" something like "the sum total of the physical laws of the universe," according to Sagan; "that is, gravitation plus quantum mechanics plus grand unified field theories . . . equaled God." If this is God, then no one can be an atheist, since it is foolish to deny the existence of laws of nature.

In fact, there is a dizzying array of religious alternatives to feast upon. There are gods that never die and gods that do. There's a smorgasbord of questions about "sacraments, religious mutilations, baptisms, monastic orders, ascetic expectations, the afterlife (yeah or nay), days to eat fish, days not to eat at all, how many afterlives you have coming to you, jus-tice in this world or the next world or not at all, reincarnation, human sac-rifice, temple prostitution, jihads, and so forth." It all seems exceedingly arbitrary—this "grab bag" of religious alternatives. Sagan estimated that in the history of the world there were tens, maybe hundred of thousands, of religions.

Richard Dawkins and The God Delusion

Richard Dawkins is one of the pre-eminent scientists in the world. An Oxford professor and paleontologist by training, Dawkins is, because of a series of vigorously argued books and numerous speaking appearances, a famous public figure. But his atheism owes not just to his hard scientific evidence. Dawkins believes that religious belief is fundamentally irrational and has ravaged mankind from the Crusades to the attacks on September 11. Religion continues to lead to war, bigotry, sexism, and child abuse.

Dawkins's books and lectures have drawn letters from people reminding him of the less extreme forms of religion, such as the views expressed in the writings of Paul Tillich and Diedrich Bonhoeffer. But he claims that the decent, understated sort of religion is "numerically negligible." What predominates instead are the likes of Pat Robertson, Jerry Fallwell, Ted Haggart, Osama bin Laden, and Ayatollah Khomeini.

FACT

Dawkins's book *The God Delusion,* to date, has spent one year on the *New York Times* bestseller list. Other books, like Christopher Hitchens's *God Is Not Great*, have enjoyed similar success. The popularity of such critical books may owe to the mixture of politics and religion that caused the September 11 attacks and some unpopular American administrations that often mix religion and politics.

It isn't just fundamentalists and fanatics who rule the roost either. There are nonviolent but fundamentalist Christians who are so passionately opposed to evolution and any science that threatens their worldview that their minds cannot be changed. He quotes Kurt Wise: "If all the evidence in the world turns against creationism, I would be the first to admit it, but I would still be a creationist, since that is what the word of God indicates."

Dawkins provides his own version of the same words: "If all the evidence in the universe turns against creationism, I would be the first to admit it and I would immediately change my mind. As things stand, however, all available evidence—and there is a vast amount of it—favors evolution."

QUESTION?

How has Dawkins advanced the cause of science?
Richard Dawkins began a new foundation in 2006—the Richard Dawkins Foundation for Reason and Science. The foundation seeks to promote scientific explanations of reality and advance the causes of rationalism and humanism.

One of the common ideas that Dawkins hears is that people need religion. Humanity has a need for comfort. But he asks: Isn't there something childish about the notion that the universe owes us comfort? In fact, he quotes Isaac Asimov in saying that if you inspect every piece of pseudo-science—from astrology and tarot cards to contacting mediums and palmistry—you will find some kind of comfort too. Asimov's remark about the infantilism of pseudo-science is just as applicable to religion. Inspect every bit of pseudo-science and you will find a security blanket—a thumb to suck on or a skirt to hold. Moreover, it is astonishing to find how many people fail to understand that *X is comforting* does not imply that *X is true*.

A related complaint to the notion about comfort is the idea that life must have a purpose. The human soul requires that X has a purpose, Dawkins's readers tell him. This provides consolation for the believer. But "the consolation content of the belief does not raise its truth value," Dawkins observes. He adds that if the consolation that religion offers is founded on the neurologically highly implausible premise that we survive the death of our brains, do you really want to defend it? Due to the failure of many people's educations to provide palatable alternatives, nonbelief is not an option.

INSIGHT

Dawkins claims that fundamentalists and scientists possess a passion. But his passion is "based on evidence; their passion flies in the face of evidence and is truly fundamentalist." To illustrate his passion he says: "Want to contradict evolution? Find me fossils of rabbits in the pre-Cambrian period."

On the matter of religious belief, an anthropologist quoted former Israeli leader Golda Meir: "I believe in the Jewish people and the Jewish people believe in God." The anthropologist added his view: "I believe in people and people believe in God." Dawkins offered up a different version: "I prefer to say I believe in people and when people are given all the information and encouraged to think for themselves very often turn out not to believe in God and lead fulfilled and satisfied and indeed liberated lives."

Dawkins has helped the public understand science and has been a merciless critic of pseudo-science. Dawkins's popular book *Unweaving the Rainbow* takes on John Keats's statement that by explaining rainbows Sir Isaac Newton had diminished them. Dawkins argues that deep space, millions of years of life's evolution, and the microscopic workings of biology and heredity contain more beauty than myths and pseudo-science.

The "Design Argument" and Other Arguments Revisited

Thomas Aquinas's fifth "proof" of the existence of God (see Chapter 8) has been received as his most thoughtful. But in recent times his design argument has drawn renewed attention. Richard Dawkins addressed this and other arguments in his book *The God Delusion*.

Thomas Aquinas's design argument—also called his teleological argument—says that things in the world, especially living things, appear as if they have been designed. Therefore, Aquinas concluded, there must have been a designer, which you give the name of God. In Aquinas's earthy analogy, the universe and the things in it moving toward a goal are like an arrow moving toward its goal—the target. This is but one of the arguments that Dawkins goes after.

Dawkins's Treatment of Thomas Aquinas's Five "Proofs"

Without hesitating, Richard Dawkins claims that the five "proofs" asserted by Thomas Aquinas in the thirteenth century don't prove a thing. In fact, Dawkins attacks Aquinas's first three arguments—the Unmoved Mover, the Uncaused Cause, and the Cosmological Argument—in one fell swoop.

Aquinas's first argument, the Unmoved Mover, says that nothing moves without a prime mover. In Aquinas's mind, however, this leads to a chain of motions going back in time indefinitely and the only escape from the regress is God. In similar fashion the Uncaused Cause argument says that nothing is caused by itself. Since every effect has a prior cause, this chain of causes will also go on indefinitely, unless God is invoked as the first cause. Finally, his third argument—the Cosmological Argument—states that there must have been a time when no physical things existed. But it is apparent just by looking around that physical things exist now. Therefore, a nonphysical entity must have brought them into existence and this can be called God.

Dawkins's rebuttal of the argument says that each makes use of a regress and then brings God into the picture in order to terminate the regress. This move assumes without proof that God himself is immune to the regress. All of this is arbitrary, according to Dawkins.

On arguments for God's existence, Dawkins writes, "To conjure up a being and give it a name is one thing. But to go further and give that being the qualities normally attributed to God—such as omnipotence, omniscience, goodness, creativity of design, listener to prayers, miracle performer, and listener to innermost thoughts—is quite another matter."

Aquinas's fourth argument is an argument from gradation or degree. You notice in the world degrees of goodness or perfection, but these degrees can only be judged by comparison with a maximum. Since human beings can be good or bad or a mixture of both, the maximum of goodness does not reside with them. So the need for a maximum brings God into the picture, since he sets the standard for perfection. The problem with this argument is that just positing a maximum of goodness doesn't bring existence to that maximum.

FACT

An outspoken atheist, Dawkins is renowned for his contempt for religious extremism, from Islamist terrorism to Christian fundamentalism. Besides taking on extremists, he has also argued with liberal believers and religious scientists.

In discussing Aquinas's fifth argument, the design argument, Richard Dawkins recounts how Charles Darwin was very impressed with the argument when he first encountered it as a young man in William Paley's *Natural Theology*. But in the years to come Darwin would pick apart the argument. Since Darwin, people no longer say that all things that look designed are designed. For evolution by natural selection produces design, from the simplest to the most complex and elegant organisms. In fact, Dawkins says, even tiny insects have nervous systems that work as if they were goal-directed systems.

The Believer's Response

It is in the nature of a believer to find some reason for believing, even when it appears most of the reasons line up on the opponent's side of the issue. Where there is some unexplained phenomenon, there is always room for the religious hypothesis to rear its head. The Greeks could not explain the wind and the rain and said that the Gods must have caused such phenomena. Sir Isaac Newton resorted to a "God of the gaps" to fill in those natural processes he could not account for.

David Nicholls, president of the Atheist Foundation of Australia, argues that Dawkins does not contend that religion is the source of all that is wrong in the world, but that it is an "unnecessary part of what is wrong." In fact, Dawkins contends that his objection to religion is not solely that it causes wars and violence, but also that it gives people an excuse to hold beliefs that are not based on evidence. Dawkins believes that the "existence of God is a scientific hypothesis like any other," and as such is subject to the same evaluation and criticism.

Further, Dawkins takes issue with Stephen Jay Gould's idea of "non-overlapping magisterial" (NOMA). In his book *Rock of Ages,* Gould laid out what he considered to be "a blessedly simple and entirely conventional resolution to the supposed conflict between science and religion." The NOMA principle is that "the magesterium of science covers the empirical realm: what the Universe is made of (fact) and why does it work in this way (theory)." On the other hand, "The magesterium of religion extends over questions of ultimate meaning and moral value. These two magesteria do not overlap, nor do they encompass all inquiry (consider, for example, the magesterium of art and the meaning of beauty.)"

Commentators have gone after Dawkins. Margaret Somerville, a professor of law and medical ethics at McGill University, has attacked Dawkins for "overstating the case against religion." Professor Somerville argues that global conflict would continue without religion from factors such as economic pressures or land disputes.

But this will not do on several levels. For one, Dawkins says the "God hypothesis"—namely that there exists a superhuman, supernatural intelligence who deliberately designed and created the universe and everything in it, including us—is a scientific hypothesis and is therefore no more exempt from scientific scrutiny than any other hypothesis. In addition, do we really want to go with Gould when he says that religion extends over questions of "ultimate meaning and moral value"? What moral value is at work in Islam when it claims that women should be stoned for committing adultery?

Evaluation and Significance

The writings of Dawkins and Sagan have had the effect of making religions substantiate and back up their own claims about the world. The high spirits of people such as Dawkins, and Christopher Hitchens, author of *God Is Not Great,* suggest that you can't go easy on religions and let them get away with unsubstantiated theses and dangerous dogmas. In recent times, no one has come near to the arguments presented by these men.

CHAPTER 23

Contemporary Metaphysics

The analytic movement influenced the treatment of traditional metaphysical problems. Questions pertaining to free will and determinism, the problem of evil, and arguments pertaining to God's existence and more were analyzed through an analytic pair of glasses. The result was a view of metaphysics different from what had been seen before.

Metaphysics in the Analytic Period

The twentieth-century analytic movement began a concentration on language and the attempt to analyze statements (or concepts). One of the tasks of analytic philosophy is forming definitions; another is to reduce expressions to their simplest logical forms. This movement impacted metaphysics.

Metaphysics is that branch of philosophy that investigates the nature of reality. Throughout most of the history of philosophy metaphysics offered a broader, more inclusive area for exploration than either physics or any of the special sciences. This is because when metaphysics investigates reality it means "all of reality," not merely physical reality, as physics, cosmology, or chemistry might do.

Included in the purview of metaphysics is all of nonphysical reality, including entities like God, souls, spirit. It can ask many things about these entities, including "Do they exist?" "What is their nature?" and "Is there immortality?" Traditional metaphysics boldly took on these questions.

You have already seen how logical positivism rejects the claims of traditional metaphysics, since it regards metaphysical statements as "cognitively meaningless." To positivists like A. J. Ayer this means that statements about nonphysical entities are not empirically verifiable. Statements talking about Gods, spirits, and immortal souls are not false, just meaningless, since you can't prove the existence of the things mentioned.

Willard Van Orman Quine (1908–2000) also rejected metaphysics. Quine thought that only science provided genuine knowledge of the external world. But Gustav Bergmann (1906–87), who like Ayer was a member of the Vienna Circle that espoused positivism, criticized positivism and Quine for their assumptions. In his book *The Metaphysics of Logical Positivism* (1954), he attacked both Ayer and Quine because their views assumed a certain view of metaphysics. The positivists, for example, presumed that only empirically verifiable statements had meaning. And the view that all that exists is spatiotemporal (i.e., things existing in space and time) and is only knowable through the sciences—known as *metaphysical naturalism*—is assumed to be a scientific theory, but is in actuality not scientific at all and is not argued for by positivists.

How Do Mind and Body Interact?

In addition to metaphysical issues dealing with the immortality of the soul, God's existence, freedom of the will, and more is the question, "How do mind and body interact?" The answer one gives depends upon on what theory of reality one accepts. There are at least two prevailing theories.

What exists? The question is clear, but several compelling answers have been offered. If an individual believes that only matter exists, that person is a materialist and accepts a theory known as *materialism*. On the other hand, if a person believes that only minds and mental states and ideas exist, then she is an idealist and she embraces the theory known as *idealism*. Finally, if a person accepts that matter and mental entities exist, then he is a dualist and accepts the doctrine of *dualism*.

Dualistic Interractionism

The name *dualism* comes from the theory that there are two kinds of reality—material and mental. Take consciousness as an example of one kind of reality. Right now you may be thinking of the page before you, but that consciousness is not solid or material. In addition, consciousness is not extended in three-dimensional space. In fact, it does not occupy space at all. In contrast to physical bodies, mental entities have no width, breadth, depth, shape, height, color, velocity, or temperature. Can you imagine someone calling a belief blue or describing an emotion as being two inches by three inches in dimension? No, nor can you imagine a thought as being porous or a notion as being hard.

According to dualism, there are bodies and minds. Bodies have one sort of existence and minds have another. Bodies are extended in three-dimensional space. But that is just a beginning. They are also observable, measurable, divisible into parts, and capable of causing things to happen according to strict laws of mechanics. By contrast, minds lack any bodily properties.

Further, your consciousness is only observable by yourself. It cannot be measured, and it isn't clear how consciousness—possessing all nonphysical properties—could cause anything. Only a person can think his own thoughts, feel his own emotions, and suffer his own pain.

As distinct as mental and physical entities are, your ordinary thinking tells you that they interact in some fashion. If a person touches a hot stove, the burned skin communicates some message to the central nervous system. This pain message would seem to have no size or shape or be public in any way. So the stove is very public, while your sustained pain is private.

QUESTION?

Is there an example of the body influencing the mind?
The mind tells us that some ointment might soothe the pain on our foot. A thought of getting an ointment precedes an act of will to go to our medicine cabinet, remove the ointment, and apply it. If mind and body interact you have dualistic interactionism.

Materialism

Thomas Hobbes, one of the early empiricists, said that nothing but matter in motion exists. According to one brand of materialism, even the mind—be it spirit, soul, or consciousness—is matter in motion. Further, materialism is a *monistic* theory, since it claims that only one kind of substance exists. Thus, matter and the universe do not in any way possess the nonphysical characteristics of mind, such as purpose, intention, awareness, intelligence, wishing, and so on.

On this materialistic view, then, there is no interaction to explain. Dualism must be false since it believes in two kinds of reality. If you trip and turn your ankle, the pain state that you feel is purely physical. It is no more nonphysical or private than the hurt ankle itself. One kind of materialism is logical behaviorism.

The English philosopher Gilbert Ryle (1900–76) held logical behaviorism to be true. In fact, Ryle famously criticized Rene Descartes's dualism as the theory that there is a "ghost in the machine." Recall that Descartes was a dualist who believed that mind and body were two fundamentally different kinds of substances. He said that minds are private, immeasurable, and so forth, while bodies are extended, public, and so on. Despite their differences, they interact. But Ryle voiced an objection to Descartes's view.

Ryle said the opinion that the mind is a substance rests on a category mistake. *Mind* is surely a noun, Ryle conceded. But it refers to no known object. So Descartes confuses the discourse about bodies with discourse about minds. Mental states like belief, desire, and intention are not internal causes of behavior, as Descartes said. Rather, Ryle thought they were just dispositions to behave in certain ways. So when you talk about mental states like thoughts, beliefs, and desires, you are really referring to overt bodily behavior. When you say "John is thinking deeply," you are not implying that this activity of thinking is taking place in some private place that only he knows of. You are asserting that you can see it in his behavior. Hence the doctrine is given the name *logical behaviorism*.

Is the Will Free? Three Positions

One of the perennial metaphysical problems of philosophy is the problem of free will and determinism. Tying this issue to the previous one about mind-body interaction, dualists are inclined to say that the will is free, since there is a mind separate from the body that is not governed by causal laws. In the contemporary debate over whether the will is free, three distinct positions have been distinguished.

Libertarianism

Libertarianism is the position that you possess free will. It says that no matter what conditions were acting on you when you decided to do some action A, you could have done some other action besides the one you did. Though you chose pistachio ice cream yesterday, you could just as easily have chosen vanilla. Libertarians believe that two arguments support the view that our actions are free. The first is the argument from *deliberation*. The second is the argument from *moral responsibility*.

When you deliberate about whether to take one course of action or another, you assume you are free to choose among the alternatives. This experience of having first deliberated and then decided is a very frequent one. The argument from moral responsibility says that you are aware of certain duties and moral responsibilities you have and the guilt you feel at falling short of those duties. You know that you have deadlines to meet, promises to keep, and that a responsibility attaches to their performance. But the only way that you can have such responsibilities is if you have choices. The argument plays out like this:

1. If determinism is true and our actions are merely the product of the laws of nature and antecedent states of affairs, then it is not up to you to choose what you do.
2. But if it is not up to you to do what you do, you cannot be said to be responsible for what you do.
3. So if determinism is true, you are not responsible for what you do.
4. But your belief is moral responsibility is self-evident (at least as strong as your belief in universal causality).
5. So if you believe that you have moral responsibilities, determinism cannot be accepted.

According to determinism, even our deliberations are the consequences of antecedent causes. If you have deliberated about having a cigar or not having one, you are weighing two desires. You simply end up acting in accord with the strongest desire. You could only have acted differently than you did if an alternative motive had prevailed at the time.

FACT

You may desire to have a cigar. But you also have another desire to hold off and not have the cigar. Many times you smoked the cigar, fulfilling a desire to taste the tobacco and smell the smoke. At other times you refrained, just to avoid the throat pain that follows. If both choices are possible, then this implies you acted freely.

Do you recognize the argument style? It is called a *reductio ad absurdum*. It goes back to Parmenides and Socrates. Whenever you say, "Let's assume what you say is true and see where it leads" and it leads to an absurd conclusion, then you have defeated the opposing view, as libertarianism has defeated determinism in the previous argument.

Determinism

Determinism is the doctrine that all actions are the inevitable results of prior causes. Put another way, there is no free will. To the libertarian's argument from deliberation, the determinist says that the feeling that you are deliberating freely is an illusory one. The determinist argument runs as follows:

1. Actions are the results of (are caused by) beliefs and desires.
2. You do not choose your beliefs and desires.
3. Beliefs and desires are thrust upon you by the environment in conjunction with innate dispositions.
4. Therefore, you do not freely choose your actions, but your actions are generated by the causal processes that form your beliefs and desires.

As regards moral responsibility, the determinist says you may *in fact* hold yourself and others responsible for their actions, but you have no *right* to do so. The belief that you are responsible for what you do is just that—a belief only. In order to be responsible for your life you need to be free as a condition of being responsible, but you're not free.

Metaphysical Compatibilism

Metaphysical compatibilism might be better known by the name *soft determinism*. Philosophers such as David Hume, John Stuart Mill, Walter Stace, and Harry Frankfurt have embraced this position, which argues that both the determinist view that all actions and events are caused and the notion of human responsibility are true. That is, your action of getting behind the wheel of your car after having three drinks is "compatible" with your being responsible for what happens afterward. Hence the name *compatibilism* has been given to this theory.

According to Stace, free acts are those that are done voluntarily. If an agent chooses to have a cigar after dinner, then he performs a voluntary act and acts freely. If a man is addicted to the taste of tobacco, then he does not act freely when he smokes. "Acts freely done are those whose immediate causes are psychological states in the agent. Acts not freely done are those whose immediate causes are states of affairs external to the agent," according to Stace.

According to compatibilism, an act is unfree if the cause for it is external to the agent. So if a store clerk is locking up at night and is approached by a robber with a gun who demands he hand over the contents of the safe, and he does as told, his act was not chosen freely and he is not responsible.

This argument could be cast in slightly different terms. We can describe actions as having to do with reasons. If an agent acts according to reasons instead of internal neurotic or external coercive pressures, then that agent acts freely. At the same time, your reasons and beliefs are not things you choose but impulses you find within yourself.

Harry Frankfurt has added to the compatibilist position. In his article "Freedom of the Will and the Concept of a Person," Frankfurt maintains that conscious beings have what he calls "first-order desires." But persons, unlike animals and other conscious beings (which he calls "wantons"), are capable of analyzing the second-order desires they have. Persons have the capacity to reflect on their desires and beliefs and form desires and judgments concerning them. For instance, you may want a third cup of coffee (which is a first-order desire), but it is possible that you also may want *not to want* this (second-order desire), since having too much coffee causes you to have gastritis and be on edge for the rest of the day.

According to Frankfurt, you *act freely* when the desire on which you act is one with which you identify. By contrast, an addict acts from a desire that he does not want to act upon. So he is not acting freely. If you desire not to drink the coffee and act on that desire, then your desire is effective and is a volition, which is a desire that moves the agent all the way to action.

Philosophy of Religion

Philosophy of religion has existed at least since the time of Socrates, who among other things used skeptical arguments to analyze statements made about the Gods. (You saw this in Chapter 2 with Socrates's conversation with Euthyphro about the topic "What is holiness?") Since that time, philosophers have debated whether it is rational to believe in God's existence, whether there are sound proofs of the existence of God, whether God's foreknowledge and human freedom can coexist, the meaning of religious language, and so on.

The philosophy of religion is concerned with the meaning and justification of religious statements. Statements about how the world is are more typical of the major Western religions, Judaism, Christianity, and Islam. The Eastern religions, such as Buddhism, Hinduism, and Confucianism, tend to concentrate more on a way of life than on ways to theoretically justify that way of life.

You have already seen how the school of logical positivism flourished in the analytic period. Positivism has deep roots in empiricism. The movement shot up in the twentieth century when a group of philosophers began meeting in the 1920s and into the 1930s at the University of Vienna. They were called "the Vienna Circle." These positivists claimed that much of traditional metaphysics, including the claim that there is a God, is incapable of support using evidence, and is therefore meaningless.

According to A. J. Ayer and other positivists, for a statement to be meaningful it must be either about the formal relations between ideas such as those found in mathematics and analytic definitions—such as squares have four sides and bachelors are unmarried men—or sensible evidence of whether a given claim is true or false. "Roses are sweet" is meaningful if and only if there is some actual or conceivable sense experience that can confirm it. Thus, religious statements like "The absolute is outside of time and space" or "Krishna is an avatar of Vishnu" cannot be verified.

Antony Flew brilliantly illustrated the same point about the baffling nature of religious belief in his article "Theology and Falsification." Flew uses a parable about a gardener in order to show that people hold religious statements as true, regardless of confirming evidence. Two men look at a plot of land containing weeds and flowers. One contends that a gardener tends to the plot, but the other insists there is no gardener. No gardener is ever seen, guard dogs never give out a cry. The believer keeps insisting: there is a gardener who tends this plot. Finally, the nonbeliever cries out in exasperation: How does your gardener differ from an imaginary gardener or no gardener at all? Flew's nonbeliever makes the same point that the positivists made: meaningful statements must be established by evidence.

The Problem of Evil

You learned about the problem of evil in Chapter 7. Philosophers through the ages including David Hume, John Stuart Mill, and contemporary philosophers have taken up the problem again. The question that "the Problem of Evil" poses is: If God is all-knowing, all-powerful, and all-good, why is there evil in the world?

One contemporary defense of evil is called "the Greater Good Defense." According to this defense, certain evils—including man-made and natural disasters—serve to bring about a "greater good" for humanity. According to this view, horrible events like the attacks on the United States on September 11, 2001, and Hurricane Katrina in New Orleans evoke in humanity virtues like generosity, courage, compassion, and fellowship. Thus tragedy brings a greater good in its wake. People give blood, time, money, and whatever help they can offer.

"The Greater Good Defense" of evil would argue that the atrocities of Nazi Germany or Hiroshima brought about a greater good. How so? Doctors tried to heal those damaged physically and psychologically by the events. Ordinary citizens showed compassion in their response to the victims. Political figures resolved that it should never happen again.

Another kind of *theodicy* or defense of God is illustrated in the philosophy of John Hick. In *Evil and the God of Love* (1978), Hick defends God against the charge of evil by saying that tragic outcomes in life are justified by people acting virtuously. In this manner, they develop virtues gradually.

The popularity of the philosophy of religion is surging. Courses once part of religion departments have been absorbed into philosophy programs. Philosophy in the analytic period will always have something to say about religions, since the analytic movement views the task of philosophy as the analysis of statements.

Evaluation and Significance

Philosophers like Gilbert Ryle, A. J. Ayer, and Antony Flew brought new life to old metaphysical issues like mind-body interaction, God's existence, and the problem of evil. Their revelations were more about the analysis of concepts and the language used than in introducing new content. But good analytic philosophy had the power to make an old presentation of a problem seem downright naive.

Antony Flew's "Parable of the Gardener" was one such case. Flew had shown by applying his concept of falsification what no philosopher unequipped with such a concept could have shown.

CHAPTER 24

Contemporary Ethics

Contemporary philosophy has been a boon period for ethics in several ways. For one, metaethics has flourished, borrowing on the analytic tradition's analysis of words and concepts. Second, normative ethical theories have been examined anew. Most notably, fields in applied ethics like medical ethics, business ethics, sports ethics, and others have gotten a foothold. Philosophical ethics has helped to illuminate problems in several fields.

24

Ethics and Language: Emotivism

A. J. Ayer had already written that ethical statements were factually meaningless but served to express favorable or unfavorable feelings toward something. So someone who said "capital punishment is just" may be expressing an attitude like "Hurray for capital punishment." "Stealing is wrong" is equivalent to saying "Boo for stealing." Charles L. Stevenson (1908–79) furthered the analytic approach to philosophy in his book *Ethics and Language* and in a series of articles.

According to Stevenson, statements making use of value predicate terms like *good* or *right* are expressions of a felt "pro-attitude" that their readers or listeners are expected to share. On the other hand, statements containing value terms like *wrong* or *evil* reveal a disapproving attitude. Stevenson's view became known as *emotivism*.

According to Charles Stevenson's emotivist theory of ethics, you can attempt to persuade others to agree with you about capital punishment or abortion or suicide or any moral matter at all, but the concept of valid argument is not applicable to moral discourse. Your beliefs will only express your emotions.

Sometimes a disagreement in attitude results from a disagreement about the facts of the case, and the conflict might disappear if an agreement on the facts is reached. At times, however, two people may agree about the facts surrounding capital punishment (or abortion, euthanasia, or some other issue), while one regards it as "state-approved murder" and the other regards it as the "highest justice." The disagreement can only be resolved by a change of attitude, Stevenson thought. The linguistic component of such changes will be "persuasive definitions," and in the present dispute about capital punishment redefinitions of *murder* and *justice*. But this process of redefinition is likely to be carried out rhetorically, and so one attitude that does not result from a mistake of fact is no more reasonable or unreasonable than another.

Metaethics

Before you answer issues in applied ethics about matters like abortion and capital punishment, it may be necessary to "back up" and handle some other questions first.

Moral philosophers have broadened the subject to include metaethics and normative ethics. *Metaethics* (the prefix *meta* means "beyond") usually deals with the meaning or origin of ethical concepts.

One metaethical issue is whether ethical issues are *relative* or *objective*. Philosophers known as *objectivists* usually believe that values exist in the external world independently of your comprehension of them. Put another way, values are real and do not depend upon our opinions of them. For instance, an objectivist might say that the statement "Capital punishment is unjust" is objectively true. That is, its truth doesn't depend upon your opinion one way or the other. The position is called objectivism because it is like saying that chairs and rocks and persons and other things exist and are "out there" whether you *think* they are there or not. Objectivists further argue that these values can be found and known by human perceivers and that they must be used as principles for human judgments and conduct.

Relativism is opposed to *objectivism*. Philosophers known as relativists say that values are relative. Their truth depends on what society you are from, what time you live in, and what conditions you are brought up in. A relativist might point out that in the "Bible Belt" region of the United States more people disapprove of abortion. By contrast, in the northeast more people approve. Neither region of the country is right or wrong, since rightness and wrongness are relative to one's culture, circumstances, and other factors. Therefore, such values are not universally applicable at all times or in all places and you cannot speak of a person's values as "objectively" correct or incorrect.

Relativists do not reject all moral values. But they deny that values have objective status—as $2 \times 2 = 4$ is objectively true or that the glass before you exists objectively. Relativists also deny that moral values are immutable *divine commands* in the mind of God. Moral values, they argue, are strictly human inventions.

Other Metaethical Issues

There are also psychological issues in metathics. This is where you analyze what is the psychological basis of morality and what, if anything, motivates you to be moral. The issue of *egoism* versus *altruism* investigates whether individuals are always motivated by *selfishness*, which is what egoists claim, or whether they are sometimes motivated by the desire to do good or act with *benevolence*, which is what altruism claims.

Egoism accepts a universal affirmative claim, namely, that *all* human actions are motivated by selfishness. It is hard to dispute that some actions are motivated by selfishness. After all, you might work hard solely for the reason that you will get a raise. You could also play a game hoping to win and draw the praise of others.

What makes egoism interesting is the claim that *all* human actions are in the final analysis motivated by selfishness. If you give to a charity, the egoist will assert that you wanted to alleviate guilt feelings, or desire the approval of others, or wished for a tax write-off. So behind even the most generous actions is a selfish motivation. Even heroic or saintly behavior might be seen as being motivated by a desire to please God.

Altruism holds a contrary view. People do act selfishly some or even most of the time, but they are still capable of acting selflessly, according to altruism. Altruism says that people can be motivated by caring for others without a thought for themselves. If parents put a child through college, they are doing it for the child's well-being and not their own. If you give money or time to the victims of a disaster, you are doing it for them because you care for their plight, not because you need to erase guilt feelings that have been with you since childhood.

The altruist may improve his position by distinguishing between selfishness and self-interest. If you go to the doctor to have a colonoscopy you are acting out of self-interest, but are you acting selfishly? It would be hard to see how. For one, in visiting the doctor you are not putting your own well-being above anyone else's. In fact, no one else's interests but yours are involved. How could an egoist say that such an action is selfish? If it isn't selfish, then the egoist's universal affirmative thesis is defeated with a single counter-example.

In the *Descent of Man* (1871), Charles Darwin provided an evolutionist account of the moral sense that is neither egoistic nor altruistic. Darwin took as "the standard or morality the general good or welfare of the community, rather than the general happiness." By "general good" he meant "the greatest number of individuals in full vigor and health." Darwin observed that when a person "risks his life to save that of a fellow-creature, it seems more correct to say that he acts for the general good, rather than for the general happiness." It would be hard to label such behavior either as selfish or altruistic.

Normative Ethics

In addition to these three metaethical concerns, normative ethics involves arriving at moral standards or "norms" that regulate right and wrong. The key assumption in normative ethics is that there is only one ultimate criterion of moral conduct, whether it is a single rule or a set of principles. Four different normative ethics are (1) virtue ethics, (2) consequentialism, (3) deontology or "duty" theories, and (4) intuitionism.

Is the Golden Rule Always Golden?

In a sense, normative ethics searches for an ideal litmus test of proper behavior. One example of a normative principle is the Golden Rule, which urges us to "Do unto others what we would want others to do to us." Since you do not want your neighbor to steal your car, it is wrong for you to steal her car. Since you would want people to feed you if you were starving, you should help feed starving people. Using this same reasoning, you believe that you can theoretically determine whether any possible action is right or wrong.

So, based on the Golden Rule, it would be wrong for you to lie to, harass, victimize, assault, or kill others. The Golden Rule is one example of a normative theory that establishes a single principle against which we judge all actions.

But be careful. Should you help another student to cheat because you would want him to help you cheat? Maybe the rule isn't always so "golden."

Other normative theories focus on a *set* of foundational principles or a set of good character traits.

Other Normative Theories

Virtue theories, as discussed in Chapter 4, stress developing character traits—or virtues—like courage, self-control, and other excellences which are essential means for achieving happiness. Consequentialist theories, like those of Bentham and Mill examined in Chapter 16, stress actions that produce good consequences. In fact, you are obligated to do that action that promotes the greatest happiness for the greatest number of people.

In Chapter 15, which explained the philosophy of Immanuel Kant, you saw the elaboration of his duty-based theory. Kant emphasized a single principle of duty, the *categorical imperative*. This is: act always such that the maxim of your action can be universalized. Kant stated this in another form, too: act always to treat persons, including oneself, always as ends, never as means.

But Kant did not explain conflict of duty situations. Suppose a person, Smith, promised to meet Miller for lunch. Kant would say that the promise binds Smith to do the promised action. But before Smith could leave for his meeting, his neighbor Jones had a heart attack and needed medical assistance. Here Smith experiences a conflict of duties. You might say intuitively that the duty to render emergency aid overrides the duty to keep a promise in this situation. If this is your conclusion, you are thinking right along with British philosopher W. D. Ross (1877–1971). Ross applied his idea of *prima facie duties* (prima facie meaning "first glance") in situations when there is a *conflict of duties*. In this instance Smith's prima facie duty would be to render emergency aid to Jones, since performing that action appears to have more rightness than the other, in that it would produce better consequences.

Applied Ethics

Contrasted with metaethics and normative ethics is applied ethics. Whereas metaethics analyses ethical concepts and ethical reasoning, and normative ethics studies the norms used in making ethical judgments, in applied ethics we employ ethical considerations to guide individual and collective conduct in areas like law, business, medicine, and sports.

Sports Ethics

Sports ethics, which is probably the newest field in applied ethics, analyzes the practices of sports leagues, teams, and individuals in order to understand the rightness or wrongness of those practices. Cheating is one practice that is frequently examined.

Cheating

Philosophers have used metaethical principles to understand and define cheating of various kinds and normative principles to evaluate the practice. One kind of cheating prevalent in sports today is the use of performance-enhancing drugs (PED). At the outset, you can distinguish the issues of the *legality* of using certain performance enhancers from the *morality* of using them.

Different sports have different tolerances toward the use of PED. So you find an almost "anything goes" attitude toward steroid use in the National Football League and, until quite recently, major-league baseball. By contrast, both cycling and track and field athletes have been subject to strict policies about PED and face extreme sanctions for their use.

Philosophers fitting in the category of formalists might claim that "games" are activities in which a formal set of rules come into play and these rules determine what is sporting behavior and good sportsmanship. So formalists, as Robert Simon has explained in his book *Fair Play,* are more likely to hold the view that cheaters don't really win at games, since games are governed by rules and cheaters violate the rules. Conventionalists disagree. They maintain that formalists hold too rigorous—perhaps even an idealized—definition of sports. After all, when Don Sutton (who pitched in the major leagues for more than twenty years) scuffed the ball illegally with sandpaper, he was still playing baseball.

Several normative positions would likely regard cheating as immoral. Kant's categorical imperative would inquire about universalizing a maxim to cheat. It could not be universalized, since—like his case about lying—no one would trust that anyone playing the game was playing fairly. Any consequentialist ethic would judge the short- or long-term consequences of an action by its results. How could those results favor cheating? Long-term the game is weakened, with the integrity of competition sacrificed for short-term "goods" like selfishness and greed.

FACT

Jose Canseco blew the whistle on some of his baseball brethren who used steroids. His book *Juiced* exposed some of the game's chronic steroid users—including himself—and led to congressional hearings on the matter before the major-league baseball season started in 2005.

Medical Ethics

Euthanasia is one philosophical issue in medical ethics. University of Alabama philosopher James Rachels sets out the following example in his book *The Elements of Moral Philosophy.*

Matthew Donnelly was a physicist who had worked with X-rays for thirty years. Perhaps as a result of too much exposure, he contracted cancer and lost part of his jaw, his upper lip, his nose, and his left hand, as well as two fingers from his right hand. He was also left blind. Mr. Donnelly's physicians told him that he had about a year to live, but he decided that he did not want to go on living in such a state. He was in constant pain—one writer said that "at its worst, he could be seen lying in bed with teeth clenched and beads of perspiration standing out on his forehead." Knowing that he was going to die eventually anyway, and wanting to escape his misery, Mr. Donnelly begged his three brothers to kill him. Two refused, but one did not. The youngest brother, thirty-six-year-old Harold Donnelly, carried a .30-caliber pistol into the hospital and shot Matthew to death.
Was Harold Donnelly's action morally justified?

Two considerations might lead one to argue that his action was moral. One, Harold Donnelly's action seems to have been motivated by mercy; he wanted to relieve his brother's suffering. Two, his brother Matthew had asked to die. Accordingly, you could say that Harold "killed" his brother. He was, after all, the agent of his death. But notice that you would be more hesitant to conclude that he "murdered" his brother. If you define murder as the "wrongful killing of a human being," then it does not follow logically that Harold's act can be classified as murder, since to make that claim you would first need to show—and not merely assume—that Harold's killing of Matthew was wrong.

Besides these preliminary moral considerations, there are at least two philosophical views about whether Harold acted morally in killing his brother Matt. One, the dominant moral tradition in our society would maintain that Harold's action was wrong. The dominant moral tradition is the Christian tradition. The Christian tradition holds that human life is a gift from God. As such, life is, in effect, entrusted to us from God and you are not at liberty to dispose of life as you wish. The thinking continues that only God can decide when life will end.

The early church prohibited all killing, believing that Jesus' teaching on the subject permitted no exceptions. Rachels explains that in later times exceptions were made, permitting capital punishment and killing in war. But other kinds of killing, including suicide and euthanasia, remained absolutely forbidden. Thus this tradition forbids what Harold Donnelly did. He intentionally killed an innocent person; thus what he did was wrong.

Dr. Jack Kevorkian, a retired physician who assisted in more than 120 suicides, could be defended by utilitarian moralists because he ended the suffering of his patients. When asked, Kevorkian said he practiced "medicide." He claimed that his intention was to "end the suffering of agonized human beings."

A second moral position does not make use of the Christian tradition. The moral philosophy known as utilitarianism bids you to undertake a kind of cost-benefit analysis and asks which of the choices available to

Harold Donnelly will produce the best overall consequences. Put another way, it asks: Which action will produce the greatest balance of happiness over unhappiness for all concerned? Surely Matthew Donnelly's happiness is central, since he is the person most affected.

If Harold does not kill Matthew, he will live on, perhaps for as long as a year, blind, mutilated, and in continual pain. Further, Matthew has already said that his pain is so great that he desires to die. Since killing him would put an end to his insufferable misery, utilitarians conclude that euthanasia may be the most merciful and morally right thing to do. Their argument might be summarized as:

1. The morally right thing to do, on any occasion, is whatever could bring about the greatest balance of happiness over unhappiness.
2. On at least some occasions, the greatest balance of happiness over unhappiness may be brought about by mercy killing.
3. Therefore, on at least some occasions, mercy killing may be morally right.

Utilitarianism shifts the focus of the debate from the issue of moral rules (e.g., about killing or obeying or disobeying God's will, whatever that is) and puts happiness (or pleasure or "well-being) front and center.

Business Ethics

Business ethics is yet another field in applied ethics. Philosophers working in this field have applied traditional ethical frameworks like utilitarianism, deontology, and egoism to a broad range of business topics. These topics include advertising and at what point the claims made by advertisers are exaggerated or lying and unethical. The ethics of affirmative action and sexual harassment are also popular topics, along with a dozen others. One perennially interesting topic is whether an employee should "blow the whistle" on the corporation or some other employee suspected of wrongdoing.

First off, is it obligatory for an employee to blow the whistle? What if blowing the whistle leads to one's own physical harm or will contribute to the corporation's losing money?

FACT

A Civil Action, starring John Travolta, was a very popular movie having to do with business ethics. Members of a small town were getting sick from the carcinogens in the local water supply, the result of chemical dumping from a large firm.

You can focus on one kind of whistle-blowing: *internal* whistle-blowing. One kind of internal whistle-blowing is where the employee of a firm reports improper activities to executives in the firm. These reports typically concern improper conduct of fellow employees or superiors who are cheating on expense accounts, or are engaging in petty or grand theft. Students have been known to "blow the whistle" on fellow students whom they see cheating on exams.

You could argue that people have a moral obligation to prevent serious harm to others if they are able to do so without doing serious harm to themselves. In fact, one could argue that as the cost of whistle-blowing increases, the obligation to blow the whistle decreases.

If by blowing the whistle you stand a serious chance of losing your job, being physically harmed, having your reputation maligned, and so on, then you must include all of this in your moral calculation.

Utilitarianism is the normative ethical theory most likely to favor blowing the whistle. This is because individuals blowing the whistle often undertake a cost-benefit analysis before blowing the whistle.

Evaluation and Significance

Contemporary ethics have added greatly to the history of ethical thinking in at least two ways. First, since ethics in the last 100 years have been a part of the analytic tradition discussed in Chapter 20, there has been increased attention to the meaning of ethical terms such as fairness, justice, goodness, and so on. In addition, there has been a boon period for applied ethics since the latter part of the twentieth century. Legal ethics, medical ethics, the ethics of sports, the philosophy of warfare, and medical ethics have grown up in response to social concerns.

Glossary

absolute:
A principle that is universally binding and thus can never be overridden, as in "I have an absolute duty not to take my own life."

absolutism:
The view that there is only one correct answer to every moral problem; truth is objectively real, final, and eternal.

absurd:
The view expressed by Soren Kierkegaard, Albert Camus, and others that life is irrational, paradoxical, or contradictory.

ad hominem (argument):
In an ad hominem argument one arguer attacks the other arguer personally, instead of attacking his ideas.

aesthetics:
The branch of philosophy that studies beauty, art, and related concepts, such as the sublime, the tragic, the comic, and so forth.

agnosticism:
A belief that we cannot have knowledge of God and that we cannot prove that God exists or doesn't exist.

altruism:
Unselfish regard or concern for others; disinterested, other-regarding action.

amoral:
Literally not moral. The term may be contrasted with nonmoral (that area in which moral categories cannot be applied) and with immoral (evil, wrong, etc.) Choosing which sock to put on first in the morning is a nonmoral act; that is, it is one that does not involve moral values. Killing a person, where such killing goes against the moral and social standards of one's society, is immoral. Killing a person without concern or regard for concepts like "good" or "bad" is amoral.

a posteriori:
Based on a Latin word meaning "later"; knowledge that is obtained only from experience, such as sense perceptions.

a priori:
Based on a Latin word meaning "preceding"; knowledge that is not based on sense experience but rather is innate and known simply by the meanings of words or definitions.

autonomy:
From the Greek for "self-rule"; self-directed freedom. The autonomous individual arrives at his or her moral judgments through reason, not mere acceptance of authority.

categorical imperative:
Kant's command that all agents should always act in such a manner that the maxim of their actions can be universalized.

causal thesis:
The view that there is no indeterminacy, that every act and event in the universe is caused by antecedent events.

Communism:
A political-economic philosophy, held notably by Karl Marx and Friedrich Engels in the nineteenth century, that holds to (1) economic determinism—that the way a society produces its wealth determines all else—and (2) the notion.

compatibilism:
The thesis sometimes referred to as "soft-determinism." Compatibilism holds that an act can be entirely determined and yet be free in the sense that it was done voluntarily and not under external coercion.

contradictory:
When one statement denies another, such that both cannot be true; an example would be the contradictory pair of statements: "It is raining" and "It is not raining."

deontological ethics:
From the Greek word *deon*, meaning duty or obligation, deontology is a normative ethic that stresses doing actions that are our duties, regardless of whether they produce good results.

determinism:
All events and actions are caused, according to the theory of determinism.

divine command theory:
The theory that holds that moral principles are defined in terms of God's commands. Thus, a morally good action agrees with God's commands.

dualism:
The view that there are two types of substances, or reality, in conscious beings, mind and matter. According to many philosophers, these two substances interact with each other, the body producing mental events and the mind leading to physical action.

egoism:
There are two components to egoism. Psychological egoism is a descriptive theory about human motivation, holding that people always act to satisfy their perceived best interests. Ethical egoism is a prescriptive or normative theory about how people ought to act; they ought to act according to their perceived best interests. The British empiricist Thomas Hobbes held this view.

ethical relativism:
According to relativism, moral judgments depend upon cultural acceptance.

hedonism:
Psychological hedonism is the theory that motivation must be explained exclusively through desire for pleasure and aversion for pain. Ethical hedonism is the theory that pleasure is the only intrinsic positive value.

heteronomy:
Kant's term for the determination of the will on nonrational grounds. It contrasts with autonomy of the will, in which the will is guided by reason.

hypothetical imperatives:
These imperatives are of the form "If you want X, do action Y." Utilitarian moralists would view such principles as moral.

intrinsic worth:
Something has intrinsic worth if it is good in itself. This can be opposed to something that has extrinsic worth or instrumental value as a means to something else.

libertarianism:
Libertarianism is the theory that human beings possess free will and the ability to do otherwise, whatever the causes of their actions.

materialism:
According to materialism, only matter and its properties exist. Even consciousness and various mental states are physical according to this doctrine.

metaphysics:
Meta means "beyond"; the study of ultimate reality beyond empirical experience. This branch of philosophy includes free will, causality, the nature of matter, immortality, and the existence of God.

monism:
The metaphysical view that all reality is one substance, rather than two or more as with dualism.

natural law:
The theory that an eternal, absolute moral law can be discovered by reason.

nihilism:
From the Latin *nihil,* meaning "nothing." Nihilism is the view that there are no valid moral principles or values.

noumenal:
Kant's idea of reality "in itself," as opposed to "phenomenal" reality, which is how it appears to us. This includes our transcendent self and what is beyond the appearances.

Ockham's razor:
This is sometimes called the "principle of parsimony," which states that "entities are not to be multiplied beyond necessity." William of Ockham, after whom the principle is named, said that we should accept the simplest scientific hypothesis that does away with any unnecessary material.

pantheism:
The view that all existing things are attributes of God.

perfect duties:
Kant divides duties into perfect and imperfect. These duties—like not lying and not taking your own life—are for Kant absolute, specific duties.

prima facie:
Latin for "first glance"; in W. D. Ross's view, it stands for a duty that will remain a duty unless another duty overrides it. Such prima facie duties contrast with actual duties.

relativism:
There are two parts to relativism. Cultural relativism is a descriptive thesis stating that moral beliefs vary across cultures. Ethical relativism is an evaluative thesis stating that the truth of a moral judgment depends upon whether a culture recognizes the principle in question. (The truth of cultural relativism does not imply the truth of ethical relativism.)

skepticism:
The view that certain knowledge is impossible. Universal skepticism holds that we can know nothing at all; local, or particular, skepticism holds that we are ignorant in important realms (e.g., David Hume on metaphysics or A. J. Ayer on theology or metaphysics). Moral skepticism holds that we cannot know whether any moral truth exists.

subjective truth:
Truth according to some perceiver; according to Soren Kierkegaard this is a truth that is more important than objective truth, since it is a truth for which one can live passionately.

supererogatory:
In ethics, an action that is "beyond the call of duty." Such an action would not be morally required, but possesses enormous value as a heroic action; e.g. saving the life of another.

teleological ethics:
Aristotelian ethics and utilitarian ethics are both teleological, since intrinsic value is not located in actions themselves, but in the consequences to be attained by them. For Aristotle, this value to be attained is happiness.

utilitarianism:
The moral theory that says an action is moral if and only if it is the best of the alternatives available to the agent.

virtue:
A good character trait, typically involving a disposition to feel, think, and act in certain morally good ways.

APPENDIX B

Further Reading

Becker, Lawrence, and Charlotte Becker, *A History of Western Ethics* (New York: Garland, 1992).

Camus, Albert, *Lyrical and Critical Essays* (New York: Vintage Books, 1968).

Camus, Albert, *The Myth of Sisyphus and Other Essays* (New York: Vintage, 1955).

Dawkins, Richard, *The God Delusion* (Boston: Houghton Mifflin, 2006).

Hitchens, Christopher, *God Is Not Great: How Religion Poisons Everything* (New York: Hachette Books, 2007).

Kant, Immanuel, *The Doctrine of Virtue* (Philadelphia: University of Pennsylvania Press, 1964).

Norman, Richard, *The Moral Philosophers* (Oxford: Clarendon Press, 1986).

Sagan, Carl, *The Varieties of Scientific Experience* (New York: Penguin, 2006).

Taylor, A. E., *Socrates* (Garden City: Doubleday, 1953).

White, Thomas, *Business Ethics: A Philosophical Reader* (Upper Saddle River: Prentice Hall, 1993).

INDEX

Abelard, Peter, 90–93
  dialectic of, 92
  life of, 90–91
  on morality, 91–92
  significance of, 94
Achilles and the Tortoise, 11
Aesthetics, 55–56
Against the Academics, 71
Alcibiades, 16
Al-Ghazali, 87
Altruism, 125, 280
American philosophy, 217–29
Analytic philosophy, 231–42
Analytic propositions, 236–37
Anaximander, 3–4
Anaximenes, 4–5
Animal rights, 190–92
Anselm, Saint, 81–87
  arguments by, 83–84
  criticism on, 118

on God, 83–87
  life of, 82
  significance of, 94
Apathy, 64
Applied ethics, 282–83
A priori statements, 178–79
Aquinas, Thomas, 95–104
  on Abelard, 92
  arguments of, 260–62
  on Aristotle, 97–98
  on Augustine, 74
  ethics of, 103–4
  faith of, 98–99
  on God, 99–103, 260–62
  life of, 96–97
  significance of, 104
Aristocracy, 37, 54
Aristotle, 44–57
  criticism on, 118
  on ethics, 50–53

life of, 44
  logic of, 44–47
  political thinking of, 53–55
  principles of, 45
  significance of, 57
Art, 39–40, 56
The Assayer, 112, 113
Atheism, 245–47
Augustine, Saint Aurelius, 69–80
  faith of, 73–75
  on God, 75–78
  life of, 70–71
  significance of, 80
  skepticism on, 71–73
Authenticity, 248–49
Averroes, 85–88
Avicenna, 85–88
Ayer, A. J., 233–37
  and logical positivism, 233–37

THE EVERYTHING SERIES!

BUSINESS & PERSONAL FINANCE

Everything® Accounting Book
Everything® Budgeting Book, 2nd Ed.
Everything® Business Planning Book
Everything® Coaching and Mentoring Book, 2nd Ed.
Everything® Fundraising Book
Everything® Get Out of Debt Book
Everything® Grant Writing Book, 2nd Ed.
Everything® Guide to Buying Foreclosures
Everything® Guide to Mortgages
Everything® Guide to Personal Finance for Single Mothers
Everything® Home-Based Business Book, 2nd Ed.
Everything® Homebuying Book, 2nd Ed.
Everything® Homeselling Book, 2nd Ed.
Everything® Human Resource Management Book
Everything® Improve Your Credit Book
Everything® Investing Book, 2nd Ed.
Everything® Landlording Book
Everything® Leadership Book, 2nd Ed.
Everything® Managing People Book, 2nd Ed.
Everything® Negotiating Book
Everything® Online Auctions Book
Everything® Online Business Book
Everything® Personal Finance Book
Everything® Personal Finance in Your 20s & 30s Book, 2nd Ed.
Everything® Project Management Book, 2nd Ed.
Everything® Real Estate Investing Book
Everything® Retirement Planning Book
Everything® Robert's Rules Book, $7.95
Everything® Selling Book
Everything® Start Your Own Business Book, 2nd Ed.
Everything® Wills & Estate Planning Book

COOKING

Everything® Barbecue Cookbook
Everything® Bartender's Book, 2nd Ed., $9.95
Everything® Calorie Counting Cookbook
Everything® Cheese Book
Everything® Chinese Cookbook
Everything® Classic Recipes Book
Everything® Cocktail Parties & Drinks Book
Everything® College Cookbook
Everything® Cooking for Baby and Toddler Book
Everything® Cooking for Two Cookbook
Everything® Diabetes Cookbook
Everything® Easy Gourmet Cookbook
Everything® Fondue Cookbook
Everything® Fondue Party Book
Everything® Gluten-Free Cookbook
Everything® Glycemic Index Cookbook
Everything® Grilling Cookbook
Everything® Healthy Meals in Minutes Cookbook
Everything® Holiday Cookbook
Everything® Indian Cookbook
Everything® Italian Cookbook

Everything® Lactose-Free Cookbook
Everything® Low-Carb Cookbook
Everything® Low-Cholesterol Cookbook
Everything® Low-Fat High-Flavor Cookbook
Everything® Low-Salt Cookbook
Everything® Meals for a Month Cookbook
Everything® Meals on a Budget Cookbook
Everything® Mediterranean Cookbook
Everything® Mexican Cookbook
Everything® No Trans Fat Cookbook
Everything® One-Pot Cookbook
Everything® Pizza Cookbook
Everything® Quick and Easy 30-Minute,
     5-Ingredient Cookbook
Everything® Quick Meals Cookbook
Everything® Slow Cooker Cookbook
Everything® Slow Cooking for a Crowd Cookbook
Everything® Soup Cookbook
Everything® Stir-Fry Cookbook
Everything® Sugar-Free Cookbook
Everything® Tapas and Small Plates Cookbook
Everything® Tex-Mex Cookbook
Everything® Thai Cookbook
Everything® Vegetarian Cookbook
Everything® Whole-Grain, High-Fiber Cookbook
Everything® Wild Game Cookbook
Everything® Wine Book, 2nd Ed.

GAMES

Everything® 15-Minute Sudoku Book, $9.95
Everything® 30-Minute Sudoku Book, $9.95
Everything® Bible Crosswords Book, $9.95
Everything® Blackjack Strategy Book
Everything® Brain Strain Book, $9.95
Everything® Bridge Book
Everything® Card Games Book
Everything® Card Tricks Book, $9.95
Everything® Casino Gambling Book, 2nd Ed.
Everything® Chess Basics Book
Everything® Craps Strategy Book
Everything® Crossword and Puzzle Book
Everything® Crossword Challenge Book
Everything® Crosswords for the Beach Book, $9.95
Everything® Cryptic Crosswords Book, $9.95
Everything® Cryptograms Book, $9.95
Everything® Easy Crosswords Book
Everything® Easy Kakuro Book, $9.95
Everything® Easy Large-Print Crosswords Book
Everything® Games Book, 2nd Ed.
Everything® Giant Sudoku Book, $9.95
Everything® Giant Word Search Book
Everything® Kakuro Challenge Book, $9.95
Everything® Large-Print Crossword Challenge Book
Everything® Large-Print Crosswords Book
Everything® Lateral Thinking Puzzles Book, $9.95
Everything® Literary Crosswords Book, $9.95
Everything® Mazes Book
Everything® Memory Booster Puzzles Book, $9.95
Everything® Movie Crosswords Book, $9.95

Everything® Music Crosswords Book, $9.95
Everything® Online Poker Book
Everything® Pencil Puzzles Book, $9.95
Everything® Poker Strategy Book
Everything® Pool & Billiards Book
Everything® Puzzles for Commuters Book, $9.95
Everything® Puzzles for Dog Lovers Book, $9.95
Everything® Sports Crosswords Book, $9.95
Everything® Test Your IQ Book, $9.95
Everything® Texas Hold 'Em Book, $9.95
Everything® Travel Crosswords Book, $9.95
Everything® TV Crosswords Book, $9.95
Everything® Word Games Challenge Book
Everything® Word Scramble Book
Everything® Word Search Book

HEALTH

Everything® Alzheimer's Book
Everything® Diabetes Book
Everything® First Aid Book, $9.95
Everything® Health Guide to Adult Bipolar Disorder
Everything® Health Guide to Arthritis
Everything® Health Guide to Controlling Anxiety
Everything® Health Guide to Depression
Everything® Health Guide to Fibromyalgia
Everything® Health Guide to Menopause, 2nd Ed.
Everything® Health Guide to Migraines
Everything® Health Guide to OCD
Everything® Health Guide to PMS
Everything® Health Guide to Postpartum Care
Everything® Health Guide to Thyroid Disease
Everything® Hypnosis Book
Everything® Low Cholesterol Book
Everything® Menopause Book
Everything® Nutrition Book
Everything® Reflexology Book
Everything® Stress Management Book

HISTORY

Everything® American Government Book
Everything® American History Book, 2nd Ed.
Everything® Civil War Book
Everything® Freemasons Book
Everything® Irish History & Heritage Book
Everything® Middle East Book
Everything® World War II Book, 2nd Ed.

HOBBIES

Everything® Candlemaking Book
Everything® Cartooning Book
Everything® Coin Collecting Book
Everything® Digital Photography Book, 2nd Ed.
Everything® Drawing Book
Everything® Family Tree Book, 2nd Ed.
Everything® Knitting Book
Everything® Knots Book
Everything® Photography Book
Everything® Quilting Book

Everything® Sewing Book
Everything® Soapmaking Book, 2nd Ed.
Everything® Woodworking Book

HOME IMPROVEMENT

Everything® Feng Shui Book
Everything® Feng Shui Decluttering Book, $9.95
Everything® Fix-It Book
Everything® Green Living Book
Everything® Home Decorating Book
Everything® Home Storage Solutions Book
Everything® Homebuilding Book
Everything® Organize Your Home Book, 2nd Ed.

KIDS' BOOKS

All titles are $7.95
Everything® Fairy Tales Book, $14.95
Everything® Kids' Animal Puzzle & Activity Book
Everything® Kids' Astronomy Book
Everything® Kids' Baseball Book, 5th Ed.
Everything® Kids' Bible Trivia Book
Everything® Kids' Bugs Book
Everything® Kids' Cars and Trucks Puzzle and Activity Book
Everything® Kids' Christmas Puzzle & Activity Book
Everything® Kids' Connect the Dots
    Puzzle and Activity Book
Everything® Kids' Cookbook
Everything® Kids' Crazy Puzzles Book
Everything® Kids' Dinosaurs Book
Everything® Kids' Environment Book
Everything® Kids' Fairies Puzzle and Activity Book
Everything® Kids' First Spanish Puzzle and Activity Book
Everything® Kids' Football Book
Everything® Kids' Gross Cookbook
Everything® Kids' Gross Hidden Pictures Book
Everything® Kids' Gross Jokes Book
Everything® Kids' Gross Mazes Book
Everything® Kids' Gross Puzzle & Activity Book
Everything® Kids' Halloween Puzzle & Activity Book
Everything® Kids' Hidden Pictures Book
Everything® Kids' Horses Book
Everything® Kids' Joke Book
Everything® Kids' Knock Knock Book
Everything® Kids' Learning French Book
Everything® Kids' Learning Spanish Book
Everything® Kids' Magical Science Experiments Book
Everything® Kids' Math Puzzles Book
Everything® Kids' Mazes Book
Everything® Kids' Money Book
Everything® Kids' Nature Book
Everything® Kids' Pirates Puzzle and Activity Book
Everything® Kids' Presidents Book
Everything® Kids' Princess Puzzle and Activity Book
Everything® Kids' Puzzle Book
Everything® Kids' Racecars Puzzle and Activity Book
Everything® Kids' Riddles & Brain Teasers Book
Everything® Kids' Science Experiments Book
Everything® Kids' Sharks Book
Everything® Kids' Soccer Book
Everything® Kids' Spies Puzzle and Activity Book
Everything® Kids' States Book
Everything® Kids' Travel Activity Book
Everything® Kids' Word Search Puzzle and Activity Book

LANGUAGE

Everything® Conversational Japanese Book with CD, $19.95
Everything® French Grammar Book
Everything® French Phrase Book, $9.95
Everything® French Verb Book, $9.95
Everything® German Practice Book with CD, $19.95
Everything® Inglés Book
Everything® Intermediate Spanish Book with CD, $19.95
Everything® Italian Practice Book with CD, $19.95
Everything® Learning Brazilian Portuguese Book with CD, $19.95
Everything® Learning French Book with CD, 2nd Ed., $19.95
Everything® Learning German Book
Everything® Learning Italian Book
Everything® Learning Latin Book
Everything® Learning Russian Book with CD, $19.95
Everything® Learning Spanish Book
Everything® Learning Spanish Book with CD, 2nd Ed., $19.95
Everything® Russian Practice Book with CD, $19.95
Everything® Sign Language Book
Everything® Spanish Grammar Book
Everything® Spanish Phrase Book, $9.95
Everything® Spanish Practice Book with CD, $19.95
Everything® Spanish Verb Book, $9.95
Everything® Speaking Mandarin Chinese Book with CD, $19.95

MUSIC

Everything® Bass Guitar Book with CD, $19.95
Everything® Drums Book with CD, $19.95
Everything® Guitar Book with CD, 2nd Ed., $19.95
Everything® Guitar Chords Book with CD, $19.95
Everything® Harmonica Book with CD, $15.95
Everything® Home Recording Book
Everything® Music Theory Book with CD, $19.95
Everything® Reading Music Book with CD, $19.95
Everything® Rock & Blues Guitar Book with CD, $19.95
Everything® Rock & Blues Piano Book with CD, $19.95
Everything® Songwriting Book

NEW AGE

Everything® Astrology Book, 2nd Ed.
Everything® Birthday Personology Book
Everything® Dreams Book, 2nd Ed.
Everything® Love Signs Book, $9.95
Everything® Love Spells Book, $9.95
Everything® Paganism Book
Everything® Palmistry Book
Everything® Psychic Book
Everything® Reiki Book
Everything® Sex Signs Book, $9.95
Everything® Spells & Charms Book, 2nd Ed.
Everything® Tarot Book, 2nd Ed.
Everything® Toltec Wisdom Book
Everything® Wicca & Witchcraft Book, 2nd Ed.

PARENTING

Everything® Baby Names Book, 2nd Ed.
Everything® Baby Shower Book, 2nd Ed.
Everything® Baby Sign Language Book with DVD
Everything® Baby's First Year Book
Everything® Birthing Book

Everything® Breastfeeding Book
Everything® Father-to-Be Book
Everything® Father's First Year Book
Everything® Get Ready for Baby Book, 2nd Ed.
Everything® Get Your Baby to Sleep Book, $9.95
Everything® Getting Pregnant Book
Everything® Guide to Pregnancy Over 35
Everything® Guide to Raising a One-Year-Old
Everything® Guide to Raising a Two-Year-Old
Everything® Guide to Raising Adolescent Boys
Everything® Guide to Raising Adolescent Girls
Everything® Mother's First Year Book
Everything® Parent's Guide to Childhood Illnesses
Everything® Parent's Guide to Children and Divorce
Everything® Parent's Guide to Children with ADD/ADHD
Everything® Parent's Guide to Children with Asperger's Syndrome
Everything® Parent's Guide to Children with Asthma
Everything® Parent's Guide to Children with Autism
Everything® Parent's Guide to Children with Bipolar Disorder
Everything® Parent's Guide to Children with Depression
Everything® Parent's Guide to Children with Dyslexia
Everything® Parent's Guide to Children with Juvenile Diabetes
Everything® Parent's Guide to Positive Discipline
Everything® Parent's Guide to Raising a Successful Child
Everything® Parent's Guide to Raising Boys
Everything® Parent's Guide to Raising Girls
Everything® Parent's Guide to Raising Siblings
Everything® Parent's Guide to Sensory Integration Disorder
Everything® Parent's Guide to Tantrums
Everything® Parent's Guide to the Strong-Willed Child
Everything® Parenting a Teenager Book
Everything® Potty Training Book, $9.95
Everything® Pregnancy Book, 3rd Ed.
Everything® Pregnancy Fitness Book
Everything® Pregnancy Nutrition Book
Everything® Pregnancy Organizer, 2nd Ed., $16.95
Everything® Toddler Activities Book
Everything® Toddler Book
Everything® Tween Book
Everything® Twins, Triplets, and More Book

PETS

Everything® Aquarium Book
Everything® Boxer Book
Everything® Cat Book, 2nd Ed.
Everything® Chihuahua Book
Everything® Cooking for Dogs Book
Everything® Dachshund Book
Everything® Dog Book, 2nd Ed.
Everything® Dog Grooming Book
Everything® Dog Health Book
Everything® Dog Obedience Book
Everything® Dog Owner's Organizer, $16.95
Everything® Dog Training and Tricks Book
Everything® German Shepherd Book
Everything® Golden Retriever Book
Everything® Horse Book
Everything® Horse Care Book
Everything® Horseback Riding Book
Everything® Labrador Retriever Book
Everything® Poodle Book
Everything® Pug Book

Everything® Puppy Book
Everything® Rottweiler Book
Everything® Small Dogs Book
Everything® Tropical Fish Book
Everything® Yorkshire Terrier Book

REFERENCE

Everything® American Presidents Book
Everything® Blogging Book
Everything® Build Your Vocabulary Book, $9.95
Everything® Car Care Book
Everything® Classical Mythology Book
Everything® Da Vinci Book
Everything® Divorce Book
Everything® Einstein Book
Everything® Enneagram Book
Everything® Etiquette Book, 2nd Ed.
Everything® Guide to C. S. Lewis & Narnia
Everything® Guide to Edgar Allan Poe
Everything® Guide to Understanding Philosophy
Everything® Inventions and Patents Book
Everything® Jacqueline Kennedy Onassis Book
Everything® John F. Kennedy Book
Everything® Mafia Book
Everything® Martin Luther King Jr. Book
Everything® Philosophy Book
Everything® Pirates Book
Everything® Private Investigation Book
Everything® Psychology Book
Everything® Public Speaking Book, $9.95
Everything® Shakespeare Book, 2nd Ed.

RELIGION

Everything® Angels Book
Everything® Bible Book
Everything® Bible Study Book with CD, $19.95
Everything® Buddhism Book
Everything® Catholicism Book
Everything® Christianity Book
Everything® Gnostic Gospels Book
Everything® History of the Bible Book
Everything® Jesus Book
Everything® Jewish History & Heritage Book
Everything® Judaism Book
Everything® Kabbalah Book
Everything® Koran Book
Everything® Mary Book
Everything® Mary Magdalene Book
Everything® Prayer Book
Everything® Saints Book, 2nd Ed.
Everything® Torah Book
Everything® Understanding Islam Book
Everything® Women of the Bible Book
Everything® World's Religions Book

SCHOOL & CAREERS

Everything® Career Tests Book
Everything® College Major Test Book
Everything® College Survival Book, 2nd Ed.
Everything® Cover Letter Book, 2nd Ed.
Everything® Filmmaking Book
Everything® Get-a-Job Book, 2nd Ed.
Everything® Guide to Being a Paralegal
Everything® Guide to Being a Personal Trainer
Everything® Guide to Being a Real Estate Agent
Everything® Guide to Being a Sales Rep
Everything® Guide to Being an Event Planner
Everything® Guide to Careers in Health Care
Everything® Guide to Careers in Law Enforcement
Everything® Guide to Government Jobs
Everything® Guide to Starting and Running a Catering
 Business
Everything® Guide to Starting and Running a Restaurant
Everything® Job Interview Book, 2nd Ed.
Everything® New Nurse Book
Everything® New Teacher Book
Everything® Paying for College Book
Everything® Practice Interview Book
Everything® Resume Book, 3rd Ed.
Everything® Study Book

SELF-HELP

Everything® Body Language Book
Everything® Dating Book, 2nd Ed.
Everything® Great Sex Book
Everything® Self-Esteem Book
Everything® Tantric Sex Book

SPORTS & FITNESS

Everything® Easy Fitness Book
Everything® Fishing Book
Everything® Krav Maga for Fitness Book
Everything® Running Book, 2nd Ed.

TRAVEL

Everything® Family Guide to Coastal Florida
Everything® Family Guide to Cruise Vacations
Everything® Family Guide to Hawaii
Everything® Family Guide to Las Vegas, 2nd Ed.
Everything® Family Guide to Mexico
Everything® Family Guide to New England, 2nd Ed.
Everything® Family Guide to New York City, 3rd Ed.
Everything® Family Guide to RV Travel & Campgrounds
Everything® Family Guide to the Caribbean
Everything® Family Guide to the Disneyland® Resort, California
 Adventure®, Universal Studios®, and the Anaheim
 Area, 2nd Ed.
Everything® Family Guide to the Walt Disney World Resort®,
 Universal Studios®, and Greater Orlando, 5th Ed.
Everything® Family Guide to Timeshares
Everything® Family Guide to Washington D.C., 2nd Ed.

WEDDINGS

Everything® Bachelorette Party Book, $9.95
Everything® Bridesmaid Book, $9.95
Everything® Destination Wedding Book
Everything® Father of the Bride Book, $9.95
Everything® Groom Book, $9.95
Everything® Mother of the Bride Book, $9.95
Everything® Outdoor Wedding Book
Everything® Wedding Book, 3rd Ed.
Everything® Wedding Checklist, $9.95
Everything® Wedding Etiquette Book, $9.95
Everything® Wedding Organizer, 2nd Ed., $16.95
Everything® Wedding Shower Book, $9.95
Everything® Wedding Vows Book, $9.95
Everything® Wedding Workout Book
Everything® Weddings on a Budget Book, 2nd Ed., $9.95

WRITING

Everything® Creative Writing Book
Everything® Get Published Book, 2nd Ed.
Everything® Grammar and Style Book, 2nd Ed.
Everything® Guide to Magazine Writing
Everything® Guide to Writing a Book Proposal
Everything® Guide to Writing a Novel
Everything® Guide to Writing Children's Books
Everything® Guide to Writing Copy
Everything® Guide to Writing Graphic Novels
Everything® Guide to Writing Research Papers
Everything® Improve Your Writing Book, 2nd Ed.
Everything® Writing Poetry Book

Available wherever books are sold! To order, call 800-258-0929, or visit us at **www.adamsmedia.com**.
Everything® and everything.com® are registered trademarks of F+W Publications, Inc.
Bolded titles are new additions to the series.
All Everything® books are priced at $12.95 or $14.95, unless otherwise stated. Prices subject to change without notice.